Reflective Practice in the Sport and Exercise Sciences

Drawing on the experiences of scientists, researchers, practitioners and teachers in a wide range of sport and exercise settings, this book explores contemporary issues in reflective practice and considers the way that reflective practice impacts upon applied practice, on research methodology and on professional development. It includes chapters on the use of reflective practice in areas as diverse as:

- delivering coach education
- sport psychology support
- working in sports physiology
- developing young players in sport
- exercise-related interventions
- physiotherapy
- working inside a professional football club
- student skills and the physical activity and health curriculum.

Based on multi-disciplinary work in education and the health sciences, and exploring the crucial interface between learning and practice, this book is important reading for all sport and exercise scientists and any professional working in sport and exercise who is looking to become a more effective practitioner.

Zoe Knowles is Reader and HCPC Practitioner psychologist at Liverpool John Moores University, specialising in the areas of reflective practice, elite sports performance and paediatric exercise science (active play). She has published extensively within international journals on reflective practice and has advised BASES, The Open University (UK) and International HEIs as regards the development and facilitation of reflective practice in curricula.

David Gilbourne is Professor of Critical Qualitative Research in the Department of Sport, Exercise and Health at the University of Hull. He initiated and co-directed the 1st and 2nd International Conferences in Qualitative Research in Sport (2004–2006), and co-founded and now acts as Advisory Editor to *Qualitative Research in Sport, Exercise and Health*. His research interests include

critical reflective practice and the practice of critical social science, and his writing explores the representation of qualitative research through creative mediums such as storytelling, auto-ethnography, poetry and theatre.

Brendan Cropley is Senior Lecturer in Coaching Science and Sport Psychology at Cardiff Metropolitan University as well as a BASES Accredited Sport and Exercise Scientist. His research has focused on effective and reflective practice in sport psychology as well as the utility of reflective practice as a means of developing life skills in young athletes.

Lindsey Dugdill is Professor of Public Health at the University of Salford. She has previously been a member of the Editorial Board for the *International Journal of Reflective Practice* and has integrated reflective practice into her teaching and research practice throughout her career.

Reflective Practice in the Sport and Exercise Sciences

Contemporary issues

Edited by Zoe Knowles, David Gilbourne,
Brendan Cropley and Lindsey Dugdill

Routledge
Taylor & Francis Group

LONDON AND NEW YORK

First published 2014
by Routledge
2 Park Square, Milton Park, Abingdon, Oxon OX14 4RN

and by Routledge
711 Third Avenue, New York, NY 10017

Routledge is an imprint of the Taylor & Francis Group, an informa business

British Library Cataloguing in Publication Data
A catalogue record for this book is available from the British Library

Library of Congress Cataloging in Publication Data
Reflective practice in the sport and exercise sciences : contemporary issues / edited by Zoe Knowles, David Gilbourne, Brendan Cropley and Lindsey Dugdill.
pages cm
Includes bibliographical references and index.
1. Sports sciences. 2. Exercise. I. Knowles, Zoe.
GV558.R44 2014
613.7'1—dc23
2013027206

ISBN 978-0-415-81492-8 (hbk)
ISBN 978-0-415-81493-5 (pbk)
ISBN 978-0-203-06654-6 (ebk)

Typeset in GoudyStd
by Swales & Willis Ltd, Devon, UK

Contents

Tables and Figures

Tables

Figures

Notes on Contributors

Mark B. Andersen, College of Sport and Exercise Science, Institute of Sport, Exercise and Active Living, Victoria University, Australia

Steve T. Barney, Department of Psychology, Southern Utah University, USA

Angela M. Coppola, Faculty of Physical Education and Recreation, University of Alberta, Canada

Diane Crone, Faculty of Applied Sciences, University of Gloucestershire, UK

Brendan Cropley, Cardiff School of Sport, Cardiff Metropolitan University, UK

Tracey Devonport, Faculty of Health, Education and Wellbeing, University of Wolverhampton, UK

Barry Drust, School of Sport and Exercise Sciences, Liverpool John Moores University, Liverpool, UK

Lindsey Dugdill, School of Health Sciences, University of Salford, UK

Orla Flannery, Faculty of Applied Sciences, University of Gloucestershire, UK

David Gilbourne, Department of Sport, Health and Exercise Science, University of Hull, UK

Sheldon Hanton, Cardiff School of Sport, Cardiff Metropolitan University, UK

Linda Hollingworth, School of Health Sciences, University of Salford, UK

Nicholas L. Holt, Faculty of Physical Education and Recreation, University of Alberta, Canada

Emma Huntley, Department of Sport and Physical Activity, Edge Hill University, UK

Lindsey Kilgour, Faculty of Applied Sciences, University of Gloucestershire, UK

Zoe Knowles, Physical Activity Exchange/School of Sport and Exercise Sciences, Liverpool John Moores University, UK

Andrew Lane, Faculty of Health, Education and Wellbeing, University of Wolverhampton, UK

Martin Littlewood, School of Sport and Exercise Sciences, Liverpool John Moores University, UK

Phil Marshall, Department of Sport, Health and Exercise Science, University of Hull, UK

Nic Matthews, School of Leisure, Faculty of Applied Sciences, University of Gloucestershire, UK

Tara-Leigh F. McHugh, Faculty of Physical Education and Recreation, University of Alberta, Canada

Stephen Mellalieu, College of Engineering, University of Swansea, UK

James Morton, School of Sport and Exercise Sciences, Liverpool John Moores University, UK

Kacey C. Neely, Faculty of Physical Education and Recreation, University of Alberta, Canada

Lee Nelson, Department of Sport, Health and Exercise Science, University of Hull, UK

Gareth Picknell, Health and Sport Medicine Centre, United Arab Emirates Armed Forces

Lorna Porcellato, Faculty of Health and Applied Sciences, Liverpool John Moores University, UK

Paul Potrac, Department of Sport, Health and Exercise Science, University of Hull, UK

Sarah Prenton, School of Health Sciences, University of Salford, UK

Alison Rhodius, College of Graduate and Professional Studies, John F. Kennedy University, California, USA

Reinhard Stelter, Department of Nutrition, Exercise and Sports Coaching, Psychology Unit, University of Copenhagen, Denmark

Hamish Telfer, Independent academic (formerly University of Cumbria, UK), Sedbergh, UK

John Toner, Department of Sport, Health and Exercise Science, University of Hull, UK

Jo Trelfa, Department of Children, Young People and Communities, University of St Mark & St John, Plymouth, UK

Carmel Triggs, Department of Sport and Exercise Sciences, University of Chester, UK

Dedications

Zoe Knowles: This book is dedicated to my daughters Anya and Caitlin, husband Dave and my wonderful family. Many events have influenced my research around reflective practice, both those apparent to all in the literature and through other experiences known only to close family and friends. I thank those who have mentored me in academic work, particularly Professors Gilbourne, Stratton, Fairclough and Dugdill; colleagues at LJMU and co-author Brendan Cropley.

David Gilbourne: To Bluebell, a gentle chicken with a wicked sense of humour.

Brendan Cropley: To my wife for her love and understanding; to my family for the motivation; to my colleagues for the inspiration.

Lindsey Dugdill: I would like to dedicate this to my parents, Derek and Mary Gee, and all my past and present students and colleagues.

The authors would like to thank all the contributors; Dr Andy Miles and Dr Andy Pringle for their constructive comments on drafts of chapters 1 and 17; and Prof. Greg Whyte for the Foreword.

By three methods we may learn wisdom: First, by reflection, which is noblest; Second, by imitation, which is easiest; and third by experience, which is the bitterest.
(Confucius: Chinese philosopher, 551–479BC)

Foreword

Given the complex interaction between individuals, each with their own subtly different agenda, the application of theory to practice or the evolution of service provision is rarely a simple task. In sport and exercise science there is a common perception that only a small number of leaders exist within a team, such as the football manager or performance director. In reality, every member of a team is a leader whose responsibility it is to deliver their optimal performance to ensure the overall success of the team, however small the task. Ensuring optimal performance is far from easy. Performance is not solely associated with knowledge or technical competence. In my experience, some of the greatest practitioners have not been the most qualified or technically adept. The interaction between individuals requires a range of skills that are not taught in a traditional educational setting. Optimising impact requires the ability to bridge the gap between theory and practice and deliver a service to a wide range of clients, that is, the coach, the athlete or client, support staff or administrators.

The ability of a service provider to translate and deliver their message in the most appropriate way will ultimately dictate success. Reflective practice provides a tool to mould and develop a service provider's professional knowledge and skills. Reflecting on what we do as practitioners allows us to understand the reasons for success or failure of a particular intervention or relationship better. My own experience as both an athlete and a practitioner leads me to believe that excellence is achieved when you are able to critically analyse performance and make the necessary, and sometimes difficult, changes to practice that result in a positive development of practice. Failure is most often seen in those who believe they are always right. An absence of introspection and self-evaluation is a flaw uncommon, nay absent, in leading practitioners. That said, self-reflection is significantly strengthened through the support of others including: fellow practitioners, coaches, administrators, and, most importantly, the athletes or clients whom you are serving. Reflective practice should not be limited to the outcome of delivery but the *process* of delivery itself. Understanding which elements of an intervention work and which do not will allow for a more comprehensive evolution of practice. To assume the process is optimal based solely on a successful end product makes replication of success difficult to achieve. Sport itself is infected by 'success by association' – the belief that successful athletes are only supported by high-quality interventions. The reality is often far from this belief, and it is only when we reflect on all aspects of support, successful and unsuccessful, that we can enhance practice and ultimately optimize performance.

Like so many approaches, reflective practice requires commitment to the process and the resultant outcomes. Reflective practice has to result in learning, development and ultimately a positive change to be truly effective. This book is a unique resource from world leaders in the field, providing the background, rationale, techniques, application and examples of best practice, which should enable the reader to implement one of the most important processes in a practitioner's development in their quest for excellence.

Greg Whyte PhD DSc FBASES FACSM

Professor Greg Whyte is an Olympian as a modern pentathlete, and is a European and World Championship medallist. He is an expert in the field of sports science, graduating from Brunel University; he furthered his studies with an MSc in human performance in the USA and completed his PhD at St Georges Hospital Medical School, London. Formerly Director of Science and Research for the British Olympic Association and the English Institute of Sport, Greg is currently a Professor of Applied Sport and Exercise Science at Liverpool John Moores University. An internationally recognised expert in the field of applied sport and exercise science, Greg has extensive professional experience in the performance enhancement of elite athletes, sporting enthusiasts and diseased populations. Greg is well known for his work with the charity Comic Relief in helping celebrities to successfully achieve feats of ultra-endurance performance.

Part One

Key principles of reflective practice

Part One

Key principles of reflective practice

1 Reflecting on reflection and journeys

Zoe Knowles, David Gilbourne,
Brendan Cropley and Lindsey Dugdill

Introducing the team

When there are four editors and all four need to contribute to the introductory chapter then usually one of the team lands the role of telling everyone's story for them! So, with that role designated my way, I (David) waited for Zoe, Brendan and Lindsey to send over their initial ideas. We had agreed that there would be a series of 'things' we must try to do. First, we decided readers should know a little of our background in all things reflective, and so we have tried to locate ourselves in that regard. Second, we wanted to try and explain what role reflective practice has played in our work more generally; this seemed, to us, to be important, particularly as our career paths have intersected from time to time. We also wanted to ensure we offered an overview of the concepts, principles and techniques that we share an affinity with as a team within the realms of reflective practice. Finally, we wanted to present to readers how we feel you could learn from reading the book, inviting you to read it not from the position of your discipline but perhaps from a location and subsequent order you would never have considered.

As an editorial team we have all, at some point in our careers, worked together, in the same institution or, on other occasions, we have found ourselves reunited by appearing on the same platform (at conferences and so forth). We have all aged a little in each other's company, and this sense of a shared history makes the task of working together on this book a real pleasure. As time has gone by we have all explored different facets of reflective practice, engaged in separate (yet interconnected) applied fields, and written commentaries on issues such as critical reflective practice in sport psychology. At this precise moment in time (April 2013) we are working on the present manuscript from a wide-ranging geography as we all now hold posts in different institutions and, despite distance, we remain genuinely connected by our interest in reflective practice and, so, here we are.

Our pathway to this point has not been necessarily smooth or straightforward. We have faced challenges and been required, frequently, to defend our ideas at conferences, through journal reviewer feedback or via personal communications. In the spirit of critical reflection these interjections and questions have been welcomed. In our collective view facing critique, even scepticism, has forced us to think through our ideas carefully, and we appreciate the need to always be under scrutiny from colleagues and practitioners. This book is designed to engage a wide community of academics and practitioners, an engagement that hopes to include those who have subscribed to the notion of reflective practice and also those who might remain unconvinced; we see little point in simply talking to the converted or becoming over-evangelical.

A final point on structure and style. As the different editors are introduced I act as a kind of narrator who introduces the other members of the editorial team. Towards the end, I hand to Zoe to talk a little about my own connections to reflection through the medium of qualitative methodology. I hope this works, let's see!

Zoe Knowles

I seem to have known Zoe Knowles for a scholarly lifetime. In fact, working along-side Zoe for the best parts of two decades just serves to reinforce the fact that I am very old, very old indeed. Unless my memory is playing tricks Zoe based her under-graduate thesis around the themes and processes of reflective practice sometime in the mid-1990s and followed this, immediately, with a Masters thesis and her PhD on the same topic several years later. Throughout all of this I was hanging around in various supervisory roles, and to my knowledge we never fell out once.

Zoe's early research writing focused on the emerging discipline of coaching science before that of sport psychology, and she is now recognised nationally and internationally for her contributions to the reflective practice literature both within these arenas and, more recently, in the area of children's play. In her early writing Zoe was mindful to embrace and, if necessary, borrow, from literature that existed in more established domains such as teaching and nursing, and some texts offer evidence of that eclectic approach (see Anderson, Knowles & Gilbourne, 2004). In the field of sport and exercise psychology, Zoe has contributed a series of reflective texts that build in both scope and complexity (see Knowles, Gilbourne, Tomlinson & Niven, 2007; Knowles & Gilbourne, 2010; and Knowles, Katz & Gilbourne, 2012). The impact of this work is evident through the inclusion of reflective practice in the training curricula of neophyte sport and exercise scientists and psychologists in the UK, and through Zoe's advisory roles with UK and International Higher Education Institutions.

Brendan Cropley

I only worked alongside Brendan for a short time (at Cardiff Metropolitan University), but whenever we found time to talk reflective practice was high on the agenda. Sometimes being members of the same institution offers little guarantee that you might work together, and our time in Cardiff is a good example of that. The programmes we contributed to were associated with different facets of the undergraduate and postgraduate structure, but despite these structural issues, we managed to share some lecture sessions. I sense we worked together more when we worked apart, sharing research platforms and workshop seminars, for example.

Brendan was first introduced to reflective practice during the Supervised Experience process that underpins the British Association of Sport and Exercise Sciences (BASES) professional accreditation training for sport and exercise scientists. Key to this process is the critical evaluation of personal practice and his doctoral research, post-doctoral inquiry and the writings that stem from these, which offer evidence of his sustained interest in the reflective practice field.

Brendan's PhD examined the *value* of reflective practice in more detail, with specific emphasis on its relationship with the effectiveness of applied sport psychology service delivery. He was keen to uncover the way in which practitioners could more successfully elicit reflective learning from their experiences and how they might be better prepared to do so. This work acted as a catalyst for Brendan's subsequent initiation, development and delivery of core professional development workshops for BASES; conducting research for Sports Coach UK (SCUK) and consulting with National Governing Bodies (e.g., British Cycling; Welsh Football Trust; British Gymnastics). These relationships have developed through Brendan's interest in the development of coach education qualifications that integrate, more effectively, reflective practice. Within the sport and exercise science domain Brendan has continued to pursue his interest in reflective practice through the supervision of PhD students who are presently examining the utility of reflective practice across a range of contexts (i.e., coach education; management development; health education), and/or utilizing reflective practice as an approach to undertaking research more generally.

Lindsey Dugdill

Lindsey and I worked together at Liverpool John Moores University, our tutor rooms a few doors apart. During our corridor-sharing years I was just beginning to get interested in auto-ethnographic writing, and, whenever I had developed an idea or drafted a little more storyline, Lindsey was always my first choice as trusted reader and critical editor. I sensed that we both shared a leaning towards the idea of understanding people in context, and that progressed in different ways towards our further and ongoing interest in reflective practice.

Lindsey began her academic training as a scientist with a first degree in Zoology and an MPhil in Exercise Physiology. However, it was as a new lecturer in Higher Education that the importance of *reflection-in-thinking* took hold, with Lindsey developing a particular interest in the pedagogic challenges associated with the theory/practice interface. While working with undergraduate Health Studies students, who were required to undertake a piece of experiential learning in the workplace, Lindsey, intuitively perhaps, utilised reflection as one of the tools to help them critically analyse their experiences and any arising implications. The students found the experience of using reflection both difficult (learning to write down one's inner thoughts) and rewarding (when they started to really understand complex situations or issues). As a consequence Lindsey began using features of reflective practice in her own PhD research, which investigated the design, development and evaluation of workplace health interventions using Participatory Action Research (PAR). Lindsey became convinced about the efficacy of reflection, for example, when used to help compile diaries and logs, and she is now an advocate of these processes in PAR helping in the process of gathering data on processes of intervention design and delivery – something often overlooked within traditional research paradigms.

Whilst completing her PhD Lindsey returned to what she describes as her 'exercise roots' and joined the School of Sport and Exercise Science at LJMU in 1998. This move allowed further opportunities to collaborate on enhancing work-based learning curricula with reflective practice concepts. To the present day Lindsey continues to use reflective practice in her own research across a range of workplace spaces, with health practitioners, PhD students and most recently physiotherapists, via *Tidy's Physiotherapy* (Porter, 2013). One final point, for all of Lindsey's energy and commitment, I can say that I have never sensed an uncritical evangelical streak, and I find that reassuring. For example, through all the years of reflective writing and applied reflective practice Lindsey has always maintained interest in the range of ethical issues that can arise during reflection (such as disclosure), and this is just one example of the complications that can be associated with doing reflection well. So, Lindsey remains a critical advocate of the empowering nature of reflective practice, a mindset that ensures that progression and promotion of reflection is always tempered with a sense of caution.

David Gilbourne

As Editorial lead I (Zoe) have been passed the baton to write about David, and I must agree that I don't think we have ever fallen out! In 1972 David began his own involvement in sport through what he describes as a 'largely ineffectual effort' at playing professional football – an experience that he has often revisited in his auto-ethnographic writing. Later, and after a short time in the domain of school-based pedagogy and outdoor education, David began to develop his research interest in sport social science, specialising in the processes of creative communication and writing-as-research. I think over time we as a duo have become synonymous with reflective practice work, and while at times have been prominent in the literature we have also taken considered time to step back and glance at the methodological landscape more widely.

Writing this book has given me time to look at what we have achieved and indeed become. David has never shied away from writing about his own journey, his own life and career experiences. He writes candidly and with a sense of authenticity that is respected. In his writing David has explored a range of critical methodologies (such as action research and auto-ethnography) and utilised techniques such as creative writing, poetry and drama. Seemingly unconcerned with critique or indifference, David has managed to provoke the sport and exercise science community to consider how we might represent and disseminate our work outside the traditional qualitative realms of interview and content analysis. Finally, I think on behalf of all the team we should point out that 'old . . . very old . . . ' is, to us, 'wise . . . very wise . . . ' We have all benefited as researchers and people from being in his company formally, on the same corridor or at the end of the phone/e-mail, and for that we are grateful.

Reflecting on reflection

So why do reflective practice?

Having introduced ourselves and how we came together to write this text in this section, we aim to set out, in essence, the why, what and how of reflective practice, or indeed the principles that we commit to as a team. The popularity of reflective practice in the sport and exercise domain has increased in recent years. Building on the support emanating from research and practice in a range of associated fields (e.g., nursing, education, management), it has been suggested that reflective practice should be a fundamental aspect of the work of professionals, and those training to be, employed in the different disciplines of sport and exercise (e.g., athletes, coaches, sport scientists: see Knowles & Telfer, 2010). Consequently, researchers, educators and practitioners alike have begun to *buy in* to the notion that reflective practice has the potential to help develop the knowledge and understanding required to function effectively in the complex and often messy reality of the contexts in which the sport and exercise professions operate (cf. Heaney, Oakley & Rea, 2010). It is within this context that the need for, and value of, reflective practice becomes evident.

Bowes and Jones (2006) have suggested that any activity involving human interaction is innately complex. Thus, building on the thoughts of Martens (1987), such activities prevent the neat application of theory to practice and require the application of other forms of knowledge and understanding. These ideas resonate with the notion of *technical rationality* (e.g., problem-solving through the exacting of solutions by applying theory and techniques derived from systematic scientific knowledge, cf. Schön, 1983), which if followed rigidly is thought to reduce practitioners to the level of technicians whose only role is to implement the research findings and theoretical models of scientists, researchers and theoreticians (Rolfe, Freshwater & Jasper, 2001). As a consequence, those attempting to solve practice-based problems through a technical rational approach are thought to be unlikely to deal with reality in a way that will ultimately render practice as effective. More recently, however, some authors have begun to question the basis of this critique, suggesting that in professional practice there are solutions to some problems that tend to 'ring true' in many different situations (e.g., Johns, 2009; Rømer, 2003). As a result, we contend that while the application of theory to practice may be suitable for well-defined and recognizable issues within the domain of sport and exercise, problems associated with practice rarely present themselves in easily definable and resolvable form. This does not mean that in order to deal with, and potentially prevent, such complex problems technical knowledge should be overlooked or ignored. Instead, it is important for trainees and professionals to transform their experiences through reflective practice in order to bridge the gap between theory and practice. Integrating prior beliefs, values, prejudices and social norms with theory and practice in this reflective process is thought to help reconstruct professional knowledge (e.g., technical, theoretical knowledge about things) and develop a way of *knowing-in-action* (Anderson et al., 2004).

Knowing- or *knowledge-in-action* has also been labeled as *craft knowledge* (e.g., Knowles, Gilbourne, Borrie & Neville, 2001) and *tacit knowledge* (e.g., Martens, 1987) and is suggested to be constructed of two parts. First, is that improving practice and professional development begins with reflecting on what we actually do, on our own experience. This reflection generates a rich and detailed knowledge base derived from practice (Ghaye, 2010). Second, this knowledge is used by practitioners in their work, and thus it becomes our *knowing-in-action*. Researchers have begun to suggest that the knowledge-in-action developed through reflective practice is the most essential form of knowledge and should constitute the fundamental body of knowledge of a practice discipline (e.g., Johns, 2009). In light of these ideas, we believe that in order for practitioners working within sport and exercise to know and understand how to do what they do reflective practice becomes an integral part of learning and ongoing development. Indeed, making sense of our knowledge-in-action through reflective practice allows practitioners to make more informed decisions in practice and about practice, and in doing so helps them to better understand and cope with the complexity imposed by the context of sport and exercise (Cropley & Hanton, 2011).

In addition to the preceding discussion, we feel that reflective practice should be seen as a meaning-making process. In this sense, we are in agreement with Rogers (2002), who has suggested that this process moves a learner from one experience into the next with deeper understanding of its relationships with, and connections to, other experiences and ideas. It is the thread that makes continuity of learning possible, and ensures the progress of the individual and, ultimately, the field in which they work. We appreciate that reflective practice is becoming a central part of assessment procedures in Higher Education (HE) and professional training programmes, and therefore many see reflecting on their practice simply as a necessity for qualification. However, we should not be constrained by assessment protocols and marking criteria and instead value the opportunity to engage in formal reflective processes. In doing this, reflective practice should facilitate the opportunity for experiential learning that has the potential to develop the knowledge-in-action required to be more critical, confident, innovative, informed and thus ultimately effective in what we do. Reflective practice should therefore become a disposition of the trainee and professional that underpins the judgement and decision-making processes associated with professional practice.

Defining reflective practice – the 'what'

Anderson, Knowles and Gilbourne (2004) argued that given the number of typologies that are available, as well as the complexity inherent in the process that involves the whole person (e.g., cognitions, emotions, behaviours), a simple definition of reflective practice is elusive. In addition to this, the definitions offered across different fields are often contradictory, meaning that understandings of reflective practice have been equivocal. This has resulted in many practitioners thinking that they are engaging in reflective practice when actually they are not (Cropley & Hanton, 2011). In order to help develop a better understanding of what reflective practice actually is, it is important to draw firstly upon Schön's (1983, 1987) depictions of the time phases of reflection. Schön considered that reflection can occur both *on-action* (e.g., explicitly drawing upon professional knowledge to review and make sense of a situation once it has ended) and *in-action* (e.g., tacitly drawing on a knowledge base as we engage with practice tasks, and therefore it is a matter of 'thinking on our feet'). In addition to these, Thompson and Pascal (2012) have offered an additional time-phase depiction of reflection in *reflection-for-action*. They suggested that this refers to:

> The process of planning, thinking ahead about what is to come, so that we can draw on our experience (and the professional knowledge base implicit within it) in order to make the best use of the time resources available to us. (p. 317)

These conceptions give us an understanding of the differences associated with engaging in reflection at different times, while also providing a platform from which we are able to better define these approaches. The discussion that follows focuses primarily on *reflection-on-action*, although we argue that the way in which we define this concept has weight in the general definitions of the others.

Following Schön's (1983, 1987) ideas, many definitions have considered reflection to be a process of 'looking back' at our experiences as a way of informing our subsequent actions. For example, Ghaye (2010) stated that reflective practice is about:

> Looking back and making sense of your practice, learning from this and using this learning to affect your future action. (p. 22)

While we agree that such definitions provide valuable insights into the reflective process, many may find it difficult to distinguish between these conceptualizations and those of other modes of thinking, such as evaluation. These issues are supported by Thompson and Thompson (2008), who indicated that a number of myths and misunderstandings have grown around reflective practice, including the tendency to take reflective practice too literally; that is, to see it as simply a matter of pausing for thought. The authors contend that it is important to go beyond this literalism to recognise that reflective practice is not simply thinking about practice in a general, loosely defined way.

In order to further clarify these issues, we suggest that examining both the process and outcome elements inherent within the array of definitions available provides a clearer picture about what reflective practice is and is not. There appear to be several key characteristics commonly reported in definitions that help to explicate the landscape of reflective practice:

First, reflective practice is a process that is *purposeful* in that it is something that we consciously decide to engage in, which distinguishes reflection from the subconscious processes of day-dreaming and navel-gazing.

Second, the process is *complex*, involving and considering the *whole self*. In this sense, reflective practice has to consider personal cognitions, emotions and behaviours, their interaction and impact on the situation, as well as the impact of the context on these.

Third, reflective practice is instigated through *questioning*, with the potential for reflective learning lying in the quality of this questioning process.

Fourth, reflective practice actively *transforms experience* into learning. Experience has traditionally been seen as an accumulation of hours of 'doing something' (e.g., Ericsson, Krampe & Tesch-Römer, 1993), but this passive process is unlikely to impact on learning in a way that reduces the likelihood of similar problems occurring in different situations. Instead, experience has to be examined through reflective practice in order to shift it to knowledge.

Finally, linked to the previous point, reflective practice has to *result in change*. Within the literature there appears to be some confusion as to what this *change* represents. However, we are in agreement with Knowles and Saxon (2010), who suggested that it represents: (a) a change in behaviour, values or beliefs; (b) confirmation or rejection of a particular theory or practice; and/or (c) a change in knowledge of the self, the context of practice or the environment in which the practitioner is working.

In light of this discussion we propose that reflective practice is:

> A purposeful and complex process that facilitates the examination of experience by questioning the whole self and our agency within the context of practice. This examination transforms experience into learning, which helps us to access, make sense of and develop our knowledge-in-action in order to better understand and/or improve practice and the situation in which it occurs.

The 'how to' – doing reflective practice

There are many approaches that can be undertaken to realize the process of reflective practice. Indeed, in view of the number of typologies available many advocate the plural term *reflective practices* (cf. Ghaye, 2010). However, it is important to recognise that becoming a reflective practitioner is more than a collection of techniques, and instead involves an all-encompassing attitude to practice that requires the practitioner to commit to professional and personal development (Anderson et al., 2004). It is also a process that requires certain skills (e.g., critical thinking, problem-solving) that can be developed through guidance and practice; therefore simply engaging with certain *practices* will not necessarily elicit the reflective learning outcomes reported in the literature.

An important consideration that should influence the decision about which approach is used, concerns the purpose for reflecting-on-practice. In considering James and Clarke's (1994) classification of *reflective levels*, reflective practice can serve technical (e.g., developing the mechanical aspects of practice), practical (e.g., understanding personal meaning within a situation), and critical (e.g., challenging habitual practices) purposes. Thus, in order to reflect at the level (e.g., descriptive to critical: see Knowles et al., 2001) required to achieve these purposes an appropriate approach should be selected. We take the same stance as James and Clarke; however, in recommending that truly reflective practitioners should operate at all three levels of reflection in order to examine and transform experience into learning that is meaningful for the individual, for practice and for the field alike. Nevertheless, we also recognise that being critically self-aware is an acquired skill that comes with experience and intellect, and that certain situations may only require a technical level of reflection, for example, when attempting to increase accountability to a client or profession. As a result of this, we advise that prior to engaging in reflective practice the *purpose for* and *method of* reflecting is thought about in a considered manner rather than blindly 'jumping on the bandwagon' and simply selecting the most available approach.

Given the understanding that reflective practice is complex and therefore a profoundly difficult thing to do, structured approaches to reflective practice are often advocated to facilitate the process (Johns, 2009). It is thought that such structure, be it formal (e.g., Johns' [2009] model for structured reflection) or informal (e.g., Rolfe et al.'s [2001] 'what, so what, now what' framework) allows for more systematic reflection, rather than the simple mulling over of an experience (Knowles et al., 2001). We propose, therefore, that structured frameworks have a positive impact on guiding people through a reflective journey towards reflective learning. Conversely, we warn against the dogmatic acceptance of approaches that may constrain the artistry of reflective practices and thus inhibit the learning that can potentially be elicited. In this sense, we agree with Anderson et al. (2004) who suggested that the practicalities of engaging in reflective practice should be flexible. Taking this into account, and building on the work of Telfer and Knowles (2009), we have provided a description of various approaches to reflective practice (see Table 1.1). These also offer an insight into how reflective practice may be captured as part of ongoing professional training and development. While it is appreciated that this is not an exhaustive list, and that the methods identified can take many different forms, it is thought that the range of options indicates the need for people to develop their own approach that may or may not be formed through a combination of those presented. By doing this we are empowered to direct our own reflective practices in a way that allows us to be more critical and move practice forward in a way that is personally significant, rather than becoming sanitized by the *norm*.

Table 1.1 Approaches to, and methods of capturing, reflective practice

Approach	Description
Journals	Written journals can be structured with specific frameworks and questions to guide the reflective writing process. This approach can help to make sense of the experience by examining the minutiae of the situation, offering a cathartic release through writing, and considering the symbiotic nature of the self, practice and context.
Mind maps	Provide a more visual representation of reflective practice through the construction of interrelated factors that may have shaped the experience. This approach can help to unpick the relational nature of practice and learning in order to make better sense of practice, self and context.
Visual sociology	The use of photographs, still video images and drawings can provide the focus and stimulation for reflective practice and reflective conversation. These images help to remind, represent and reconstruct experiences from which new meanings and understandings can be created.
Recorded narrative	The use of digital voice recording media can help to capture thoughts, feelings and behavioural outcomes both *in-action* and immediately post-action. Such procedures help to 'bank' these things for consideration at a later date.
Communities of practice	Reflecting with others in homogeneous groups in both a non-structured (conversational) or a structured (framework of questions) manner can help to generate creative and innovative thinking. This is done by adding new knowledge from different experiences and discussing the potential for the development of practice.
Reflective conversations	Usually focused and structured conversations with 'critical friends' that help to challenge self-perceptions by examining the 'how' and 'why' of practice. Conversations are designed to stimulate thought by adding new knowledge and exploring practice more critically through the use of interview techniques.

A guide to the chapters ahead

Having set out who we are and what we do by way of defining what reflective practice means to us, we now set out the position and structure of the book and how you might go about reading it. The book is designed to embrace and explore contemporary issues in reflective practice and considers the ways that reflective practice impacts upon applied practice, research methodology, learning in higher education and professional development. Contributions have been designed to challenge and contest, to offer innovative and critical perspectives, and to communicate differential points of engagement with reflective practice. The structure and aims embrace a grounded and pragmatic perspective allowing the dilemmas and challenges faced by reflective practitioners to be shared in a way that is practical and helpful.

Each chapter offers a distinct perspective on reflective practice. Contributors have been invited for their impact and contribution to developing reflective practice to date, their ability to stimulate applied debate and to encourage different thinking on applied research directions. At this point it is timely to thank them formally for their contributions. As editors we have thoroughly enjoyed working with all on this venture. The editors and contributors align in the view that there is much to be learned from practice in other disciplines and are deliberate in their inclusion of a multidisciplinary applied practice section and the perspectives of educators and students/supervisees to encourage readers to explore practice and expertise from 'less familiar' others. The book is structured in a way that allows contributors to present their views on reflective practice through a range of writing approaches. Chapters are free-flowing in design, although each will offer a short position statement with regard to definition and experiences with regard to reflective practice. Some tell stories from their own experiences, others compile their arguments through reference to draw from more traditional research-based data, and some express their ideas through reference to domains such as dance, poetry and drawing.

Part Two: Critical perspectives within reflective practice

The aim of this collection is to offer contemporary debate as to reflective practice from its historical and traditional origins to what we see in sport and exercise domains through widening application within, and for, a range of populations (i.e., coaches, sport psychologists, children). The contributions explore the value, ethical and practical considerations of reflective practice together with appraisal and comment to date on empirical evidence. Authors also provide suggestions for future research that will contribute to the notion that reflective practice 'works'. This section is designed, therefore, to offer perspectives, to contest, to advance critical debate and to progress knowledge in the field.

Part Three: Pedagogical approaches to reflective practice

Reflective practice is now an established mechanism within applied sport and exercise practice and is central to many areas of professional accreditation and training across disciplines such as sport psychology, sports physiology, exercise-based practice physiotherapy and sports coaching. This collection is written by authors with experience of designing, delivering, facilitating and evidencing reflective practice. Authors write and represent the perspectives of the educator and the student/ trainee practitioner and thus provide critical insights into 'both sides' of the educational process.

Part Four: Applied practice: reflective practice in action

Despite the global deployment of reflective practice in applied sport practice our understandings and appreciation of reflective practice processes are perhaps still formative. This section brings together ideas and experiences from a number of sports practitioners who have engaged with reflective practice in order to better understand themselves, to better understand others who they might work alongside, and to improve, ultimately, the ways they might deliver and, possibly, intervene.

Part Five: Reflecting forwards

A final chapter offers contemporary views and sketches out future directions appropriate to researchers, practitioners, educators and consumers of reflective practice. Here the editors set out to explore some of the dilemmas faced by those attempting to practise and utilize reflective practice in challenging real-world settings and to present new possibilities on the way reflective practice might be contextualized, presented and shared now and in the future.

Summary

This textbook aims to challenge both academic and practice-based audiences with regard to the utility, research and representation of reflective practice. We have introduced ourselves, our journeys and our position in terms of reflective practice. We have attempted to *set the scene* by considering the importance of reflective practice in the development of the knowledge required to improve the effectiveness of practice within the varied disciplines and professions of sport and exercise. We have suggested that in order to cope with the complex and often messy realities of learning and teaching, professional practice and sporting performance that reflective practice must form a fundamental aspect of what we do. Additionally, we have attempted to dispel a variety of myths surrounding the definition of and approaches to reflective practice. We acknowledge that a full discussion of many of the issues inherent within these areas goes beyond the scope of this section, and so we now hand over to our contributors to take matters forward through three sections across critical perspectives, pedagogical approaches and applied practice. However, we hope that by laying a foundation of our insights into reflective practice and situating it at the heart of professional practice we will ignite interest, further understanding and open the door for the diverse range of chapters to follow.

Part Two

Critical perspectives within reflective practice

2 Using reflective practice in the development of exercise-related interventions

Orla Flannery

Introduction

The increasing prevalence of diseases such as obesity, cardiovascular disease and type II diabetes (Health Survey for England [HSE], 2012; Department of Health [DH], 2011) has resulted in an increase in the demand for effective Public Health interventions. In relation to the above diseases, physical inactivity and sedentary behaviour have been identified as a contributory factor (Lee et al., 2012) with physical inactivity also recognised as the fourth leading cause of death worldwide (Kohl et al., 2012). As a result there is a need to understand how to develop and deliver effective exercise and physical activity interventions, as they have been identified as an important aspect of Public Health agendas to address a number of health issues (Lee et al., 2012). Conversely, the development of Public Health interventions is an issue of much debate. One of the key problems with Public Health interventions is the 'gap' between best practice and clinical care (Grol & Wensing, 2004; Leykum, Pugh, Lanham, Harmon & McDaniel, 2009; Watson, Dugdill, Murphy, Knowles & Cable, 2012), and a contributing factor to the gap is the challenge associated with the evaluation of interventions.

This chapter aims to firstly consider the use of reflective practice in the development of Public Health and exercise-related interventions; provide an overview of Public Health interventions in relation to exercise, physical activity and obesity; discuss current frameworks for evaluating complex interventions, including the MRC framework; consider the role of reflective learning in the developmental process, in order to allow aspects such as multi-professional working, intervention delivery and team effectiveness to be explored; focus on the 'how' interventions are delivered in order to contribute to the development of best practice interventions by using the views of staff and service users; consider reflective practice in the context of childhood obesity interventions and finally provide a summary of current practice and areas for future research.

Overview of Public Health interventions (exercise and obesity interventions)

In general the aim of Public Health interventions is to promote and protect the health of both the community and population (Rychetnik, Frommer, Hawe &

Shiell, 2002). The increase in the prevalence of long-term health conditions for which physical inactivity is a contributory factor (HSE, 2012; DH, 2011) has resulted in an increase in the demand for effective exercise and physical activity interventions. However, while the National Institute for Health and Clinical Excellence (NICE) (2006) has identified the need for evidenced-based interventions, there is a paucity of research on successful interventions in the UK (Hillsdon, Foster, Naidoo & Crombie, 2004). In the past few decades, exercise and physical activity interventions have become a key part of the remit for Public Health interventions (Heath et al., 2012). Public Health interventions should be regarded as complex interventions, and have been defined as interventions that contain a number of interacting components (Craig et al., 2008). According to Craig et al., complex interventions include the following: the amount of interacting components with an intervention; the amount and complexity of the behaviours that are required either by those who are delivering or receiving the interventions; the number of groups or organizational levels that are targeted by the intervention; the range and number of outcomes, and the degree of flexibility or tailoring within the intervention.

In the context of childhood obesity, the focus of this chapter, the challenges of the evaluation are inherent in the problem itself. Childhood obesity is regarded as a complex issue (Wyatt, Winters & Dubbert, 2006), as the causes and treatment are interchangeable and incorporate a wide range of factors including diet, physical activity, the environment and parents (DH, 2011; NICE, 2006). Thus, interventions developed to address childhood obesity are complex, and determining their success is dependent on a number of contributing factors, including the individual, type of intervention (e.g., individual, group, family), the environment and setting of the intervention (e.g., community, primary care), and the range of allied health professionals involved (e.g., GP, school nurses, dieticians, exercise professional). As a result the evidence of effective Public Health interventions (particularly in the context of childhood obesity) is deemed to be limited (Waters et al., 2011; Watson et al., 2012).

Evidence-based practice

Evidenced-based practice has been defined as an approach to problem-solving in clinical settings (McKibbon, 1998; Rosenburg & Donald, 1995). The development of evidence-based practice is deemed as crucial for effective health promotion (Berentson-Shaw & Price, 2007), and refers to the utilization of evaluation and research in the design, delivery and measurement of the impact that the intervention has had. There is a need to distinguish between evidence-based practice (EBP) and effective evidence (McKenna et al., 2004). While effective evidence may demonstrate whether an intervention has worked and achieved its aims, EBP tends to provide a more detailed overview of the intervention and the factors that may have supported or hindered its success. The main purpose of evaluation is to inform the decision-making process and the development of evidence, although the increasing demand for evaluation is due in part to funding agencies requiring accountability (Crone & Baker, 2009; Habicht, Victoria & Vaughn, 1999). Thus, evaluation has become a key aspect of Public Health, where without it, resources are wasted on unsuccessful interventions (Vaughn, 2004).

Evaluation frameworks

The development of Public Health interventions is widely debated, which is in part a reflection of the lack of consensus on 'how' to evaluate complex interventions. In 2000 the Medical Research Council (MRC) developed a framework for the evaluation of complex health interventions (Campbell et al., 2000; MRC, 2000) (see Figure 2.1). While recognizing the importance of randomized controlled trials (RCTs), the framework acknowledges the difficulty in evaluating interventions that require behaviour change or involve health promotion. The framework for complex interventions follows a phased approach and incorporates both qualitative and quantitative methodologies. The four phases in the approach range from preclinical to Phase IV and include theory, modelling, exploratory trial, definitive randomized control trial and long-term implementation. While Campbell et al. advocated the use of RCTs in terms of the development of 'gold standard' evidence, the framework illustrates the importance of evaluation in the developmental stages of an intervention.

However, since the publication of the MRC framework in 2000, a number of authors have questioned whether complex interventions can or should be standardized in order to adhere to the principles of RCTs (Hawe, Shiell & Riley, 2004; Seers, 2007; Watson et al., 2012). According to Hawe et al. (2004), the content of complex interventions should not be standardized, in order to allow for the development of an intervention which that can be tailored specifically to the target population and the needs of the local area. However, they maintain that the process and function of the complex intervention can and should be standardized (Hawe et al., 2004).

The MRC framework was revised to provide more suggestions for flexible use, and proposes that before a definitive trial can be carried out, researchers need to ensure they: define and understand the problem and its context; develop and understand the intervention; and develop an appropriate evaluation (MRC, 2008; Craig et al., 2008). Craig and colleagues purported that the revision was a result of a number of recent publications, which identified some limitations with the MRC framework in 2000. For example, in the context of Public Health, RCTs may lack external validity as a result of the environment created to minimize confounding factors to ensure internal validity (Habicht et al., 1999). Dugdill, Graham and McNair (2005) supported this notion where, in the context of physical activity interventions, they argued that RCTs may yield limited data as a result of failing to capture the complexities of physical activity behaviour. Furthermore, within a Public Health framework the causal chain between cause and effect is complicated as a result of the complex relationship between the agent and the outcome (Cesar, Habicht & Bryce, 2004). Patterson, Baarts, Launso and

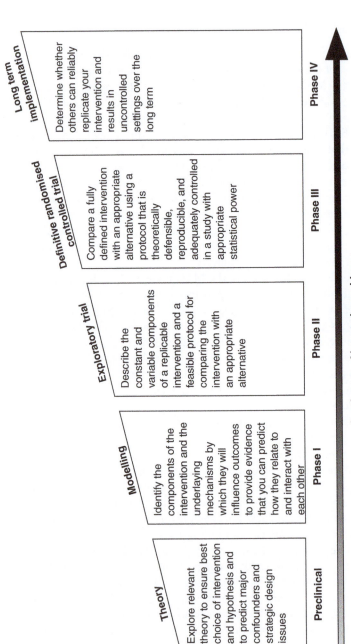

Figure 2.1 A framework for development and evaluation of RCTs for complex interventions to improve health (MRC, 2000) (Reproduced with permission of the Medical Research Council)

Verhoef (2009) argued that by just focusing on the 'outcomes' of an intervention, which tend to be quantitatively driven, important information such as the users' experience, contextual factors and the long-term benefits of the intervention are omitted. There is a need to explore other ways of evaluating Public Health interventions (Cesar et al., 2004), and McKenna, Cutliffe and McKenna (2000) suggest that a range of methodological approaches are needed. This is further supported by the World Health Organization [WHO] (2001) guidance for the evaluation of Public Health interventions, where the recommendations highlighted the importance of participatory approaches to evaluation; where the views of stakeholders and services users are captured; and a combination of process and outcome measures are used to evaluate all Public Health interventions.

Thus, the revised MRC framework (see Figure 2.2) reflects the recognition that in practice the evaluation of complex health interventions is not linear and is influenced by a wide variety of factors, including staff, setting, time and available tools (MRC, 2008; Campbell et al., 2008). For example, in the evaluation of an obesity intervention in the community, issues such as access to the intervention setting by local transport may impact on the adherence to an intervention, particularly in lower socio-economic areas (SES) areas, and this can be captured if the pilot stages of the intervention are evaluated. The revised MRC framework places a greater emphasis on 'process evaluation' and tailoring the intervention to the needs of the local area, thus highlighting that RCTs are not always appropriate.

Changing times: Health and Well-Being Boards and Public Health England

Recent changes to Public Health in the United Kingdom (UK) have heightened the need for developing effective interventions. The current White Paper *Healthy Lives, Healthy People* (DH, 2011) and the Health and Social Care Act (2012) (DH, 2012) require Public Health interventions to address the needs of the local community. This, in part, is a result of the recognition that gender, SES and the local environment are contributing factors in a number of Public Health issues, including obesity (DH, 2011). Health and Well-Being boards aim to provide a more 'integrative' and 'localized' service (DH, 2012). As a result there will be considerable change to the development and delivery of Public Health interventions, with a range of professionals required to come together to design and deliver services that address the needs of the local area. In the context of physical activity, the drive for collaborative working is a result of the need for financial accountability and a weak evidence base (Crone & Baker, 2009).

Collaborative working and multi-disciplinary teams

The advocacy of multi-disciplinary teamwork within the National Health Service [NHS] (DH, 2000), and indeed the recent changes to Public Health provision in

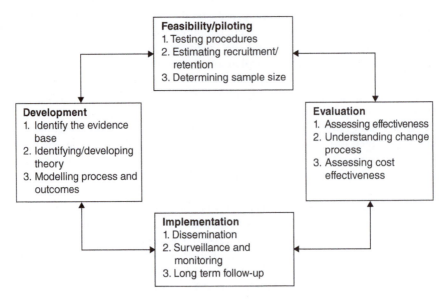

Figure 2.2   Key elements of the development and evaluation process (MRC, 2008)
(Reproduced with permission of the Medical Research Council)

the UK, have resulted in the requirement of collaborative working (DH, 2012) and have contributed to the impetus for the adoption of reflective practice. In general, the literature supports multi-disciplinary teamwork, as it is regarded as an important aspect to current healthcare in the UK (Atwal & Caldwell, 2006). Xyrichis and Lowton (2008) suggest that it is needed in order to improve the health of the population and improve service effectiveness, but, despite this recognition, it is not always achieved. These authors' review of the literature indicated that there are a number of barriers that hamper its potential, including team size and composition, team meetings, organizational support, and clear goals and objectives (Xyrichis & Lowton, 2008).

In the context of childhood obesity, multi-disciplinary teamwork is advocated as a key element of intervention design and delivery (NICE, 2006). Interventions that include dieticians, exercise professionals, GPs and behavioural therapists have been advocated (NICE, 2006; Nowicka, 2005). However, such a wide range of professionals will have very different views about the causes and treatment of childhood obesity, and they will also use a variety of methods to facilitate weight loss. Thus, ensuring that the multi-disciplinary team has a coherent approach to the intervention is crucial for long-term success. While there is generally a paucity of guidance on how it should be done, the use of reflective practice and participatory action research [PAR], when used alongside RCT design, can result in an approach that highlights the complexity of healthcare organizations and the need to understand the processes involved in intervention delivery (Leykum et al., 2009).

Heneghan, Wright and Watson (2013) have explored group reflective practice in a clinical setting, and their findings have particular significance given the changes to Public Health in the UK and the need for multi-disciplinary team-work. These authors' findings indicated that group reflective practice was ben-eficial particularly in terms of teamwork and staff well-being. However, there were a number of challenges to reflective practice, including engagement and a lack of management. Further research is needed to understand how groups work together, and there is a need to understand how groups can use reflective practice to inform practice (Heneghan et al., 2013).

The successful delivery of Public Health interventions for obesity and physical activity requires an understanding of the views of both health professionals and service users in order to understand the facilitators and barriers for effective ser-vice delivery. The use of a qualitative methodology would allow for the collection of these issues (WHO, 2001). Information gained through this process can pro-vide a valuable insight into the success or failure of an intervention (Livingstone et al., 2006). The use of a mixed-method approach (qualitative and quantitative data) was advocated for the evaluation of complex interventions (Dugdill et al., 2005; WHO, 2001).

Reflective practice and participatory research in health interventions

Reflective practice means creating a learning situation and ensuring that the 'learning outcome is a combination of previous experience, specific contexts and the theory that guided practice' (Peden-McAlpine et al., 2005, p. 49). Fleming (2006) outlined reflection as the process involved in gaining a greater understanding of specific issues, as a result of analyzing and generating new knowledge. There is an established recognition and indeed requirement in Public Health to obtain the views of the service user and provider in order to tailor the intervention to the needs of the local community (DH, 2000). In addition, it is expected as part of continuous professional development (Jaya-tilleke & Mackie, 2012). Jayatilleke and Mackie (2012) found that although there is no definitive model used for reflective practice in Public Health, the evidence indicates that it can improve practice. A number of models have been developed over the years for reflective practice, including those by Gibbs (1988) and Johns (1995). Fleming (2006) (see Figure 2.3) developed a typology for reflective practice in health promotion, which focuses on three domains: (a) the role of the self which includes the individual and teams; (b) the context of programme planning, which refers to the influence of the wider environment, including political, environmental and socio-economic fac-tors; and (c) issues relating to the processes and planning of interventions. Furthermore, it also highlights how reflection can occur, pre-, during and post-intervention.

Fleming (2006) highlighted that there are a number of barriers to reflection, which include motivation, time and lack of support. However, the benefits to practice and indeed the individual should outweigh these barriers. Using reflec-tive practice has been shown to improve care and practice in nursing, where Peden-McAlpine et al. (2005) explored the effectiveness of reflective practice

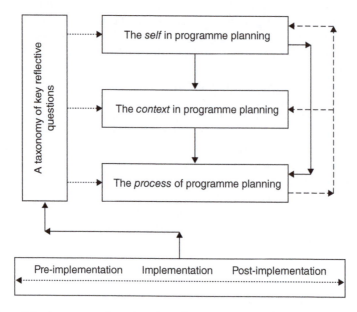

Figure 2.3 A conceptual typology for reflective practice in health promotion planning

interventions in family care. Their study with eight practice nurses involved in pediatric care revealed that reflective practice interventions gave rise to double-loop learning, which resulted in a change in attitudes and led to an improvement in relationships with families and an improvement in care with families.

Benefits of reflective practice and Participatory Action Research

There is a growing body of evidence that highlights the importance of using reflective practice for the duration of the intervention. As highlighted in the revised MRC framework, piloting and evaluation at each stage of the intervention are crucial for an effective intervention. Using reflective practice as part of this process will help identify the barriers and facilitators to service provision. De Silva-Sanigorski et al. (2012) conducted a process and impact evaluation of ROMP and CHOMP, an obesity prevention intervention in a pre-school setting in Australia. As a result of the process evaluation, a number of important findings were identified in relation to the delivery and challenges of implementing a preventive intervention. For example, determining the impact of an intervention is challenging when it is delivered as part of a wider health promotion scheme in terms of establishing what caused the effect. Watson et al. (2012) outlined how the use of reflective practice in the development and evaluation of GOALS, a childhood obesity intervention, was important in order to bridge the gap between research and practice. In particular, they highlighted the importance of the 'feedback loop' for the continuous development of an effective intervention. Jagosh et al. (2012) reported that PAR can increase recruitment to interventions, increase capacity over time, increase the sustainability of projects beyond funding, help change the systems, and potentially lead to the development of new interventions. Two practical examples of how reflective practice can be used to improve intervention design and delivery are outlined below.

Case study 1: Fit4Fun: a family intervention for childhood obesity

Outline of project

Fit4Fun was developed as a family-based intervention for obese children in Wigan. Based on the principles outlined by NICE (2006), the intervention targets children and their parents, and focuses on nutrition, physical activity and behaviour change. The aim of the intervention is to support families to make changes to their lifestyle, and provides parents and children with support in making changes to their diet and physical activity levels. The intervention runs for 12 weeks, and parents and children attend for 2 hours once a week.

Reflection as a continuous process

The intervention was evaluated as part of a PhD thesis from 2005 to 2008 (Flannery, 2009). The intervention delivery team, which consisted of a psychologist, dietician and physical activity coordinator, met formally on a regular basis to discuss the development and delivery of the intervention. However, staff involved in the delivery of the intervention also reflected immediately post the delivery of the weekly sessions, to discuss any issues that may have occurred and what worked well. In addition, meetings were held quarterly with stakeholders (e.g., school nurses, dieticians, pediatricians) to discuss the intervention. Focus groups were conducted with staff, parents and children pre-, mid- and post-intervention, which highlighted the 'process' and in particular the barriers and facilitators of the intervention. Throughout the meetings, staff were asked to reflect on the issues affecting the delivery of the intervention. The evaluation results from the PhD thesis (e.g., the focus groups with parents) were provided for discussion during these meetings.

Outcomes of evaluation

Outlined below are examples of the findings that emerged as part of the reflective process. These key issues were identified by staff and service users, which were addressed in subsequent cohorts of the intervention.

> **Referral**: *Issue*: Staff and parents reported that referral on to the intervention was inconsistent across the Borough.
> *Action*: Relaunch event to a wide range of health professionals to promote the programme, including radio and newspaper advertising.

Content: *Issue*: Parents and staff identified a need for more practical content. *Action*: More cookery demonstrations, parents involved in activity sessions.
Setting: *Issue*: Parents were uncomfortable when the intervention was delivered in a commercial gym setting.
Action: Intervention was delivered in a community setting (e.g., school, local leisure centre).
Delivery: *Issue*: Parents reported that they would like to participate in the physical activity session with the children.
Action: Piloted a 12-week intervention where parents participated in all the activity sessions with the children.

Application to practice

Data from Fit4Fun indicated that continuous reflective practice (both informal and formal) including participatory action research is crucial to developing effective obesity interventions. Ensuring this is a continuous process helps ensure long-term success as barriers to the delivery of the intervention can be dealt with in a timely manner.

Case study 2: LEAP4Life (Learn Eat and Play)

Outline of project

Leap4Life was developed as a family- and community-based healthy lifestyle intervention for children (under the age of 5) and their families in Tameside. The pilot study was developed in 2010/2011 in response to the increasing prevalence of obesity and oral health issues in the area.

Intervention development

The intervention brought together a range of community-based professionals to deliver a healthy lifestyle intervention. The aim of LEAP4Life was to support and empower families with children under the age of 5 to promote healthy eating, good oral health and active play, and promote healthy weight for children and improve long-term health. The pilot study was initially rolled out to eight families.

Reflection as a continuous process

The aim of the pilot study was to establish the feasibility of Leap4Life as part of a wider remit of weight management services. Regular team meetings were established to develop the intervention. Throughout this process staff from a range of organizations met regularly to develop the key elements of the intervention. Focus groups were conducted with the staff post-delivery of the pilot to establish the main facilitators and barriers to effective delivery of the intervention.

Outcomes of evaluation

Staff support: *Issue*: Staff reported that delivery of the intervention by only one member of staff was too challenging.
Action: Future programme ensured two members of staff were involved in the delivery.
Referral: *Issue*: Staff reported that they were not involved in the recruitment of participants, and this affected the initial relationship with parents. They felt it was important to have established a relationship prior to the start of the intervention.
Action: Future programme involved the delivery team in the recruitment of participants to the intervention.

Application to practice

While the pilot was only delivered to a small number of families, the reflective process highlighted a number of key issues that were addressed in the roll-out of the main programme.

Conclusion and implications for practice

The aim of this chapter was to explore the use of reflective practice in the development of Public Health interventions. The increase in prevalence of long-term health conditions has led to the subsequent need for effective Public Health interventions. In addition, recent changes to the delivery of Public Health in the UK have resulted in the development of multi-disciplinary teams who will be tasked with developing and delivering effective interventions that address the needs of the local area. Furthermore, the need for financial accountability will only add to the pressure to develop effective interventions, in order to ensure that resources are used effectively.

While it is recognised that RCTs are the gold standard in terms of evidence, their use in a Public Health context is not always appropriate. The use of reflective practice, particularly within the early stages of intervention design, is crucial in order to develop effective interventions both in the short and long term. Two different case studies have demonstrated that reflective practice is crucial throughout the intervention cycle, but particularly in the early stages, as it can help identify the factors that may hinder or facilitate successful delivery. Reflective practice can highlight a number of issues around the delivery of an intervention, including settings, staff skills, lack of knowledge and confidence of delivery staff, which, if addressed, may lead to more effective use of time and resources. Practitioners should ensure that they allocate a sufficient amount of time for reflective practice in order to improve practice and help develop a greater evidence base of Public Health interventions.

3 Where's the evidence?

A review of empirical reflective practice research within sport

Gareth Picknell, Brendan Cropley,
Sheldon Hanton and Stephen Mellalieu

Introduction

The importance of reflective learning is frequently noted in the professional development literature, with reflective capacity being regarded by many as an essential characteristic for developing individuals' expertise within a variety of fields (e.g., Newman, 1999; Mann, Gordon & MacLeod, 2009). The relationship between reflection and expertise stems from Schön's (1983) influential work within the education literature, where he noted that practitioners make judgements and decisions based largely on *knowledge-in-action* (otherwise referred to as *tacit* knowledge). According to Schön, this knowledge-in-action is acquired from the practice settings that professionals operate in, whereby the simple application of theory may be insufficient for effective practice. Further, Schön contended that knowledge-in-action, while an automatic feature of repetitive and stable professional practice, is developmental insofar as practitioners are cognizant of the complex nature of human interactions that present unusual phenomena (i.e., unexpected problems or unexplained outcomes), which may not always fit within the boundaries of what has come to be viewed as 'normal'. Accordingly, practitioners are able to develop their knowledge-in-action, or *professional artistry*, from their diverse range of practical experiences following engagement with two distinct learning processes referred to as: *reflection-in-action* (takes place during the situation) and *reflection-on-action* (takes place following the completion of an event).

As a result of Schön's (1983) initial work, and subsequent support from various domains, reflective practice has received increased interest within the sport and exercise domain over the past decade (see Cropley & Hanton, 2011; Cushion, Nelson, Lyle, Jones, Sandford & O'Callaghan, 2010). Indeed, the acceptance of reflective practice within sport and exercise has evolved as a result of two significant concerns: (a) the professionalization, and increased accountability of sport practitioners (e.g., sport scientists, coaches); and (b) criticisms that formal education programmes and professional body-endorsed qualifications underprepare practitioners for the complexities of operating in real-world sporting environments. Whilst promising, the inclusion of reflective principles as a means of generating professional knowledge and learning from experiences is currently primarily grounded on theoretical debate and anecdotal accounts (Cropley &

Hanton, 2011). This has resulted in a paradox for advocates who contend that reflective practice 'should work', based on logical theoretical reasoning, yet are unable to conclusively demonstrate whether it 'actually works', with empirically supportive evidence.

Similar concerns have been noted previously within other domains, including nurse education (e.g., Peden-McAlpine, Tomlinson, Forneris, Genck & Meiers, 2005), medical professions (e.g., Mamede, Schmidt & Penaforte, 2008) and health sciences (e.g., Mann et al., 2009). In these fields, the paucity of empirical evidence regarding the usefulness of reflective practice resulted in scholars exploring various experimental research programmes, their intention being to contribute to the advancement of an evidence base that aimed to increase professionals' confidence and adoption of reflective principles into education programmes and practices. Such developments addressed Newman's (1999) concerns regarding accepting the values of reflective approaches without questioning the evidence upon which claims are made. Whilst the sport and exercise domain has made progress towards developing an empirically validated evidence base, with research identified in the coaching (Knowles, Gilbourne, Borrie & Neville, 2001), applied sport psychology (Cropley, Hanton, Miles & Niven, 2013) and athletic development literature (Jonker, Elferink-Gemser, de Roos & Visscher, 2012), more is needed to understand the role of reflective practice in developing professionals' reflective skills, and whether these enhanced skills result in positive changes to practice.

To provoke thought among researchers and practitioners as to increasing the value of reflective practice within the applied disciplines of sport and exercise this chapter will be divided into two main sections. The first section will consider the purported benefits of reflective learning, developing reflective skills and becoming a reflective practitioner based on empirical research within the wider literature. The second section will address limitations that presently exist within sport and exercise, using studies from other domains to unearth future research avenues for furthering our understanding of reflective practice. In doing so, it is hoped that progress can be made within the sport and exercise domain towards developing an empirical evidence base that facilitates practitioners' confidence, acceptance and adoption of reflective practice as part of their everyday professional activities.

Reflective practice: an empirical research review

The intuitive appeal of reflective practice, with its proposed benefits for practitioners in a range of domains, has resulted in researchers attempting to understand how its principles can be integrated into education programmes and ongoing professional practice. However, in line with the limitations identified within the sport and exercise domain (see Cropley & Hanton, 2011), there continues to be a paucity of empirical evidence examining whether reflective practice actually works (Duke & Appleton, 2000; Mann et al., 2009; Peden-McAlpine et al., 2005). To overcome this lack of experimental research, preliminary programmes have been developed with the intention of reviewing whether reflective practice interventions are able to 'bridge the gap' between discipline-specific abstract theory content and the particulars of unique and complex situations in professional practice settings (Forneris & Peden-McAlpine, 2006).

Research examining the efficacy of reflective practice interventions can be grouped into two broad categories: (a) *process-oriented* and (b) *outcome-oriented*. Process-oriented investigations are concerned with the development of reflective skills among participants following their involvement on education programmes which involve activities designed to provoke reflective thinking (e.g., Duke & Appleton, 2000; Sobral, 2000). The intention of this broad research is based on the assumption that enhanced reflexivity will ultimately improve professional practice. Research designs have employed both qualitative and quantitative methods to determine alterations of the levels at which individuals are able to reflect or their self-perceived use of reflective thought. Duke and Appleton's (2000) research is recognised as the first to quantitatively investigate the development of reflective capabilities within the health sciences, and assessed the changes in levels of student nurses' reflective skills over the course of an academic year. Levels of reflective skills were gauged following the authors' development of a marking grid, adapted from the extant literature (e.g., Wong, Kember, Chung & Yan, 1995), which was subsequently used while assessing reflective-based coursework. The findings provided some initial support for the notion that reflection is developmental (cf., Mann et al., 2009), as enhanced reflective skills linked to the description and analysis of practice, as well as the synthesis of relationships between theory and practice were evident.

The notion of development within reflective skills was further supported by Sobral (2000) who studied medical students' appraisals of self-reflection in learning following their involvement in a study skills course. The research design was deemed more rigorous than Duke and Appleton's (2000) as a control group of individuals not enrolled on the study skills course, and thus not exposed to the reflective practice intervention, was used to compare pre- and post-test appraisals of self-reflection. While both groups were considered homogenous with respect to their initial self-reflection appraisals, a significant difference was noted between the experimental group pre- and post-intervention scores, whereas the control group scores remained similar over the same time frame. To elucidate the positive relationship between the education programme and its impact on the use of reflective practice by students, key features of the course that encouraged and developed reflections included: (a) self-appraisal of current learning practices and outcomes; (b) discussion of learning strategies with peers and allowing learners to come to decisions by themselves; and (c) constructive feedback linked to learning goals and inviting learners to monitor their progress. Sceptics may argue that such a structured programme for promoting reflective practice could result in reflections that are not spontaneous, but deliberately stimulated by the educational context (Edwards & Thomas, 2010). Indeed, this approach has received criticism within the pedagogical literature, whereby researchers emphasize that forcing reflective practice raises unavoidable moral and practical issues including strategic, rather than open and honest responses (Hobbs, 2007). Although it seems likely that events occurring naturally in an authentic professional context would stimulate similar responses to those outlined in the available literature, further investigation is needed to demonstrate this.

These studies, although few in number, support the view that reflective skills may develop in association with certain interventions (Mann et al., 2009). It also appears that the development of reflective skills may be related to other aspects of learning and professional development. Indeed, Sobral (2000) identified positive associations between self-reflection and perceived competence for self-directed learning, and meaningfulness of the learning experiences encountered. However, without further investigation it is difficult to deduce the association of these purported relationships. In addition, limited research within the process-oriented research category has incorporated a comparison group for determining differential influences of reflective practice interventions on reflective ability. In light of this limitation within the wider reflective practice literature, the transferability of the interventions and results into the domain of sport and exercise is unclear.

Outcome-oriented research typically examines reflective principles as independent variables and their impact on discipline specific outcome measures (e.g., Mamede, Schmidt & Penaforte, 2008; Mamede, van Gog, van den Berge, van Saase, van Guldener & Schmidt, 2010; Peden-McAlpine et al., 2005). This area of research has been of particular interest to researchers in domains where decisions can be classified as either correct/accurate or incorrect/inaccurate, with limited margins of error (i.e., diagnostic accuracy by medical practitioners). The purpose of this type of research has been to raise practitioners' confidence in using reflective practice, by highlighting the relationship between reflective reasoning and enhanced professional practice competencies. Mamede et al. (2008) and Mamede et al. (2010) attempted to illustrate this relationship by examining whether medical students' diagnostic accuracy could be enhanced following reflective reasoning. Both studies reported that when confronted with complex medical cases, reflective reasoning facilitated the probability of accurate diagnoses. Indeed, Mamede et al. (2008) reported that while there were no significant differences for accuracy of diagnosing simple cases following non-analytical (automatic) and analytical (reflective) reasoning ($p < 0.05$), accuracy for diagnosing complex cases significantly increased by 200% ($p > 0.05$) when participants used reflective practice. In addition, reflecting on complex cases appeared to counteract the potential negative consequences of automatic reasoning, namely *availability bias* (overestimation of the likelihood of a correct decision based on the ease with which it comes to mind; Mamede et al., 2010), that has been recognised as a developmental artefact associated with expertise (Ericsson, 2003).

While promising, such research within the medical sciences literature does have its limitations. Specifically, studies have recruited medical students from the clinical training element of formal education programmes, with the rationale for using this cohort being two-fold. First, novice practitioners are unlikely to be contaminated by the pressures of real-world practice, and thus, are more likely to be open-minded regarding the inclusion of reflective practice as part of their decision-making process (Mamede et al., 2010). Second, it is recognised that diagnostic errors are inevitable, although more likely to occur during initial training, and thus learning strategies that attempt to minimize or reduce these errors at the outset of career initiation have warranted further investigation. Taken together, researchers have agreed that owing to the highly cognitive nature of early career practice (Ericsson, 2003), and the analytical approach to dealing with unfamiliar scenarios that reflective practice affords, calls for the initial empirical evidence base within the medical and health sciences to be developed with trainee clinicians are appropriate. This is not surprising, or at odds with that of other professional domains, including sports coaching, when considering the discontent many have with education programmes that leave novice practitioners underprepared for the realities of professional practice (Cassidy, Jones & Potrac, 2009). It seems logical, therefore, that strategies incorporated into education programmes aimed at enhancing experiential learning opportunities of novice practitioners should be developed on evidence obtained from individuals engaged with their early professional training. However, focusing solely on neophyte practitioners has led to questions regarding the potential extrapolation of beneficial outcomes of reflective practice for those professionals already operating in their field.

Peden-McAlpine and colleagues (2005) provided some evidence of the value of reflective practice for professionals already operating in their fields of work. The research examined whether incorporating elements of reflective practice into participants' ongoing professional development would promote a shift in attitude and behaviours regarding the inclusion of family interventions into critical-care practices. Participants had an average of 13 years of critical-care experience, so one would perhaps assume that much of their practical work was driven by automatic reasoning associated with the development of expertise over a prolonged number of years (cf., Ericsson, 2003). Following participants' involvement in a reflective practice intervention, three interrelated themes emerged, which were indicative of the learning outcomes achieved: (a) acknowledging and reframing preconceived ideas about practice; (b) recognizing theirs and others emotions associated with their practice; and (c) incorporation of new ideas and initiatives into their practice. This acceptance and initiation of new practice ideas is akin to Gibbs' (1988) cyclical model of reflection, which suggests that individuals orient themselves for future action following the acquisition of knowledge and learning through systematic and critical thought processes. Indeed, the few available studies within the outcome-oriented research category support this contention, in that the learning opportunities that reflective practice affords not only generate new, but also activate existing, knowledge and understanding from experiences (Mamede et al., 2010). Thus, it is the assimilation of newly constructed knowledge into existing memory schemas that promotes alternative and more favourable outcomes regarding future practice decisions.

In summary, the available literature outside of the sport and exercise domain provides empirical evidence that reflective practice is a fruitful experiential learning strategy for practitioners. Indeed, a glance at this work shows support of the benefits proposed in the sport and exercise literature through theoretical debates and anecdotal accounts, which in turn should enhance researchers' and practitioners' confidence for justifying their inclusion of reflective practice. This conclusion derives from two categories of research that have: (a) examined the influence of reflective practice for developing reflective skills and levels at which individuals are able to reflect, and (b) investigated the influence of reflective practice on outcome measures that provide insight into practitioners' decisions and behaviours.

Future research directions for sport and exercise

Having reviewed the developing evidence base within the wider literature this section offers directions for future research to enhance sport and exercise practitioners' confidence for adopting reflective practices. In doing so, we hope to address concerns about the dominance of anecdotal accounts for promoting the benefits of reflective practice in a domain that traditionally prides itself on rigorous scientific inquiry (Knowles, Gilbourne, Tomlinson & Anderson, 2007). The proceeding discussion regarding potential research avenues within the field of sport and exercise science can be categorized into three main areas: (a) examining the development of reflective skills; (b) links between reflective skills and service delivery changes; and (c) impact of enhanced reflexivity on client-support programmes.

Development of reflective skills

The general consensus within the extant sport and exercise literature is that reflective practice is a highly skilled activity that can be developed over time (Cropley & Hanton, 2011; Cushion et al., 2010; Knowles et al., 2001; Mann et al., 2009). In light of this, the lack of research examining the measurement of reflective skills following a reflective practice intervention is of concern. This is particularly so when considering the exhaustive efforts made within the sport and exercise domain to understand the developmental nature of other cognitive skills following interventions that incorporate various psychological techniques (cf., Mellalieu & Hanton, 2008). The notable exceptions of evidence that exists within the sport and exercise domain (e.g., Cropley et al., 2013; Knowles et al., 2001) have assessed participants' reflective skills following their involvement in educational programmes including reflective processes. In both studies the level at which individuals could reflect were determined by qualitative techniques (i.e., visual inspection, content analysis), which dominate the examination of reflective practice within the literature.

However, such approaches have two key limitations for convincing the domain about the usefulness of developing reflective skills. First, while qualitative research designs have been encouraged in the sport and exercise domain, Smith and Sparkes (2009) warned that this should not be at the expense *of*, but rather in conjunction *with*, quantitative methods in order to allow for elaboration of certain issues and stimulating further thought on the topic under investigation.

To the authors' knowledge there is currently no psychometric assessment tool available within the sport and exercise domain that provides an insight into levels at which individuals are able to reflect. However, as with other conceptual developments within the domain (see Fletcher, Hanton & Mellalieu, 2006), it may be difficult to make significant advances in sports practitioners' understanding, and build on the body of knowledge regarding reflective practice, without valid and reliable measures.

Second, relying predominantly on qualitative research designs may constrain the generalizability of findings without the scrutiny that control groups afford for demonstrating the impact of interventions on dependent variables under investigation (Weinberg & Comar, 1994). Cropley et al. (2013) attempted to overcome this issue by utilizing a single-subject multiple-baseline design, where in essence, participants act as their own control, so that any observed changes to behaviour were attributable to the reflective practice intervention and not other extraneous factors. This research design has previously been labelled as an *effectiveness method* and is considered useful for evaluating practice (Anderson, Miles, Mahoney & Robinson, 2002). However, Anderson et al. (2002) argued that *evaluation of practice* designs should be balanced with *evaluation research* that utilizes experimental methods (e.g., control groups) with the intention of enhancing the domain's confidence regarding cause-and-effect relationships between support programmes (i.e., reflective practice interventions) and measurable outcomes (i.e., enhanced reflective skills).

Efforts to overcome these limitations have been made within the medical sciences by comparing differences between an experimental (thus 'exposed' to a reflective intervention) and control (not exposed to the reflective intervention) groups' self-appraisal of reflection using a questionnaire that assessed individuals' reflective levels (e.g., Sobral, 2000). While the characteristics of the control group in Sobral's study were open to criticisms relating to placebo effects and the questionnaire not being previously exposed to rigorous psychometric testing, the study has been commended for adding to the already existing observational, anecdotal and analytical research relating to reflective practice. Without this type of research the transferability of interventions and findings of reflective practice across contexts will remain limited (Mann et al., 2009).

The relationship between reflective skills and practice

Effective reflective practice has been conceptualized as a purposeful learning activity that results in positive changes to practice (cf. Cropley & Hanton, 2011). As such, while the development of reflective skills allows for more advanced, critical levels of reflecting-in and reflecting-on action, unless the purpose of achieving these higher skills (e.g., critical thinking and problem-solving) is to enhance practitioner effectiveness, attempts to convince the sport and exercise domain to 'buy in' to the benefits of reflective practice will remain futile. Future research needs to examine the relationship between enhanced reflective skills and outcome measures that indicate change and improved effectiveness. Knowles and Saxton (2010) specified that change could be represented by three aspects of practice: (a) changes in values, beliefs or behaviours; (b) confirmation or rejection of particular theories or practices; and/or (c) changes in knowledge of the self, the context of practice or the environment in which individuals operate.

Numerous anecdotal accounts exist within the coaching (e.g., Peel, Cropley, Hanton & Fleming, 2013) and applied sport psychology (e.g., Tod & Bond, 2010) literature regarding the evolution of professional philosophies following engagement with reflective practice. A common feature within this literature is the enhanced sense of self-awareness and adoption of alternative approaches as a result of altered values, beliefs or behaviours that reflect practitioners' attempts to align what they do in practice with their professional philosophy. Indeed, developing such professional congruence is regarded as a critical feature of effective practice (Poczwardowski, Sherman & Ravizza, 2004) yet presently, there remains a dearth of empirical evidence to support these contentions. Further, the research that has employed experimental designs (e.g., single-subject multiple-baseline) has failed to provide tangible quantitative evidence regarding the beneficial outcomes of achieving higher levels of reflective skills (Cropley et al., 2013). Cropley and colleagues noted that while social validation interviews provided insights into practitioners' perceptions regarding improvements to their practice, changes in quantitative measures were not statistically significant from pre- to post-intervention. However, despite this constraint, the quantitative element of this study should be commended as a refreshing addition to the reflective practice literature in sport and exercise.

Researchers and practitioners interested in the relationship between reflective skills and changes to practice are directed to the medical profession literature where empirical evidence exists from carefully considered qualitative and quantitative experimental methods (see Mamede et al., 2010; Peden-McAlpine et al., 2004). For example, Peden-McAlpine and colleagues employed a phenomenological research approach to provide evidence that enhanced reflexivity resulted in nursing actions that aligned their values and beliefs with those of families they encountered, creating a more caring environment in the intensive-care unit. Additionally, Mamede and colleagues noted improved accuracy of diagnostic decision-making following reflective reasoning. Taken together these studies provide evidence of changes to practice and support the contentions reported in the social validation element of Cropley et al.'s (2013) research. The dilemma for researchers in the sport and exercise domain is how to measure and report improved outcomes of reflective processes objectively given the multidimensional nature and complexity of applied practice contexts. For example, Richards, Collins and Mascarenhas (2012) reported findings regarding the development of mental models of coaches as an outcome measure, yet the information from which conclusions were drawn is vague and ambiguous for the reader in that no evidence is presented to illustrate the nature of change to coaches' thought processes. We acknowledge that other professions may be better suited to determining effectiveness of practice objectively using outcome measures (e.g., decisions), as these are typically categorized as either correct or incorrect with little room for error, and therefore changes to practice can be considered conclusive. Indeed, Martindale and Collins (2007) raised concerns that such evaluation models may be difficult to develop in sport, but that this predicament should not restrain future exploration of their potential. Until such changes to practice following the development of reflective skills are examined with experimental research methods, scepticism regarding the usefulness of reflective practice may well remain.

Reflexivity and client-support programmes

Recently, the sport and exercise domain has outlined the potential for reflective practice to facilitate practitioners' adoption of client-centred approaches (see Cropley & Hanton, 2011). Such approaches are grounded in humanism where the recipients of support services are encouraged to develop their self-awareness to better perceive their ability to control thoughts, emotions, decisions and behaviours. The premise that enhanced reflexivity may benefit the client is of particular interest to practitioners within the domain when considering Hardy, Jones and Gould's (1996) viewpoint that effective procedures for providing athletic support should be prioritized. Initial evidence for incorporating reflective practice into support services indicates the potential for enhancing self-efficacy and managing competitive anxiety (Hanton, Cropley & Lee, 2009), maintaining effort (Hanrahan, Pedro & Cerin, 2009) and empowering self-regulated learning (Jonker et al., 2012). While encouraging, limitations of these studies include a lack of insight into researchers' attempts to develop reflective skills, and the likelihood that participants received appropriate support from suitably trained reflective practitioners, without which conclusions regarding whether participants' thought processes were indicative of critical reflection remains limited. This research within the sport and exercise domain should, however, be commended for leading the way in considering the contributions of reflective practice for benefiting clients. Indeed, most of the empirical research across domains has lauded reflective practice for enhancing practitioners' effectiveness. Yet, in line with Hardy et al. (1996), we contend that for reflective practice to be truly valued as a worthwhile contribution to the development of sport and exercise the advantages that it offers recipients of support services, whether through enhanced satisfaction, or facilitating positive performance changes, should be of paramount concern for researchers' and practitioners' future endeavours.

Concluding remarks

This chapter has reviewed the empirical evidence that exists for reflective practice in the sport and exercise domain. Given the limited experimental designs within sport and exercise, literature searches from other domains were conducted in order to explore and evaluate how these professions have utilised numerous research programmes to cultivate an evidence base that encourages practitioners to adopt reflective practice as part of their effectiveness endeavours. In doing so, we have identified three general research foci that we believe will build on the body of reflective practice knowledge that exists within the sport and exercise domain. These include: (a) examining the developmental nature of reflective skills; (b) determining the relationship between reflective skills and practitioner effectiveness measures; and (c) investigating the impact of enhanced reflexivity on clients receiving support services. Previous literature reviews have offered more global future directions that attempt to provide researchers with direction about *what* should be investigated – for example, whether reflective practice should be conducted in isolation or through shared reflections with others (e.g., Knowles et al., 2001), who should undertake reflective practice (i.e., neophyte trainees and/or experienced practitioners; e.g., Friesen & Orlick, 2010), and the modes of reflective activity (i.e., reflective writing) for effectively generating knowledge and learning from experiences (Knowles et al., 2007). It is not our intention to dismiss these suggestions, as there is indeed much to learn about reflective practice. Instead, we have provided suggestions about *how* researchers may attempt to develop an empirical evidence base that supports or challenges the abundant beneficial claims that exist within the sport and exercise literature based on anecdotal accounts and theoretical debate. In doing so, researchers within the domain will overcome Newman's (1999) concerns about adopting reflective practice without questioning the evidence that assertions are based, and can be more confident in the notion that reflective practice actually works.

4 Reflecting forward

Exploring reflective methodologies with and for children

Lorna Porcellato and Zoe Knowles

Introduction

Research *with* and *for* children is becoming increasingly accepting of the children's world as a legitimate, lived reality, and yet also accepts the significance of constant change and growth that occurs in childhood (Shaw, 1996). Children are now recognised as 'active agents' who are 'experts in their own lives' and have valid views that are worthy of being heard and acted upon (O'Kane, 2008). This reconceptualization of childhood was inspired by policy changes at both national (UK Children Act, 1989) and international level (United Nations Convention on the Rights of the Child, 1989), which acknowledged children's rights and led to the evolution of innovative child-friendly approaches that facilitate listening and actively engage children in the research process (Alderson, 2001; Alderson & Morrow, 2011).

Despite this recognition, there is still an under-representation of children's voices to be both heard and represented in sport and exercise science research. In a bid to redress this deficit, the authors of this chapter were brought together via a mutual interest in child health – Porcellato via health promotion and school-based research (e.g., Porcellato, Dugdill & Springett, 2002; 2005), and Knowles by way of the role of active play and its psychological and physiological benefits for children (e.g., Boddy, Knowles, Davies, Warburton, Houghton, Mackintosh & Fairclough, 2012; Knowles, Parnell, Ridgers & Stratton, 2013), to explore the use of reflective methodologies with and for children.

Many of the 'child-centred' methodologies used in health research or educational pedagogies develop a child's understanding and critical thinking skills and allow children to consider why and how they do what they do. Although this process simulates what we may recognise as reflective practice, it is not conceptually embedded within the evidence base as 'reflection'. This chapter aims to consider the practicalities of using reflective methodologies with children by considering, firstly, if children can be reflective, and secondly, how can reflective practice be integrated into sport and exercise science-based research with children?

For some time researchers in the sport and exercise science domain have commented on the role of reflective practice as being essential for the self-awareness, development and effectiveness of the practitioner (e.g., Cropley, Hanton, Miles & Niven, 2010; Knowles, Gilbourne, Tomlinson & Anderson 2007). More recently, the use of reflective practice with adult athletes, and how their involvement in reflection may occur, has been explored, which in turn has located the athlete as an active contributor to the reflections of the practitioner as well as to that of their own performance review (e.g., Faull & Cropley, 2009). It is perhaps now pertinent to the sport and exercise science-based community to understand via reflection the experiences of children. This may, for example, allow exploration of behaviour change associated with exercise adoption and maintenance or experiences within an elite sport developmental system, academy framework, or as recipients of sports science support. Indeed, Ryba (2008) noted that exploring qualitative methodologies that would provide us with insights into how young athletes make sense of the sporting aspect of their lives is especially important. As Piaget observed, children differ from adults not only quantitatively, in terms of the *amount* of knowledge in their possession, but also qualitatively, in the way they *organize* knowledge (Piaget & Inhelder, 1969).

The child as a reflective practitioner

The world of the child is shaped and influenced by adults around them in professional roles such as teachers, coaches and health professionals. There are distinct representations of reflective practice within the training of these professionals that is embedded within their day-to-day practice. For example, early years practitioners (CWDC, p. 7), teachers (QTS standard 29, TDA, 2012), social workers, physiotherapists and psychologists (HCPC, 2012, p. 5) in the UK are, by virtue of their training, reflective practitioners. In essence, these professions see both value and benefit from the postulates of reflective practice, and this is apparent within post-registration award criteria. In sport and exercise sciences, reflective practice is apparent in professional accreditation in sport and exercise science (e.g., BASES, 2009, p. 6) and sports coaching awards (SportscoachUK, 2012, p. 23).

Despite the centrality of reflective practice for professionals working with children, there is very little in the evidence base around the concept of children as 'reflective practitioners' in their own right, other than Newcomb (2004) who considered primary school children (aged 7–11 years) operating as reflective practitioners within the classroom. This dearth begs the question of whether children can indeed reflect. The general consensus, even with limited supporting evidence, is that reflection is not only possible but beneficial for children and that active engagement should be encouraged.

In the context of childhood, reflection is one of several learning activities oriented around exploration, thinking and questioning (Price, Rogers, Scaife, Stanton & Neale, 2003), to increase depth of learning and enhance understanding. Reflection for children is 'remembering with analysis', and engaging them in the process enhances the development of higher-level thinking and problem-solving skills:

> When we engage children in reflection, we encourage them to go beyond merely reporting what they've done. We help them become aware of what they learned in the process, what was interesting, how they feel about it, and

what they can do to build on or extend the experience. Reflection consolidates knowledge so it can be generalized to other situations thereby leading to further prediction and evaluation.

(Epstein, 2003, p. 2)

McVittie (2012) asserts that the inherent internal conversations children subconsciously have with themselves while playing or trying to work something out constitute reflection. However, she maintains that children need to be actively encouraged to externalize this internal dialogue, to share what they think and feel, and identify what was learned. Reflecting spontaneously is difficult for children without encouragement, thus reflection needs to be a facilitated, highly structured process mediated through a range of intentional strategies such as reading, writing, talking, listening and acting. To engage in reflective processes, children need:

- understanding, which can be encouraged by asking them to 'explain', 'discuss', 'describe' and 'interpret' events, situations and feelings;
- analytical skills, which can be developed by asking them to 'compare', 'examine', 'identify' and 'investigate'
- evaluative skills, which can be enhanced by requiring them to 'justify', 'determine', 'assess' and 'judge'
- creativity, which can be fostered by asking them to 'imagine', 'devise', 'create' and 'compose'.

Further, by listening attentively, commenting on and writing down children's reflections, adult practitioners not only encourage children to consider the 'what' and 'why' of their actions and experiences but validate them as well (Epstein, 2003).

Enabling children to reflect is complicated and contingent upon diverse factors including the characteristics of the learner, the environment and the task itself (Gustafson & Bennett, 1999). Developmental and individual differences between children mean their capability to reflect will vary, so opportunity for time and space within a coaching session or during/post-intervention must be factored in to develop reflective skills. Effective reflection also requires a conducive physical environment, one that provides opportunities to use reflective techniques and promotes social interaction. Within the realm of sport and health, this could be accomplished after sessions of sports training or exercise, completion of a sports science support programme, or as a component of evaluation following, for example, a physical activity school-based intervention. Finally, the type of reflection that children are asked to undertake – be it 'reacting', 'elaborating' or 'contemplating' (Surbeck, Park Han & Moyer 1991), the methods used to nurture the process (e.g., verbal or written) and the adult response to it – can all influence the development of children's reflective skills (McVittie, 2012).

Whether children can be 'taught' to reflect is somewhat undetermined. McVittie (2012) suggests that reflection cannot be taught, only encouraged and supported. Finlay (2008) believes that it can, but acknowledges that by its very nature reflective practice is difficult to teach and encourage. What we do know from the more general reflective practice literature with/for adult populations is that reflection is very much a personal process, and this is true with children; similarly, reflection also comes naturally to some but not all children (McVittie, 2012).

Benefits of and barriers to reflective practice with children

There are significant benefits to be had for children who engage in reflection. Evidence suggests that providing children with reflective opportunities results in behaviour that is more 'purposeful' and leads to improved academic performance (Epstein, 2003). Reflection not only helps children apply knowledge and understanding to find answers but improves their problem-solving skills, nurtures lifelong learning and builds confidence and self-awareness. Importantly, the reflective process provides children with the means to express their own views, to have an active role in decision-making and to potentially influence and improve programmes or interventions (Parrillo, 1994).

Reflective practice is of particular significance to those of us in the field of health improvement. By listening to and engaging with children, we are able to understand where they are at in their thinking about physical activity or health, and as a consequence, we are better able to develop effective interventions accordingly, leading to improved and sustained health and wellbeing. This aligns with key facets of National Institute of Clinical Excellence guidance on behaviour change (NICE, 2007), which emphasises the importance of involving the target population in intervention development. Taking these principles into the sport domain, reflective practice could allow practitioners to understand experiences of early specialism sports, (whereby children are chronologically immature yet have a high training age), engagement in talent development systems and encounters with sports science interventions.

As reflection can be difficult for children to accomplish, its value may not be understood or appreciated, and may make children uneasy or uncomfortable, especially if perceived to be hard work or boring. Children need to be motivated to reflect, otherwise they may be reticent to embrace the process. Embedding reflection within a range of perceived 'fun' activities is likely to increase engagement and also serves to accommodate developmental differences and individual learning styles.

Role of the practitioner

As a facilitated process, the role of the practitioner is fundamental in guiding children to varying levels of reflection. It requires planning, time, effort, resources and a willingness to encourage reflective practice. Moreover, reflection needs to be an explicit activity, which is endorsed and modelled, whereby children see and hear adult practitioners using reflection (Queensland Studies Authority, 2011).

As a unique example of this, Barratt and Kerman's (2001) counselling study with children noted the role of the therapist's own reflective practice as a stimulant for the children to think about their feelings and actions, how this impacted on others and how it resulted in the children's improved reflective capacity.

Adult practitioners who are engaging in reflective practice with children also need to be aware of the ethical challenges that may arise and ensure that they proceed with sensitivity (Kirk, 2007). Confidentiality, privacy, informed consent and professional relationships all need to be considered (Finlay, 2008). Asking children to reflect on their experiences can be emotive, has the potential to be harmful and could lead to disclosure and safeguarding issues. The creation of a safe space for reflection, one that meets children's needs and enables them to feel safe and communicate openly, without fear of criticism or reprisal, is essential. Established ground rules that have been co-produced with children themselves are useful in providing parameters for open dialogue around sensitive issues.

Techniques for facilitating reflection

Having established that children do indeed have the capability to reflect given the right circumstances, we now consider how best to facilitate reflective practice with children. Given the dearth in the sport and exercise science evidence base, examples of best practice must be drawn from other disciplines where expertise in reflective practice with and for children is well established. In the field of education, for example, a plethora of strategies are used to promote reflection within the classroom environment. Equally, in participatory research with children, a range of child-centred methods are adopted for 'knowledge production' and facilitation of reflection (Veale, 2011). Participatory research is defined as:

> a process of systematic reflective enquiry where researchers and participants actively engage in collaboration to set the research agenda, collect and analyse data and disseminate the findings so that 'those studied become full participants as active agents in the research'.
>
> (Bernard, 2000, as cited in O'Brien & Moules, 2007, p. 388)

Such techniques are primarily qualitative in nature and enable us to engage meaningfully with children around issues of importance to them. For example, in the Liverpool Longitudinal Study on Smoking (LLSS), semi-structured interviews, focus groups and the Draw and Write Technique were used to explore children's knowledge, attitudes and behaviour around smoking (Porcellato et al., 2002; Porcellato et al., 2005; Milton et al., 2012). Engaging children in dialogue not only increased understanding of the issue but underpinned the development of an evidence-based smoking prevention intervention for UK primary school-children. Within the sport and exercise domain Knowles has used interviews to elicit perspectives from young children as to experiences of active-based natural play within Forest Schools (Ridgers, Knowles & Sayers, 2012); to explore PST in elite youth gymnasts (e.g., Torres-Faggiani, McRobert & Knowles, 2012); and use formative focus group research to inform school-based physical activity interventions (e.g., Boddy et al., 2012). Other sport psychology-based authors have used conversational techniques to examine the sources of enjoyment and non-enjoyment among younger and older children in the sampling years of sport participation (McCarthy & Jones, 2007), stress in youth sport (e.g., Knight, Kneeley, Casey & Holt, 2011) and the motivational climate and role of social agents experienced by young athletes (e.g., Keegan, Harwood, Spray & Lavallee, 2009). As authors working with young populations both in research and in practice we have developed a sense of dissatisfaction with methods that rely on conversation alone. Below we consider a range of child-centred methodologies that could be adapted for use in sport and exercise science to facilitate reflective practice with and for children.

Traditional approaches

Writing / journals / diaries

Although the effectiveness of reflective journals has been questioned within the literature, it is a common tool used in the educational setting to engage children in reflective practice. It entails using a series of questions to guide children in their thought processes. Responses are then recorded in a variety of formats and styles including diaries, learning journals, story books, and life maps. Writing is an easy and effective means of recording thoughts and feelings, but as a self-reported exercise it can feel like 'school work' and thus may be challenging for some children. As such, children should be encouraged to use diagrams, notes and pictures to capture their reflections.

An emerging area is that of multiple media to capture children's reflections. High technology strategies such as blogs, websites, voice threads, video confessionals and digital presentations are currently being used to foster reflection within the educational milieu (Boss, 2009). Clark (2005) suggests digitally recorded reflections may be more novel and appealing to children who lack confidence in or dislike writing. Similar technologies may well have currency and application in the sport and exercise domain.

Reflective dialogue

A popular method for gathering children's views and experiences is face-to-face dialogue. This can be practitioner-led or peer-led. Children can be prompted to engage in thoughtful learning experiences using open-ended 'thinking' questions. Asking children 'What might happen if. . . . ?', 'What other ways can we do this?', 'So what?' or 'Now what?' are strategies for fostering reflective dialogue as it makes them consider what they already know and what they want to know (McVittie, 2012).

The small group format can also be used to encourage reflective dialogue. This is a facilitated process based on questions posed by the adult practitioner, providing children with the opportunity to articulate their experiences, opinions and knowledge, and highlight learning. Although the group environment provides 'safety in numbers', which potentially minimizes the inherent power differentials in child–adult relationships, there is a danger for some children to 'get lost in the crowd' so that their views and experiences do not get heard (Porcellato et al., 2002).

Creative approaches

While traditional approaches can be effective in nurturing reflection in children, McVittie (2012, p. 26) argues that reflection supports the use of creative learning approaches. These tend to be visually based and participatory in nature, vesting ownership of the process with the children themselves. They are 'intrinsically' motivating (Veale, 2011), and given the need to motivate children to engage in reflection, justifies their use in reflective practice. As demonstrated below, there are a range of creative techniques that provide children with the opportunity to convey what they did and how they did it, visually rather than verbally. Photographs, arts-based activities such as drawings and diagrams, painting, crafting, cartooning, modelling and projective techniques such as role play, sorting, ranking and mapping can all be used by children to highlight experiences, give meaning and demonstrate learning (Veale, 2011). These methods tend to be 'fun', 'engaging' and 'empowering', and can be used with children of all ages, though they are especially beneficial for use with children who experience difficulty in expressing themselves verbally or in writing, or when applied in ethically sensitive research. Some tools can be used singularly and others are used collectively as in the Mosaic approach (see Clark & Moss, 2011).

Photographs

Digital, disposable or video cameras have been used effectively in photo voice, a process in which children take their own pictures, thereby reflecting what matters to them (Johnson, Fister & Vindrola-Padros, 2013). For example, photographs taken by young children influenced decisions to change the play environment in work undertaken by Johnson, Fister and Vindrola-Padros (2013). Burton and Medcalf (2011) used photo voice methodology to assess English children's perceptions of motivations and barriers towards physical activity participation in rural and urban environments. For photo elicitation, pictures taken by someone else can be used as prompts for dialogue and reflection. Bhosekar (2009) used reality-based photographs taken by a street educator as a 'graphic aid', to assess how street children could be prompted to reflect and discuss their experiences. Valkanova (2004) used digital video editing as a tool to encourage self-reflection in children in a classroom project called 'Filming in My Science Class', and found that filming children's learning process led to changes in classroom behaviour and potentially influenced the children's sense of self as learners.

Drawing from these examples, there are opportunities in sport whereby children's photos could influence learning of skills or tactics in sports training, influence coaching practice or inform the practice of a sports scientist. There are significant benefits to using photographs as a means of fostering reflective practice. The process gives children ownership and responsibility for what they photograph, it enables them to discuss the issues they feel reflect their own experiences, and it has a high novelty factor, which is likely to keep children interested for a longer period of time (Fargas-Malet, McSheery, Larkin & Robinson, 2010). Einarsdottir (2005) found photography a valuable tool for obtaining information on children's views of their lives in a pre-school setting, but cautioned that the photographs must be accompanied by the children's own narrative to articulate the personal meaning within. Some skill is required to use the cameras properly, and not all children will be comfortable using it or taking pictures. There is also the potential issue of 'appropriateness' to consider when children take their own pictures.

Drawings

Children's drawings are widely used as a means of capturing children's views, experiences and reflections, although it is in listening to children talk or write about their drawings that important insights are revealed (Clark, 2005). Both authors have used the draw and write technique with primary school children to ascertain children's understanding of smoking and how it impacted on them (Porcellato et al., 2005) and more recently to explore recess physical activity-based experiences (Knowles et al., 2013 – see Figure 4.1).

Perry and Dockett (2005) asked young children to reflect on how they had changed over the course of their first year in primary school. Documenting their experience through drawings and annotated comments, the children were able to detail their experience with a view to influencing and improving service provision. Kostenuis and Ohrling (2008) used drawings to understand Swedish children's lived experience of well-being within the context of school-based health promotion activities. Specifically, a reflective process was embedded within an

Figure 4.1 Drawing from Year 6 girl illustrating a range of playtime activities and labelling (Knowles et al. 2013)

opportunity for 10 and 11 year olds to draw, exhibit and analyse their own and other children's drawings, which provided a positive and empowering experience. Although drawing is an easy and familiar activity and a good way to establish rapport, developmental appropriateness needs to considered. By virtue of its focus this tool is better suited to younger children, it prompts recall and gives children time to reflect on their own ideas (Miles, 2000). However, not all children enjoy drawing, and older children are often less keen to engage in the process.

Projective techniques

Projective techniques are an indirect method of questioning based on the premise that individuals often find it easier to express themselves by projecting what they are thinking or feeling onto or into something else. Projective techniques are used to generate insights, discussion and reflection in both individual and group discussions (Billsberry & Godrich, 2010). They can be used on their own or in conjunction with other methods (e.g., focus groups / interviews), and include a range of different strategies such as mapping, role play, word or picture association, bubble drawings, collage, storytelling, sentence completion, cartooning, ordering and ranking exercises. Clarke (2004) advocates the use of child-friendly projective techniques that enable children to explore their thoughts and feelings in a fun, safe and enjoyable way such as puppetry or play acting. Although projective techniques were originally developed for use in the clinical setting, current application extends to marketing, education and health research, and now offers researchers the opportunity to consider the utility of such techniques to explore experiences of children in sport and exercise settings.

Conclusion

The authors of this chapter concur that children have the capability to move beyond description of experiences to that of reflection. By way of definition the authors agree with Epstein (2003 – see above). By engaging in reflection children can become active agents who express themselves and offer valid views to influence decisions and the world around them. For children, reflection needs to be facilitated by adults who role-model this process and engage children in structured, developmentally appropriate techniques that are reflective in origin but creative by design.

5 Keeping the cat alive

'Getting' reflection as part of professional practice

Jo Trelfa and Hamish Telfer

Introduction

Since Schön's work of the 1980s, which brought to prominence reflection as bearing *on* and *in* practice, sport and allied health professions have witnessed a rise in the use and scope of reflective practice to the extent that it has become embraced in what Horgan calls 'A wave of euphoria' (cited in McGarr & Moody, 2010, p. 580). We argue the rapid pace at which it has been embraced has meant that critical issues have emerged at the heart of *doing* and *using* reflection. The principal challenge is to ensure that individuals 'get' reflection.

Knowles, Borrie and Telfer (2005) have described what professionals *do* within sport as possessing *craft skills*. The ability to describe and make sense of practice when engaging with the range of decisions and actions that characterize this craft (from the mundane to the more complex, including moral and ethical considerations) is problematic. Supporting and enabling individuals to engage with craft skills requires practitioners to examine their personal, reflective accounts-on-action, based on the assumption this will be transposed into their actual practice. Within training and education[1] emphasis is given to these accounts being written, on the assumption that trainees/students will write to learn, in contrast to learning to write, which characterizes the majority of their education experience (Allen, Bowers & Diekelmann, 1989). At the same time, these reflective accounts are used to assess their competencies. The combined effect impinges on what individuals write, and sets up a position–power dilemma of professional mentor intrusion into the personal and often emotional accounts, which militates against honest, self-reflective testimony.

Against this backdrop, this chapter argues that reflective practice risks becoming a technical-rational activity, framed by a normative value system (Bleakley, 2000) and an ideology that controls students, rather than allowing freedom of expression in relation to their experiences. We draw on semi-structured interviews with students to examine their experiences and the impact of reflective practices (Trelfa, 2010a)[2] and use the analogy of *Schrödinger's cat* to determine whether reflective practice has been killed off by the process of engagement despite being central to student experience and learning.

The relevance of the reflective practice 'box' in relation to vocational practice

Schrödinger's cat is a conundrum describing a cat in a sealed container. While the box remains shut the cat is both alive *and* dead, both are possible simultaneously, and one can only discover which upon opening it. Using this analogy, while reflective practice is in a sealed box, it is both alive and dead, and unless we open and critically examine the concept and practice we cannot know which, nor breathe life into the significant contribution it can make to supporting craft skills. The central question is whether individuals 'get' reflective practice or if they simply learn 'how to do it'.

Our understanding of reflective practice is that of a process through which practitioners, individually and in their communities of practice, consider, explore and develop their craft, skills and knowledge alongside a deepening appreciation of intuition (Atkinson & Claxton, 2000), improvisation (Harris, 2012), and set within a context and purpose of professional agency, understanding, knowledge and change (Eraut, 1994) that includes socio-political awareness and self-transformation (Cranton, 2006).

Being able to 'do it' does not necessarily evidence the ability to critically reflect. This is at odds with claims for using reflection as a central, key skill with which to interrogate vocational and practice readiness. Reflective practice is often also combined with benchmarking requirements of professional bodies. While the drivers and political rhetoric behind this are complex and contested (see Usher, Bryant & Johnston, 1997), it has always been of paramount importance to invest in ways of interrogating practice with a view to ensuring that future sports professionals audit, develop, understand and critique what they do, and how they do it. It helps ensure professionalism, and 'fitness for purpose', as much as it develops practice.

Uncertainty and risk are key characteristics of sport practice; practice is fluid and situationally dependent (Cassidy, Jones & Potrac, 2009). In such contexts there are no formulae for individuals to fall back on (Schön, 1987). Thus, there is a need for those engaged to be able to decide how practice should be in any given situation relative to their own skills and competencies. Lyle (2010) developed this idea of practitioners[3] being able to make rapid decisions that are contextually relevant and technically correct. These processes become tacit and therefore notoriously difficult to articulate. In essence, the practitioner has to be capable of working with, and in, a 'stream-of-consciousness flow' (Lyle, 2002, p. 212).

In all practitioner interactions there are key moments that involve ethical, moral, technical and procedural decisions (Banks & Nøhr, 2003). These practice dilemmas are further complicated as sport and physical activity becomes increasingly required to address socio-political agendas through initiatives relating to social policy. These dilemmas are described by Schön (1987, p. 42) as 'swampy lowlands' that individuals need to be able to navigate, and reflective practice supports the disentangling of practice milieu. Moreover, as Philippart (2003) observed, 'practice becomes increasingly complicated as society itself becomes more complex. . . . many conflicting interests, interpretations of reality, moral and ethical standards, visions and hopes for the future exist next to each other' (p. 70). Development of a deeply engaged analytical capacity is therefore a necessary skill to embed in training and education programmes, undertaken through the facilitation of reflective practice (Cropley & Hanton, 2011). This complex environment is characterized by competing ideas from above or outside sport pertaining to what it is to be professional and what a professional act involves, risking excessive external or managerial and bureaucratic control (Evetts, 2003). With its focus on responsibility, autonomy and interpretation, reflective practice is an important 'from within' opposing force (Furlong, 2000). It offers an avenue through which to respond to and manage these drivers and should be valued as a legitimate autonomous view.

Reflective practice: both 'alive-and-dead'

Some consider the role of reflection in learning with regard to *how* people learn from their experiences and thus develop (e.g., Boud, Keogh & Walker, 1985; Burnard, 1991). Others view the process from the perspective of critical thinking and experience to achieve an overview (e.g., Mezirow, 1990; Moon, 1999). When applied to professional practice, reflection becomes a 'specialised tool' (Moon, 1999, p. 4). Schatzki, Knorr Cetina and Von Svigny (2001) explained how *practice* in relation to professions refers to performance in specific settings, as well as preparation and repetition to improve. Repertoires of skills and judgements are emphasised as important, as is the role of critical analysis in determining the best action for any given moment (Moffatt, 1996, p. 75). Thus, it would appear the concept of reflective practice is very much alive.

We contend, however, that reliance on reflective practice in professional sports and related education programmes masks an alternative reality, one that suggests a confused concept and questionable practice. Part of the potency of reflective practice is in the notion that individuals will question previously held assumptions and decisions regarding their practice, leading to change (Jarvis, 1992). However, the grounds for this claim are confused. For instance, Mezirow (2000) contends that learning can be newly acquired or an extension of established learning, gained with or without challenging personally held assumptions, whereas previously he argued the latter had to take place for learning to happen (Mezirow, 1985). Moon (1999) argued that a change in perspective is only one of a range of possible outcomes, while Boyd and Fales (1983) and Jarvis (1992) discuss it as an inevitable consequence.

Stages of reflection that are end points in themselves representing different ways of thinking and acting could be a solution here. Van Manen's (1977) three levels of reflectivity could be valid according to the circumstances the practitioner is working in and with. Thus, *technical rationality* focuses on efficient and effective means to achieve certain ends; *practical action* is reflection that unpacks the means, so considering underpinning assumptions and outcomes; while *critical*

reflection involves reflection that results in a change in perspective that incorporates moral and ethical considerations. These levels are important for practitioners to grasp when moving between outcome and process goals. However,
stage models are typically considered hierarchically, with individuals showing
engagement in critical reflection being more highly rewarded through assessment
as long as they are able to articulate it (Placek & Smyth, 1995). To add further
confusion, writers disagree on the number of stages. In contrast to Van Manen
(1977), Zeichner and Liston (1987) propose four, King and Kitchener (1994)
seven, while Perry (1970) discusses nine. This confusion lies at the heart of discussion around *non* and *effective* reflective practitioners (e.g., Cowan, 1998), the
former being those who do not engage in reflective practice, and effective, being
sharply (and negatively) contrasted with more sophisticated practice in terms of
action, outcome, values, ethical and moral considerations, and the capacity to
question and disrupt or unsettle existing power relations (Fook, 2002). Clearly,
then, an examination of theory about reflective practice shows it to be both
alive-and-dead.

The confusion in 'getting it'

It is not altogether surprising that a key theme arising in interviews with post
and present students regarding their experiences of engaging in reflective practice is that of 'getting it', questioning whether they had correctly understood the
purpose of reflective practice and were doing it properly (Trelfa, 2010a). The
transition from merely acting on a requirement to engage in reflective practice,
to individuals experiencing it as something of intrinsic worth, value and significance has been highlighted elsewhere (e.g., Johns, 2009). However, rather than
reflective practice being the way they make meaning and create and draw on
professional knowledge, the respondents said that sometimes nothing happened
to reflect on, or certainly nothing they deemed as worthy enough. This indicates another dynamic at play. Mirroring the confusion in theory, they located
their views and understanding of reflective practice as being reliant on big, worthy events leading to fundamental change. Emphasis given to journal writing as
evidence of engaging in reflective practice compounded their confusion; they
related engagement in journal writing as a key purpose of reflective practice. In
isolation, these could be taken as an indication of poor facilitation of reflective
practice, but it is an experience more widely shared (Trelfa, 2010a; 2011).

Reflective practice: 'Opening the box'!

We contend that the way in which reflective practices are delivered, facilitated
and used are the principal issues here. The interface between reflective practices
as a learning tool and the various ways and purposes to which it is used is damag-
ing the potency of its original purpose and undermining learning. The distinction between reflection *as* learning and reflection *for* assessment seems central

to student understanding and engagement. Research respondents have related how they lied, exaggerated and censored accounts of practice in reflective journals forming evidence toward qualification, and a number now consciously avoid engagement in any reflective process in their professional life (Trelfa, 2010a). Similarly, within sports settings, student practitioners detailed how they had fabricated reflective logs for qualification and accreditation (Telfer, 2002). As a result, it could be argued that reflective practice has become detached from professional craft, skills and technique. It is therefore important that we consider the three themes of evidence, assessment and the uses of reflective practice.

Reliance on reflective journals (e.g., diaries, logs) as evidence of engagement is problematic when pro-formas and guidance direct towards 'acceptable' format, content and writing style. This is both confusing and contradictory, a clash between what is deemed to be academic style with a focus on learning to write sitting alongside cognitive reflections where the focus is on writing to learn (Allen et al., 1989), a genre that in contrast looks more like free associative thoughts than anything that satisfies course learning outcomes. Individuals speak about having profound learning experiences, but the task of writing them down to fit what is required is an *'ordeal'* that effectively *'puts a brake on'* the reflective process.[4] Since practitioner reflective recordings are emotionally significant to them, it is often difficult for others to see or feel the relevance; yet rambling over a period of time can allow things to evolve. The learning to write genre within reflective practice also involves individuals linking practice to theory, articulated as *'right, now I've got to find someone else who says something that relates to something I did'*. The inference is that their learning is insufficient in its own right.

How can student writing to learn be given comparable consideration to learning to write? Furthermore, as soon as this personalized account is shown to someone else, it creates an audience for which their writing is now wittingly or unwittingly addressing, thus making it different. This audience also examines accounts for evidence of student competence to assess ability to qualify in their profession. Individuals speak of writing in ways and about things that will allow them to pass. This experience finds support in other accounts in the literature (see Trelfa, 2010b). Hargreaves (2004) identified only three key narratives that are viewed as plausible by assessors and reflectors, hence real reflectors are not likely to emerge from such a system.

Contexts for reflection are integral to the process, but individuals involved mostly referred to being required to engage in personal therapy that is unwanted (Trelfa, 2010a). The genre of self-confession in reflective spaces such as coaching, supervision and personal journals is underpinned by assumptions and discourses that have largely gone unquestioned; the ethical implications of scrutinizing them has gained little attention (Pollard, 2008). In such circumstances, it is arguably a wise student that delivers what s/he thinks is required of them, performing according to the explicit and implicit surveillance. Reflective practice becomes *'a task to be done rather than to be embedded in practice'* and *'a hoop'* to jump through within a wider *'culture of hoop jumping'*.

Finally, individuals recount experiences in the workplace of how reflective practice serves to '*cover*' them, a place where they '*get their story right*'; and, of how organizations use reflective practice as a way to '*put more of an onus on individuals*' within a wider blame culture, as a tool to police employees and a way to '*institutionalize people into spaces and keep them there*'. In other words, reflective practices are being used as performance reviews or appraisals to guide and influence impressions, which subsequently form opinions about others (thus pejoratively). This (unsurprisingly) encourages the individual towards a more conservative, less emotionally laden approach. Reflective accounts are written to reflect the requirements of the institution or organization but not those of the individual. Rather than Schön's (1987) original notion of practice as engaging in hot streams of consciousness, reflective practice becomes ticking boxes, performing appropriately and meeting targets. The thoughts of individuals become limited and isolated to private, secret moments, thus lacking equal intrinsic validity to organizational requirements.

Personal exploration and honesty in the discovery of knowledge (or lack of it) rather than justification of actions and decisions will lead to more robust lines of enquiry into self and practice. Practitioners need not only to know, but also to be able to say honestly when they don't know. Individuals should be encouraged to be unique and relevant in the way they think about their own practice as well as thinking accessibly when their practice is about others. However, this sits uneasily with assessment and the managerial processes.

Keeping the cat alive: what we want practitioners to 'be', rather than what we want them to 'do'

How do we breathe life back into reflective practice? With student practitioners we need to remove the perception that it's all about assessment and 'getting through'. The idea that it can be a tool for professional growth often escapes them. We need, therefore, to develop different ways of using and rethinking the assessment of individuals through reflection in order to be able to use reflective practices more effectively and formatively. It also needs to be reviewed from an ethical position. Can and should reflective practices be used for assessment, since by their very nature they are highly personal and emotionally laden? Seldom is the relative maturity and emotional development of the reflector taken into account, with some individuals finding the demands of reflective practices difficult to master, even in gaining the most rudimentary of skills.

The inherent contradiction between using reflective practice to improve practice, while at the same time emphasizing the ethical underpinning that invariably frames practice based on the moral functioning of the practitioner, is a critical interface in determining how and why we use it. One person's values and sense of moral practice may be different from another's, while at the same time the profession will have organizational cultural values embedded (both implicit as well as explicit), which all involved are expected to recognise and subscribe to.

Sports practitioners are also subject to professional and public scrutiny and audit. Therefore, we have the inherent contradiction between openness and honesty on the one hand and the possibility of our self-disclosure being wrong, at fault or contradicting others on the other hand. The tendency therefore is to say what *needs* to be said, as opposed to what *should* or *could* be said. The assessment of someone else's moral or ethical dilemma is in itself an ethical issue.

Even after all this, there is little or no follow-up. Thus, assessment becomes the end point, not part of a continuous process. This also presents an ethical issue of how strong and revelatory reflection is dealt with, both in terms of support for those involved (the reflector) as well as the obligations of those in power positions dealing with it. The paradox of this should not be lost on those who know reflective practice processes and skills since they are meant to edge practice ever higher. This does not sit easy with assessments, which are too often *end point*.

Consequently, student practitioners carry out reflective practice instrumentally, making up accounts of their performance, and seeing little reason to develop reflective practice once qualified. Reflective practice *is* complex; in trying to convey what it is and encourage a leap of faith to use it there are clearly a number of gaps that need to be filled (Trelfa, 2005). A range of ways of engaging in reflection may need to be offered to individuals and used in differing contexts (Trelfa, 2010a). Consequently, trainers, educators and coaches must be challenged to consider their roles. They must bring the practitioner to a point of saying 'who am I?' as well as 'these are my preferences', with the ability to identify or locate the ideologies, theories and understandings underpinning them. Ranges of methods from which individuals can evaluate their needs and approaches (how they work for them, how they use them) can be utilised, while not shaping content. Curricula should contain elements of simulated practice to which reflection can be applied (e.g., ethnodrama). As practice is fluid, dynamic, emotional as well as situationally specific, the search for strategies to sit alongside assessment of practice need to nudge nearer the nuances of practice (including emotional connections).

Understanding and making sense of this extensive landscape makes demands on those who are the gatekeepers of professional practice and those who teach reflective techniques and facilitate reflective practice. Not all will be able to offer such extensive and deeply focused skills. Concomitantly, the impulse to put reflective practice in professional and educational activity at every turn needs to be resisted despite it being a vogue activity. Reflective activities as well as assessments have grown, but the validity of many of the experiences is questionable. There are, however, individuals who do 'get it'. They use methods such as voice recorders, mind maps, diaries, shared dialogue and group discussions. They understood that the exercise was to get them as individuals to think around, through and about their practice. They can also question what effective practice *is*, and for whom it is effective (client, practitioner or both). Even so, unstructured journals that are excellent accounts of exploring around, through and about practice that do not meet academic practice demands, and 'talking to camera' reflections-on-practice, run the risk of 'not fitting in'. Therefore, unless the means to achieve an assessment outcome looks like all other means to achieving assessment outcomes, it isn't satisfactory and ultimately nothing satisfactory is achieved. This is of course central to an understanding of the use and purpose of reflective practices as a means or an outcome. It has to look like a cat, and meow like a cat!

Control and turning out in our own image

Reflective diaries, portfolios and discussions are *de facto* policing of practice. It is a fine line between developing the student according to their professional skills and in our own image as 'experts', and developing them as rational, free thinking, autonomous professionals, given the pressures to produce 'oven ready' practitioners. This takes learning, understanding and application out of the hands of the students precisely when we need to encourage them to develop autonomy of practice. It no longer becomes 'about them', but about control 'of them'.

Over the years evidence-based practice has determined that more concrete evidence from student practitioners is required rather than their mere perception of events. Anything rooted in how they felt (insight) about this becomes difficult to deal with, both in ethical and practical terms, despite many of the reflective methods and processes asking for exactly this kind of engagement. This reduces the role of training and educating practitioners to that of policing, as indeed is the role of using reflection as part of appraisal and continuing professional development. This said, practitioners must be 'fit for purpose'. If reflective practices are used in the process of professional accreditation, how is the veracity of the work established? Does the system encourage us all to lie by justifying practice in hindsight? This is, of course, at odds with a key practitioner ethic of building trust with 'the other'. Time is houred; less formal discussion with student practitioners and what we do in that time pressurizes the student/mentor interface, and therefore the process is often reductionist. The richness in engaging with the development of practice in the moment is lost on all parties who should be absolutely central to that process, creating a number of tensions, not least between the need to obtain hard evidence and that of individual growth.

The clash of constructivist philosophies around craft skill development versus assessing the nature and content of those constructions is evident. Systems have become mechanistic where there is a requirement to provide evidence for *everything* we do. This includes students, and where they recount evidence of practice we have no way of knowing whether their experiences are real or imagined. The only decision we make is whether they are plausible.

Conclusion

Opening the box of reflective practice raises the important question of have they 'got it?' A greater discussion is needed to establish what the use and nature of reflective practice should be for and about. The debate also needs to focus on the vexed question of the ethics of using reflective accounts, emotionally charged as they are, for assessment purposes, especially within such a power relationship as that of assessed and assessor. In this chapter we have suggested that what we want of our future practitioners are intellectually and professionally curious professionals. However, the practices we use would seemingly not support this.

Does or should reflective practice allow us to 'get at' practice? Who decides this and in what context? Is the content of our work in reflective practice too methodologically laden but author-evacuated (Brown, Gilbourne & Claydon, 2009)? Has reflective practice become, or has it always been, downright nonsense? Are we in a better position now to supply an answer that can help Schrödinger discover whether his cat (called Reflective Practice) is indeed dead or alive? Perhaps it has escaped and is now something else entirely without anyone noticing. Or is it in fact now so traumatized by its experiences that it ceases to exist in any meaningful way and is merely a shell of its original self?

Notes

1 Training and education is intended to include National Governing Body of Sport professional training programmes, Higher and Further Education as well as those learning opportunities provided by other provider organizations. Trainees and students are considered those within these structures, and for simplicity will be referred to as 'students' throughout the chapter.
2 Trelfa's (2010a) research was carried out with students on two UK professional programmes in Youth and Community Work, and ex-students working in the field. The findings entirely parallel those of Telfer's experience of working with individuals on sports-related programmes, reflected in this chapter.
3 We use the generic word 'practitioner' throughout to cover the variety of contexts that include coaching, teaching and instruction related to sport and physical activity. For further reading on this issue, see Lyle and Cushion (2010).
4 References in italics and speech marks here and throughout the remainder of this chapter are the words of research participants taken from Trelfa (2010a).

Part Three

Pedagogical approaches to reflective practice

6 Sink or swim

Case study reflections from an undergraduate football scientist

Martin Littlewood, James Morton and Barry Drust

Introduction

This chapter aims to present how a reflective approach to learning has been adopted and integrated within the curriculum of the BSc (Hons) Science and Football degree programme at Liverpool John Moores University (LJMU), UK. It specifically addresses how reflective processes have been embedded into the curricula and assessment practices of a Level 6 (Year 3) applied placement module to promote students' personal and professional development, while also illustrating how a reflective learning culture is developed and promoted within the module. A single student case study is utilised to illustrate a student's reflective journey on his vocational placement, and in doing so, outlines the complex personal challenges and critical moments that can be encountered when delivering applied sports science support in the unique world of elite professional football. The case study is represented using creative non-fiction excerpts from a reflective diary and seeks to capture the daily existence of practitioners, players and self in the context of the workplace. In locating the context of the chapter, it is important to provide the necessary information in relation to the degree programme and academic framework that underpins the learning process.

Background to the programme and module

The BSc (Hons) Science and Football degree programme at LJMU is arguably the only science-based course that exists within the UK, and internationally, that specifically aims to educate and develop students for employment in the football industry (from community to elite level domains). Established formally as a recognised degree programme in 1998, the course recruits around 35–40 students annually and possesses a mixture of UK, European and international students. The last 15 years have seen a marked rise in demand for sports science graduates in professional sport, and more specifically in the professional football industry. The introduction of the recent Elite Player Performance Plan in 2012 within UK professional football also means that demand for suitably qualified and competent graduates within the football industry will continue to rise in future years. In that sense, we would argue that Sports Scientists, or Football Scientists as the term may be, who are able to understand the complexities of the player development process, organizational structures and the particular nuances associated with the occupational practices of the professional football environment are ideally positioned to progress into employment within this industry.

The programme is multidisciplinary in nature with a progressive learning experience throughout the levels of study, and it is in the final year of the students' programme that they engage in the 'active' delivery of sports science support in a work-related learning context. More specifically, this occurs in a Level 6 module termed Applied Science and Football 3, which aims to: (a) critically explore how sports science is being used within football to enhance player development and performance; (b) develop an awareness of the craft skills and knowledge required to successfully provide sports science support within a football organization; and (c) critically appraise the importance of reflection to applied practice.

Students are exposed to a variety of applied practice literature from a multidisciplinary perspective (e.g., Morton, 2009; Nesti, 2010; Nesti & Littlewood, 2011) that is delivered through a range of teaching and learning strategies (i.e., seminars, workshops, industry lectures, Q&As) to promote both *professional* and *craft* learning of the football setting. The unique cultural features of the professional football environment that shape practitioner experiences in the applied setting are examined through the work of Parker (2000, 2001, 2006), Roderick (2006), Gilbourne and Richardson (2006), and Nesti (2010). Reflective practice is also embedded into the curricula at specific junctures to promote students' knowledge and understanding of its role in personal and professional development. The work of Knowles and colleagues (2007, 2012) is used to frame the processes of reflective practice within the applied context and to support students' applied development journeys. In light of this, the programme adopts a definition of reflective practice that suggests it is a process that assists in facilitating personal and professional growth through systematically challenging one's developing knowledge of assumptions, prejudices and critical moments.

The students are assessed via a combination of oral presentations and a reflective essay across the academic year. It is the reflective essay, however, that allows the students to communicate their unique and personal fieldwork experiences in a highly authentic and emotive manner. To develop the final reflective narrative, students are encouraged to extract entries from their reflective diaries to illuminate key moments that informed their personal and professional development. These extracts are subsequently reworked creatively into a series of thematic narratives that provide rich contextual insight into the lived experiences of the students during their applied placements. The production of the narratives is framed against the writing principles advocated by Sparkes (2002) and Van Maanen (1988), and adopt a confessional approach. Reflective seminars are built into the module outline as a pedagogic strategy to facilitate shared reflection (Knowles et al., 2007) and to strengthen the meaning and understanding of student experiences in relation to knowledge-of-self and others (Cropley, Hanton, Miles & Niven, 2010).

The context of the applied environment in which the placement activity occurs offers a multitude of unique cultural features indicative of the football industry. Indeed, it is these very features that often influence and shape the nature of the reflections that the students typically integrate into their essays. We argue that an understanding and appreciation of culture in the applied setting is perhaps one of the most critical factors that influences effective applied practice. The cultural features of the applied setting consequently form an area that the module team focuses exclusively on within the group seminars that we operate to stimulate a reflective learning environment. Yet, we would contend that the lack of writing in this area, particularly those approaches that are represented with creativity and authenticity, are vitally important for the future development of applied practitioners.

Context of the applied environment: professional football

Insights into the world and inner working practices of professional football are somewhat rare within the academic community, and, as previously noted, accounts from applied practitioners that operate in this industry are even rarer. The difficulty for neophyte practitioners who are aiming to learn about the nuances of applying science in this world are therefore very difficult without any form of real, informed and meaningful accounts to guide learning and knowledge. There are a variety of reasons that explain the dearth of accounts into practice within this setting, ranging from gaining access (more prominent for academic researchers) to the reluctance of full-time practitioners in clubs not wanting to share their experiences to outsiders for fear of judgement, and even job security.

The academic material that has explored football culture has typically been framed around themes such as masculinity (Parker, 2006), identity (Nesti & Littlewood, 2011) and occupational practices in the role (Roderick, 2006). If we trace some of the earliest insights into the world of professional football, Hunter Davies (1972) provided an insider account of Tottenham Hotspur FC during the 1971/72 playing season. He aimed to explore the realities of the occupation and commented on the distinct features of *insecurity*, *loneliness* and *rejection* that framed the role of a professional football player.

These clearly resonated with the later work of both Parker (2000, 2001, 2006) and Roderick (2006), who both conducted sociological examinations of the professional football environment. More specifically, Parker (2001) aimed to explore the distinct features of masculine construction within a group of youth trainees at one football club in the early 1990s, and identified the professional football environment as a key location for the demonstration and reinforcement of traditional working-class masculine values. Parker explained how the identities of the youth trainees were shaped and constructed in unity with a series of official and unofficial institutional norms, values and assumptions. In that sense, reference was made to the players' experiences and perceptions of the menial chores that they had to engage in, the coaching style and strategies of the youth team coach, the authoritarian club culture, and education. He suggested that these cultural facets all served to shape the youth trainees' life inside the professional football club.

Roderick's (2006) more recent work similarly makes reference to the peculiar norms, values and assumptions that inform the occupational conditions under which professional football players operate. Indeed, it is these particular features that form the basis of a very powerful and dominant culture that influences behaviour of the people who reside in this setting, and contribute to organizational socialization. We contend that this unique culture is not exclusive to only the players in the clubs, but also extends to staff and practitioners who also reside in these social worlds.

The account that is provided in the student case study aims to illustrate the impact that culture had on one individual who 'practised' in an elite-level professional football setting. Furthermore, it demonstrates the importance of introducing culture as a topic of learning that new and existing practitioners need to better understand to support the development of effective practice.

Student case study: reflections on applied practice

The following section introduces a series of reflections from a student's applied experiences that we have been fortunate to supervise in our roles as academic tutors on the programme. The narratives that follow have been developed and revisited through a series of group seminars aimed at promoting the principles of shared reflection to reach a deeper sense of personal knowledge and meaning (see Cropley et al., 2010). In doing so, we feel that these examples provide a sound pedagogical strategy for disseminating professional practice about the unique individual challenges and critical moments that students may encounter in delivering applied sports science support in elite-level professional football.

Reflective narrative 1: acceptance – 'big arm'

I had eventually been given some form of specific role from Chris (Head of Academy Sports Science), one of which was to assist with the injury prevention sessions for the reserves and lead the 'core station'. This was around about the sixth consecutive time I had assisted with this session so I felt that the lads were finding a degree of consistency with regard to my attendance in the gym. During that time, there had been other opportunities where I had to assist with sessions. These had taken place on the pitch or over at the recovery gym and meant that interacting with the lads was fundamental. On this occasion, it was a cold, wet and windy Monday morning and the general mood around the Academy was pretty glum.

'Tom, can you lead the core station for me please? I'll be over in the gym in 10 minutes, so if you could just get set up for me as well that would be great', says Chris. I replied, 'Yeah that's fine Chris, I will see you in there.' The session got started and the banter was flowing amongst the lads, there seemed to be a frequent chuckle every few minutes, which showed me that they found my company enjoyable at least. Around five minutes into the session a quick and decisive voice echoed from across the gym, 'OK Tom, you can go back to the office now, I can deal with this from here.' It was Ben the Academy Sports Scientist. Unsure about why he had said that to me, when Chris had specifically told me to take the session, I replied in a somewhat surprised tone, 'Oh, OK, I will see you in a bit then.' As I began to make my way back to the office, the reserve team captain leaped to my defence and fired a snappy question to Ben, 'Why are you telling Tom to go? He always takes part and leads this session! And look at the size of his arms! We are gonna listen to him more than you.' A few of the lads chuckled and joined in on the banter by pointing and laughing at the physique of Ben in contrast to mine. After hearing the reserve captain defend me like that I felt a sense of 'acceptance' from that point on and I walked out the gym with a sense of relief and a smile on my face.

What kept playing on my mind was why I had been defended over a full-time senior member of staff, when I thought I was just perceived as an unimportant 'student', who generally has nothing to offer than lap dog service. I understand that the lads may not fully appreciate the words of Ben with regard to gym work, as his body type (slim) doesn't really allow him to practise what he preaches. Whereas I on the other hand present a more masculine frame, and one that has clearly benefited from continuous gym work, and therefore it would seem appropriate for them to listen to me over him, even if I am 'just a student'.

This reflection resonates with the work of Potrac et al. (2002) who suggested that respect in the football environment was enhanced by the information, or logical argument that practitioners present to players in order to influence a change in opinion and behaviour and more specifically, to the concepts of informational and legitimate power. I additionally realized the amount of contact that I have with the players must play a huge role in forming positive relationships. I felt that the more contact time I had with them [players] resulted in getting to know them individually, and also provided an opportunity for them to get to know me. I found that getting to know them took a little longer than them understanding me; however, this was expected, as Nesti (2010) suggested that elite level professional footballers often surround themselves in a protective barrier as they see everyone else as a threat. Baring in mind the players were a similar age to me, I found that we had plenty to talk about, with lots of things in common. As they got to know me personally, they found out that I had played football to a fairly decent standard myself (semi-professional), which provided further common ground to relate to. A growing sense of acceptance had seemed to formulate quickly when the lads found this out, and this observation was further noted by Nesti (2010) who suggested that if the sport psychologist has played football to a high standard, there will be a greater acceptance of their role and function. As time passed, the relationships I built with the players became stronger and stronger, and a sense of friendship more than anything seemed to be apparent. However, this concept proved to not always necessarily be a good thing, as the next passage demonstrates.

Reflective narrative 2: Acceptance – 'friend or coach?'

A dominant issue that I had was concerned with understanding the balance between treating the players as their *friend* or as their *coach*. This became increasingly difficult throughout the placement and I found it a constant challenge within my time at the club. One of my roles was to lead recovery sessions at the local fitness gym that was based around the corner from the Academy. These sessions specifically consisted of cycling at a low intensity, performing stretches on power plates and implementing recovery methods in the pool based around dynamic and static stretching. Chris (Head of Academy Sports Science) had asked me to take two groups during the course of the morning.

The first group ran very smoothly and according to plan, whereas the second didn't. Instead of meeting me in the gym, the second group decided to get changed in the pool area and wait for me to escort them straight to the pool instead. As I was looking for the lads, I found them at the pool, all changed and looking rather anxious about what my reaction might be. I said to them, 'Lads, what are you doing changed? Have you been on the bikes upstairs yet?' Expecting them to say no, I was shocked to hear, 'Yeah lad, been up there and done 10 minutes on the bike and done a few of them stretches on the power plates.' The voice of this player was breaking up and his tone was supplemented with a grin on his face and so I knew very well he was lying, but the question now was, 'what do I do?'

This was one of the hardest decisions I had to make at the academy during my placement. All I could think about was weighing up the pro's and con's of the decision I was about to make. The lads were talking to me, but you wouldn't have thought I was listening due to my vacant facial expression. Subconsciously, all I was doing was thinking about the implications of my next action whilst trying to continue the conversation. All I could think about was 'this is a very awkward position, what should I do, what are the implications of my actions, why are the lads testing me, should I make them go on the bikes and risk losing the respect I have gained from them, is there anything worse than "being busy" in a football environment, should I let it slide just this once and become more popular with them?' Questioning myself this much, in such a short space of time, made me realize that sometimes in football you have to act based upon what you think is right at the time and not what is right further down the line.

I had worked hard to gain the *respect* from the players and so I decided to let it go on this occasion and allow them to go straight into the pool. I wasn't happy about it, but I based the decision on a suggestion from Potrac et al. (2002) who stated that if you want to be successful as a coach, you need to be regarded as easily approachable and must be able to relate to the players as footballers, but more importantly as people. At the time this seemed a good idea because it showed that they thought I was easily approachable and I also thought I would have gained further respect from the lads. However, after reflecting upon the situation, and discussing this further within the context of the independent learning environment within the module, I was unconsciously allowing the players *to call the shots*, when that should have been my role.

I later came to understand that not only could the players feel like they possess power over me, but they also have *ammunition* against me if the relationship deteriorates in the future. This is also reinforced by Potrac et al. (2002), who noted that when players feel too comfortable, and you don't have any power over them, it is very difficult to ever get that back. As a consequence, I ultimately considered my decision a mistake, as it put me in an awkward position and would have had a massive effect on my experience if Chris were ever to find out. I later referred to a statement of Osterman and Kottkamp (1993) in order to frame the decision that I had made in this situation, as they noted that learning is most effective when it begins with an experience, specifically a problematic experience. Now I understand there is a potential negative outcome to allow things to slide with regard to players in this particular culture, I subsequently decided to change my approach slightly and become somewhat firmer in my management of the players.

Reflective narrative 3: player treatment – 'get in the ice bath'

It was game day and I had been put in charge as the Head Sports Scientist for the day. What a great feeling this was and one that I feel I had worked hard to achieve. I also needed to collect some data for a study that I was conducting, so I set up an ice bath and targeted four players to get in the ice bath immediately after the game to allow me to collect *good* data. The game ended with a 3–0 win, the spirit amongst the lads was good and the mood was very positive. During the cool down, I asked the targeted lads to get in the ice bath for 2 reasons: (1) as a favour for me; and (2) because they are supposed to as part of their individual recovery method.

'Lads, I need you four to get in the ice bath for me when you go back in, is that OK?' One of the lads Charlie replied, 'Yeah, sound Tom mate, no problem, only five minutes isn't it!' After hearing that response I thought to myself that went well and there were no problems there. After I finished the cool down, I went and had a little chat with the U18's manager Tony to discuss the game and what he thought of it. After having an in-depth chat about how we could have been more clinical in the second half I walked back into the Academy and made my way to the changing room. As I entered, I noticed only three players in the ice bath, so I said, 'OK lads, this is only going to be five minutes so not too long, where is Charlie?' A grouped response from all three players stuttered due to the coldness of the ice bath and one of the boys shouted, 'Oh he has gone Tom, he said he will do it for you next time and that he knew you'd be sound about it.'

Unhappy about Charlie leaving, I decided to take action and go find him. Moments later I saw him in the corridor, changed and ready to go home. I approached him reasonably quickly with a slight frown on my face and aggressively said, 'Charlie, what's all that about? I thought you were getting in the ice bath for me?' He replied, flustering his words with a sheepish look on his face and said, 'Oh yeah sorry about that man, I didn't fancy it so I will do it next game for you deffo mate.'

The thought of being undermined and not taken seriously was playing on my mind and so I decided to take a stand and do something about the situation. I thought that if I let this situation slide, then it might get round to the other players and they will think it's OK to skip the ice bath when I'm in charge. 'No lad, go and get changed, you're going in it now like the others did, it's not up for debate either so hurry up' was my response. The end product was Charlie entering the ice bath with no questioning or arguments.

Reflective case study summary

In addition to finding the balance of treating and communicating to the players as friends, as well as maintaining a sense of authority, I have also come to understand that the football culture is not one to challenge. I found it difficult to work with one colleague in particular throughout the placement and have since revisited and questioned my discipline. I chose not to disclose my personal reflections based on this colleague, as the treatment that I was given was by no means personal. Nevertheless, I have come to better understand that the pressures of the culture that frame the working conditions of people in this environment causes people to behave in various manners towards newcomers in the industry. This can be related to the notions of dominance, power, and fear surrounding ones position within the environment (Potrac et al., 2002). One area that I was particularly pleased with was concerned with the way that I integrated myself into the environment, even though it was a well-known highly pressurized environment (Parker, 2001; Nesti, 2010). I attempted to achieve this by making myself known instantly around the environment and effectively 'putting myself out there' for others to see. I believed that doing this would allow me to overcome my anxiety quicker, rather than just 'going with the motions' of fitting in. Throughout the placement, I believe that both personal and professional development was established as I now have a strong knowledge and understanding of how sports science is implemented within professional football. I have vastly improved my craft skills and practical knowledge as a consequence of increased levels of confidence.

Final thoughts

What we have attempted to capture within the series of narratives in the chapter is an insight into the complexities and challenges faced by one student who entered the world of elite professional football. The emergent cultural issues of power, respect, identity, insecurity, role conflict and masculinity that dominate the commentary are one student's interpretations of the situations that he experienced in the placement setting. Nevertheless, these are the very features that students have typically weaved into their narratives over the years to frame their development as applied football science practitioners. The students have also critiqued the role of sports science in professional football and commented on the technical skills and proficiencies required in the integration and application of certain scientific field-based protocols.

Indeed, while it is clearly beneficial and important that students are able to articulate their knowledge and understanding of such scientific principles, we are, however, principally in the business of developing graduates who should be able to navigate the contours of the professional football industry. In this regard, we believe that it is fundamental that our students progress from the programme with an in-depth and critical understanding of *self* in the context of the *workplace* culture of professional football. This is clearly even more significant and important in light of the rather unique and unpredictable nature relating to the occupational practices evidenced by staff and players within the industry (Roderick, 2006). Moreover, we would contend that the approach to articulate this self-knowledge and developing self-awareness is positively enhanced through the process of reflection and critical confessional writing. It is our belief that the manner of writing that integrates highly personalized and meaningful accounts of practice can help to stimulate and facilitate a depth in learning for students throughout the placement process.

In returning to the emergent concepts momentarily (i.e., power, respect, identity, insecurity, role conflict and masculinity) and the student's interpretation of these within the narrative, we as staff often discuss how different individuals appraise and react to these distinct occupational features. We are also intrigued by the continued display of these norms within the football industry, and why it is that individuals create this particular climate for neophyte practitioners. We should note at this point, however, that the history of our placement provision spans a number of different professional club levels and settings (i.e., inclusive of Academy and 1st Team environments), and that the arguments that we are locating in the chapter are not exclusive to this student case study and particular club setting. The challenge that this provides for us as staff in preparing students for the placement centres upon the notions of understanding self, through the process of reflective practice, to identify important craft skills and knowledge. We believe that the students evidence a greater level of critical self-knowledge through being exposed to the range of situations in the placement setting and making sense of these through the writing process.

The applied situations outlined in the narrative undoubtedly test the resolve and strength of character of the students that are exposed to these, and while we believe that some students are able to manage these challenges, we are also acutely aware that for others, the journey will be much more difficult. Our role in that sense is to support and encourage critical reflection on the cultural features that engender the values of the industry, such that the placement experience does not become one that means the 'football world is not for them'. For course educators in particular, it is worth noting that the incorporation of a reflective element into the curriculum is not without its challenges.

What we often find is that many students struggle initially with the basic concept of reflection (i.e., *what* it is and *how* to do it). Furthermore, students are often not sure of what issues they should be reflecting on or at what level of reflection (i.e. technical, practical or critical issues) they should be engaging in. Additionally, we often find that students can be at very different stages of their reflective journey, in that some are naturally self-aware and of the environment they are in (such as the case study provided herein) whereas others often need their learning 'signposted' throughout their applied experiences.

Finally, for students usually trained in quantitative research methods and hypothesis-driven research, actually writing reflectively does not come easily. Despite these initial challenges, by the end of the placement all students typically have a different perspective of the value of reflection, and moreover the writing process itself. They often consider that the physical process of documenting their reflections on paper, as well as the continual elements of shared and staged reflection with peers and supervisors, leads to a re-evaluation of the benefits of reflection in terms of becoming more competent and well-rounded practitioners. Although this approach to learning requires hard work, honesty and trust from both student and supervisor, we are convinced that it goes some way in making the student a life-long learner. Surely, learning to swim in the real world is, after all, our ultimate educational goal?

7 Enhancing the skills of students through the use of reflective practice in a physical activity and health curriculum

Lindsey Kilgour, Nic Matthews and Diane Crone

Introduction

In this chapter we argue for reflective practice being an effective pedagogic approach in the delivery of physical activity, exercise and health programmes in Higher Education (HE). The aim here is to demonstrate how students' skills can be enhanced and engendered through the taught curriculum. As well as providing a critique of the evidence base supporting the use of reflective practice in HE, supporting content from contributors elsewhere in this section of the book, emphasis is placed on the importance of how reflective practice is embedded, delivered and assessed according to the subject matter and level of study. Moreover, the need and relevance of connecting with local, external partners is attributed as being fundamental to establishing successful reflective practice opportunities within taught programmes. Without these connections, students would not have access to the authentic 'environments' that provide these testing grounds for theory and how it translates into practice.

Reflective practices and reflective practice per se has been prevalent in HE settings since the 1980s, though this propensity was limited mainly to sociology-based and teacher education settings (Bolton, 2005; Russell, 2005). Settings such as these prioritize experiential learning as the main style of learning (Kolb & Kolb, 2005). That is, students have direct experience of the settings relevant to their chosen vocation, and in doing so develop the skills necessary to respond to the varied contexts presented to them, as well as the myriad behavioural issues that they may encounter when operating in those contexts (Hobbs, 2007). Indeed, Kolb (1984) depicted reflection as an inherent part of the experiential learning cycle, where the individual reflects on the dynamic interface between learner and environment that experiential learning presents. More recently, the need for students to be reflective and hone the skills underpinning the reflection process became more widespread in HE, and was highlighted initially as integral to practitioner-based learning (Moon, 2001). In 2001 the Quality Assurance Agency for Higher Education (QAA) formalized reflective practice as a component within all subjects. As a consequence, Higher Education Institutes (HEIs) were encouraged to disseminate reflection, or provide opportunity for reflection, in their programmes through Personal Development and Planning (PDP) (QAA,

2009). Put simply, PDP formed a structured process by which students became responsible for their learning by reflecting on their learning experiences for future gains with regard to employment and career prospects. It is argued that, 'the process of PDP can strengthen the capacity of learners to reflect upon their own learning and achievement and to plan for their own personal, educational and career development' (QAA, 2009, p. 2).

Characteristics of reflective practice

The wealth of evidence to support the use of reflective practice in HE originates predominantly from educational practitioners and researchers (Hobbs, 2007). These authors provide comprehensive debates around the do's and don'ts of reflective practice, creating scenarios where opportunities for reflection can be realized. A number of conceptual, theoretical and practical assumptions have been proposed, which serve as guides for those wishing to embed reflective practice into taught programmes. In following this guidance, the importance of reflective practice in the teaching and learning process (and for the students' PDP) is confirmed. This serves to illustrate the many ways in which students can develop reflective practice skills pertinent to their field of study.

In terms of support for reflective practice, commentators agree that it forms an important part of the teaching and learning strategy and a fundamental skill for those studying for careers where professional competence is central (Mann, Gordon & MacLeod, 2009). Resounding agreement also exists to support the notion of reflection as a methodical process, with various models depicting this process. Accordingly, the learner is able to adopt a step-by-step approach to reflection prior to them entering the practice-based context (Moon, 2001). In considering the various approaches and models of reflective practice and specifically in light of the reflection aspects of PDP in HE, Moon developed an input/outcome model that allows for some interpretation of what constitutes reflection, according to the different academic disciplines/area in which it can be used. This model is useful as it encompasses the range of possibilities available when asking students/ learners to reflect. For example, it considers that 'inputs' to reflection, for example, thoughts, feelings, experience, knowledge and theories, can be standardized regardless of the discipline/area of study. Similarly, the list of possible outcomes serves to encompass potential benefits that can be gained by incorporating aspects of reflection into taught programmes.

There are a number of aspects to reflection, and using reflective practice within taught programmes, that have been the subject of extensive scrutiny and debate. Cautionary tales relating to the question of whether reflection practice can actually be taught are prevalent (Russell, 2005). Questions are raised regarding the inclusion of reflective practice within taught programmes implying that the process can be forced, and therefore a negative or resented aspect of learning to the students involved (Hobbs, 2007) (see also this book, Hollingworth et al., chapter 10). Moreover, widespread debates exist within the literature regarding the timing of the integration of reflective practice within taught programmes

Figure 7.1 An input–output model of reflection (Moon, 2001)

(e.g., Hobbs, 2007; Russell, 2005), the academic level at which it is included within the curriculum (e.g., undergraduate, postgraduate), and most importantly, how it is assessed (e.g., Mann et al., 2009). The most widely used approach in assessing reflective practice tends to be journals and diaries, and according to Moon (1999) they have been used successfully in most disciplines. However, William and Wessel (2004) explored the authenticity of the content of journals and diaries when used to assess reflective practice and reflective thinking, concluding that students were conscious of writing what they thought their lecturers wanted to read as opposed to writing candidly and expressively.

In their systematic review of reflective practice in health professions education, Mann et al. (2009, p. 610) stated that reflection 'fulfills several functions, including making meaning of complex situations and enabling from learning experience'. In summary, they offer guidance on what the evidence suggests facilitates reflection and reflective practice most effectively: an authentic context; a supportive learning environment; a mentoring support programme; accommodation for individual differences in learning style; free expression of opinion and time for reflection. In addition to this is the ongoing debate regarding the best 'time' to use reflective practice within the teaching context. As Hobbs (2007, p. 406) is eager to emphasize, 'being critically aware is an acquired skill that comes with experience and great intellect', which calls into question the effective use of reflection and reflective practice with novice learners and practitioners. Indeed, Bloom's (1956) taxonomy depicts how criticality, via evaluation and synthesis, is not normally assessed until the final year, in most cases the third year, of undergraduate study (in the context of this chapter, Level 6). Moreover, Gadsby and Cronin (2012) emphasize the need for student teachers to develop the skills to reflect critically, and also self-reflect, only in their move from undergraduate- to postgraduate-level study (Masters level, in the context of this chapter, Level 7).

The consideration of these varied aspects of reflective practice will be revisited later in the chapter for the purpose of detailing their use in taught modules within a physical activity and health curriculum. Specifically, the case is made for how students are able to see the benefits of reflective practice in skill development once they leave their studies. The next section will contextualize the professional and academic background of physical activity and health in order to demonstrate how the features of the context lend themselves to the features of reflective practice.

The physical activity and health context: considerations for the taught curriulum

The 1990s marked a significant change in terms of policy for health and public health provision and practice in most developed countries, with many public health organizations publishing statements regarding the pitfalls of sedentary living (Marcus & Forsyth, 2003). Before the Second World War, 'public health was changing to focus on chronic non-communicable diseases and the modification of individual behaviour' (Hardman & Stensel, 2003, p. 4), and the dawn of the twenty-first century was characterized by rising levels of obesity, an increasing ageing population and inactivity in children. This shift in the 1990s was supported by four decades of epidemiological-based evidence that supported the relationship between physical activity and health (e.g., Baecke, Burema & Frijters, 1982; Blair et al., 1995; Morris et al., 1953; Paffenbarger et al., 1986), and the contemporary academic fields of study that now exist (i.e., Physical Activity, Exercise and Health, Physical Activity and Health, Physical Activity and Public Health) are testament to this relationship.

Integral to all these fields of study is the role of the health professional/ practitioner, and in some cases a significant proportion of the taught content of these courses can be practical or experiential in nature. For example, it is not uncommon for courses within the physical activity and health context to be interdisciplinary in nature, focusing on physiology and nutrition, as well as psychology, behaviour change and policy. These various disciplines provide a breath to the curriculum, which lends itself to diverse learning contexts, skills development and assessment methods. During their course of study, a student may find him/her self engaging in skills-based practicals focusing on cardio respiratory fitness (e.g., Cardiac Rehabilitation) or dietary analysis, while in other modules examining policy guidelines and exploring the effectiveness of these guidelines when transferred to the practice context. So, while the successful completion of the degree does not depend solely on being an effective practitioner – with the exception of modules such as Cardiac Rehabilitation – having experience of the practice-based context during the learning process certainly strengthens a student's profile and provides more credibility for future employment.

Similarly, working in the physical activity and health/public health area requires skills such as problem-solving, working in multidisciplinary teams and having an awareness of the role of the various partners involved in promoting physical activity for health improvement. Typically work in this area is characterized by programmes or interventions that are set up to improve health for various population groups (see Flannery et al., chapter 2). Often these programmes or interventions take place in community-based settings including schools, sheltered housing, workplaces, local neighbourhoods, leisure centres and parks, as well as in primary and secondary health care contexts. Thus, employees (and therefore graduates) need to have experience, knowledge and skills of applied working practices that are multifaceted and involve inter- and multi-disciplinary working with a variety of other health professionals. These professionals are typically GPs, nurses, public health specialists, fitness instructors and volunteer walks leaders, who are working with people with health problems (either physical or mental), children and older people. The point here is that students need to develop confidence though experiential learning to be able to comfortably converse with such professionals and operate competently in different areas of the community as a whole. These facets combined relate directly to the authenticity of the context as outlined by Mann et al. (2009).

Embedding reflective practice within physical activity and health curricula is further supported by the successful application in closely related subjects of sports coaching (e.g., Carson, 2008; Faull & Cropley, 2009) and sports psychology (Cropley, Hanton, Miles & Niven, 2007, 2010), where the effectiveness of the practitioner is paramount to the practitioner–performer relationship, as well as the performance and success of the sports personnel they are working with. The following section will draw on two approaches to reflection embedded in modules delivered at the undergraduate (UG), Level 6, and postgraduate (PG), Level 7. The case studies serve as examples of how students' skills of reflection can be enhanced through engagement with a range of tools/techniques. In turn, they illustrate the role played by experiential learning, reflective writing, self-reflection and critical reflection in a physical activity and health curriculum. These approaches are indicative of the many ways students can be introduced to and be encouraged to appraise elements of professional practice. Moreover, justification is provided for the contrasting expectation of students' undertaking reflection at the different levels of study, reinforcing the variation of module content, modes of delivery and assessment methods.

Case study context

It is important that HEIs prepare graduates at undergraduate and postgraduate level for the reality of working as a health professional and the diversity that such a career path might offer. For students the opportunity to be introduced to and experience a range of settings in which professionals are located can be invaluable. They can observe the application of concepts such as evidence-based practice, evaluate the implementation of activities such as social marketing (Bauman, 2004) and also see the translation of theory into practice in regard to areas such as behaviour change. Understanding how these aspects of their studies operate in professional contexts and how they themselves might apply them requires an appraisal of their knowledge and understanding and current skills base. In line with the foundations of PDP set out by the QAA and HEIs, students are encouraged to see reflective practice as the basis for career development into the long term. Developing students' ability to problem-solve and have confidence to consider how to do things differently are important employability skills. Students typically plan to work in (or, in fewer instances, are working) local government leisure and health departments, in positions such as Physical Activity or Lifestyle Development Officers, and for the NHS as leads on child weight management programmes, Health Trainers or Lifestyle Advisers. Other opportunities are in health and lifestyle promotion in areas such as education and the public and private leisure sector.

Case study 1 (undergraduate, Level 6)

Aim

The purpose of this section is to set out how undergraduate students on a sport and exercise programme are introduced to the principles of reflective practice. As a multidisciplinary degree programme the curriculum is inevitably drawn from across the natural and social sciences; the breadth of the curriculum reflects the range of professional environments the students might find themselves working within. As part of a single-semester module *Contemporary Concepts in Exercise and Health Practice*, final-year students are offered the opportunity to engage with local practitioners delivering community health and physical activity initiatives. The module aims to critique the role of the exercise and health professional within multi- and inter-disciplinary working environments and to appraise the implications of contemporary contexts of health provision for the students' continuing professional development. For students in their final year of study it is important that their curriculum has an 'external' focus as the students themselves will be considering the next phase of their personal development.

Embedding reflection

The students choosing this module are tasked with undertaking a block of experiential learning attached to a local physical activity or health-related initiative.

The assessment is to then complete a reflective commentary. In line with the characterization of effective reflection on practice offered by Mann et al. (2009), the teaching team for this module recognise the need to offer students the opportunity to experience, among other things: a supportive learning environment; an authentic context; time to reflect; and freedom of expression.

To take these in turn, the first step is to introduce students to the fundamentals of reflective practice and work with them to go through examples and scenarios that help to highlight the principles of reflection before they are tasked to do it for themselves. In short, they should see it as a skill that can underpin their continued professional development. The emphasis is on shifting attention away from formal or traditional channels of knowledge transfer towards individuals identifying learning opportunities that emanate from their own experiences. However, that transition to become a self-critical professional with the capacity to examine their own values and actions can be challenging.

Using a reflective writing exercise, *The Park* by Moon (2004), the students are introduced to different levels of reflection. The exercise includes four different accounts of the same incident that takes place in a park. Each account is progressively more reflective in its tone allowing the students to see a qualitative distinction between the styles of writing. This class-based activity allows discussion of the key characteristics of reflective commentaries. Each of the four accounts builds on the last and challenges the student to recognise shifts in style from the inclusion of extraneous, descriptive information, through to the acknowledgement of multiple perspectives, the place of values and beliefs within the commentary and finally consideration of how these beliefs may influence behaviour. On completion of the task, students work in small discussion groups to share their understanding of different levels of reflection, and how this shapes reflective practice.

Taking the principles of reflective writing out of the classroom and into a practical context is the next step. Mann et al. (2009) argue that authenticity is important if students are to be encouraged to see the value in self-reflection and to subsequently cast a critical eye over the professional environment. Understanding the relationship between actions and values, recognizing contrasting viewpoints and substituting description for substantive observations can be difficult for experienced health professionals. Asking early-career practitioners to audit their skills and offer insight into practice is therefore not to be taken lightly. That said, it is important that students do have the opportunity to appraise their skills *in situ*. Students in this instance have the chance to attend exercise referral schemes (i.e., Phase IV cardiac rehabilitation and GP referral), health walks, school- and community-based healthy lifestyle initiatives with children and young people, during a four-week 'mini-placement'.

The range of placements is indicative of growing interest in physical activity-based initiatives and the increasing complexity of the modes of delivery. Students get to see the reality of a field of practice that is reliant on partnerships, diverse funding streams and a mix of volunteer and paid workers. Seeing projects over an extended period of time (up to a month) affords students the time to reflect on their experiences, which in turn encourages a full and informed expression of those views. Site visits undertaken in isolation will not result in the depth of evaluation sought from reflective activities. Engaging with projects over a longer period allows students to pick up on the effect that issues such as funding and restructuring have on workforce morale, the impact that health professionals can have on a client's willingness to change their health behaviours and start to understand how national policy is translated once it reaches those delivering programmes. For many undergraduates this will be the first time they are seeing policy and its consequences in practice. The challenge is to encourage the students to capture the reality of professional life by recognizing both good and bad practice, and how this impacts on the delivery of programmes. It is noted that in the early stages of reflection, undergraduate students experience difficulty in identifying and critiquing poor or ineffective practice.

Case study 2 (postgraduate, Level 7)

Aim

The purpose of this second case study is to provide two examples, from postgraduate study, of how reflection and experiential learning have been embedded into a taught programme. The aim of embedding reflection and experiential learning into the assignments of these modules is to assist the learner (the postgraduate student) in gaining knowledge, skills and competencies, which are difficult to experience in the confines of a traditionally taught postgraduate degree programme. The experiential learning in this case study adopts Hinett's (2002) interpretation, which includes four stages including: understanding what is known now; identifying what needs to be undertaken; feedback and evaluation; and integration of the new knowledge into practice. These examples focus on providing experiential learning within partnership working and reflection on their own role in group work, which can emulate some aspects of partnership working. Experiencing partnership working and reflecting on their role are critical requirements in the workplace, and central to physical activity and health promotion work in practice. This aspect of the modules enhances the need for authenticity when adopting reflective practice in taught programmes (Mann et al., 2009).

The modules

PHYSICAL ACTIVITY AND HEALTH POLICY

This module aims to provide students with a critical examination of the principal policies that have informed contemporary physical activity and health practice. While the central tenet of the module is the exploration of policy, it provides an opportunity to consider the roles and working practices of key health organizations and their partners involved in public health, and the interrelationships between policymakers, purchasers and providers in physical activity and health. As such, it is the students' first exposure to partnership working, specifically the importance and prevalence of multidisciplinary and interdisciplinary working practices. The assessment focuses on the challenges of partnership working, but from the students' perspective as they are required to reflect upon their own role in the development and presentation of a group project.

PHYSICAL ACTIVITY AND HEALTH: EVIDENCE-BASED APPROACHES
TO PRACTICE

This module aims to develop a critical appreciation of evidence-based practice within physical activity and sport contexts, specifically relating to healthy lifestyle behaviours and mass participation. This module exposes students to a range of interventions within the community and health care for the improvement of public health. It challenges the evidence underpinning such interventions. This example tackles the problem of how best to use evidence to develop practice through an experiential learning task, which comprises of an audit of physical activity provision, undertaken in partnership with a local government Leisure and Sport Development Service from Cheltenham Borough Council. Findings from the task can then be used by the Borough Council to inform their future practice.

Embedding reflection

In *Physical Activity and Health Policy* students are required to work together in a group, to develop a health initiative that involves some element of physical activity for the attainment/maintenance of health. This initiative must be designed for a specific target group that is, older people, people with mental health problems and within a recognised health locality area, namely, Gloucester. Assignment 1 is a group presentation where students present to deliver the initiative to module staff, as if bidding for a contract to the NHS. The reflection element is introduced in assignment 2 and requires them to reflect, using a model of reflection (Gibbs, 1988) provided by the module team, on the design and preparation of the initiative, its presentation and the questions (posed by the assessors) following the presentation of their initiative.

Embedding experiential learning

Physical Activity and Health: Evidence-based Approaches to Practice requires the students to work in collaboration with Cheltenham Borough Council to audit one of eight geographical areas of the Borough and assess physical activity opportunities available in the area. This audit is undertaken through market research and critical intelligence-gathering for a mapping exercise of the area and its facilities/opportunities. A number of investigative methods are used, including:

- Visits to the locality, i.e., town halls, church halls
- Scouring the Yellow Pages and the internet for clubs and classes
- Telephone calls to the deliverers of these activities, i.e., a local yoga teacher.

The audit needs to be undertaken thoroughly to ensure they have the required data to analyse their findings with a market segmentation approach, to identify potential gaps and duplications of provision in their geographical area. The students are then required to contextualize these findings into the broader public health policy and practice context in the local area and in the UK generally. The intelligence they develop provides Cheltenham Borough Council's Leisure and Sport Development Service with useful evidence on which to base their practice and service developments in the coming year.

Conclusions

This chapter aimed to demonstrate the potential for skills development of students through the embodiment of reflective practice in a taught physical activity and health curriculum. As well as interpreting the evidence underpinning the area and reviewing the application of key tenets to the taught curriculum, pragmatic steps were taken to ensuring the successful delivery of the modules in question. Collaborating with external Physical Activity and Health practitioners enabled us to provide invaluable opportunities for students by embedding aspects of reflective practice within modules and assessments. Ghaye and Lillyman (2006) suggest there are numerous models of reflection, yet despite this diversity there are qualities that are common across them all. Most noticeably they are practitioner-focused, they support efforts to overcome 'professional inertia' (p. 16), they encourage individuals to assign meaning and values to their practice and they encourage the planning of future actions by those engaging in a reflective cycle.

For undergraduate students in the final stage of their programme the opportunity to enhance their skills of reflection and situate that learning within contemporary work settings can only serve to enhance their employability. Similarly for postgraduate students, the continued enhancement of reflective practice skills facilitates personal and professional development and fosters meaningful experiences that can be transferred into the workplace. Reflective practice per se can provide a structure that supports the learning process, as well as aiding the development of imaginative and practitioner-based assessments that foster inter- and multi-disciplinary working practice and provides students with the following employment-related requirements:

- opportunity to engage with experiential learning
- to develop recognition of how policy and evidence is applied and transferred into practice
- to provide opportunities to take an active and influential part in applied practice
- enjoyment and engagement of students in learning, and
- improved employability.

Clearly, there are lessons to be learned regarding lecturers' expectations of students' ability to learn and hone skills inherent to reflective practice, both at modular and programme level. In particular, do the lecturers address the theoretical and evidence-based aspects of reflective practice during taught sessions? Further, do students have awareness of their abilities to move from descriptive reflections to more critical reflections and considerations of how this is assessed (Gadsby & Cronin, 2012)? Ultimately, there is the question of the importance of when, where and how to embed reflective practice and opportunities for experiential learning needs and how these are prioritized at curriculum development level, maximizing a specific skill set for students and linking directly to explicit career-focused pathways.

Acknowledgements

The first author would like to thank Gavin Chesterfield for his advice and guidance.

8 Reflections on reflection
Some personal experiences of delivering higher education coach education

Phil Marshall, Lee Nelson, John Toner and Paul Potrac

Introduction

The last two decades have witnessed significant growth in the academic and prac-tical attention given to the preparation and ongoing development of coaches (Cushion, 2006; Knowles, Borrie & Telfer, 2005; Knowles, Gilbourne, Borrie & Nevill, 2001; Lyle & Cushion, 2010). In many ways, reflection has arguably become, at least in a rhetorical sense, the 'grand idée' (Jay & Johnson, 2002, p. 73) that underpins much of the education and continuing professional devel-opment (CPD) of coaching practitioners (Cassidy, Jones & Potrac, 2009; Nel-son & Cushion, 2006; Gilbourne, Marshall & Knowles, 2013). Indeed, there has been an increasing recognition of the benefits of helping coaches to learn from their practical experiences in a meaningful and productive manner and, relatedly, to combine theory with practice in ways that might avoid the pitfalls associated with both 'technical rationality' and the 'fallacy of theoryless practice' (Cassidy et al., 2009). In this respect, numerous coaching scholars (e.g., Cassidy, Potrac & McKenzie, 2006; Cassidy et al., 2009; Gilbert & Trudel, 2001, 2005; Jones, 2006, among others) have promoted critical reflection as a valuable educational tool for helping to prepare coaches for the often dynamic, messy and ethically demanding challenges of practice.

While we believe that critical reflection provides a potentially powerful way of thinking about coaching practice, our attempts to foster the philosophy, values and intellectual processes associated with critical reflection among our students have not been a straightforward and unproblematic experience. We have been both pleasantly surprised and, at times, bitterly disappointed by the consequences that have emanated from our collective decision to embed and formally assess critically reflective work in our coaching degree programme. Encouraging stu-dents to develop their *open-mindedness, wholeheartedness* and *responsibility* is any-thing but a straightforward activity (Dewey, 1916; Cassidy et al., 2009). Like educators in other fields of practice (e.g., Cranton, 2002; Freese, 2006; Ward & McCotter, 2004), we are worried about the willingness of some of our students to delimit their critical thought to solely identifying other people or events as the root causes for all of the problematic experiences that they may have had in practice settings. There has been, in some cases, an almost complete refusal on the behalf of the students to acknowledge their own actions, knowledge bases, philosophies and choices as potential contributors to the difficult situations that have arisen. This is perhaps not surprising, as Tinning (1995, p. 50) noted that 'if becoming reflective were simply a rational process then it would be easy to train . . . teachers [read coaches] to be reflective'. As we can firmly attest to in our pedagogical work, achieving this goal is not so simple as many of the issues that coaches might be asked to reflect upon are 'not merely a matter of rational argument' but, instead, 'have a large measure of emotion and subjectivity embedded within them' (Tinning, 1995, p. 50).

We also have concerns regarding the 'studentship' (Graber, 1991) that learners on our programme may engage with in order to obtain what they consider to be a 'good mark'. The problem from our perspective is certainly not the striving for high grades per se, but instead how the outcome (i.e., the mark awarded to assessed work) is increasingly viewed as being far more valuable than the process of developing one's ability to engage in critical thought. We can very much relate to the findings that have problematized the assessment of coach learning in the wider coach education literature (e.g., Chesterfield, Potrac & Jones, 2010). Finally, and in a related vein, we have come to recognise how our desire to help students achieve 'a good mark' in the context of an increasingly marketized and consumer-orientated higher education sector (Hussey & Smith, 2010; Molesworth, Scullion & Nixon, 2011) has led us to engage in practices that may sometimes encourage and reinforce studentship in our learners. These collective issues and the irony that perhaps surrounds them have made some of our teaching team meetings uncomfortable. Although we have no answers to these issues at this stage, we believe that the sharing of our experiences may at least stimulate discussion on some of the problematic aspects of trying to facilitate and assess critically reflective thought.

More specifically in this chapter we wish to share our thoughts, experiences and concerns on these topics as they relate to a final-year work-based learning module (*Professional Practice in Coaching and Performance*) that forms part of our coaching degree programme. In structural terms the initial section of the chapter will provide background information relating to the underpinning pedagogical philosophy, structure, delivery and assessment of the module. Following this introductory information, the focus will then shift to exploring the thoughts, choices and experiences of Phil, the module leader and his interactions with Danielle, a student on the module. The chapter will then go on to explore the experiences of Mark, a student who achieved a first-class degree, with direct reference to his engagement with the reflective process on this module. Finally, in the concluding section, we provide our own reflections on the issues and tensions that have arisen as a consequence of the problematic interplay between increasingly dominant discourses of marketization and consumerism in higher education and our own efforts to facilitate the development of critical reflection in our degree programme.

Professional practice in coaching and performance: a module overview

In acknowledgement of the benefits increasingly ascribed to development of reflective coaching practitioners, we, as a programme team, decided to design a Level 6 work experience module (*Professional Practice in Coaching and Performance*) that had theory of reflection at its pedagogical core. Our intention here was not only to provide the learners on our programme (*BSc Sports Coaching and Performance*) with an opportunity to practically implement the knowledge and skills that they had started to develop through their engagement with Level 4 (Year 1), Level 5 (Year 2) and Level 6 (Year 3) modules, but also to encourage them to think critically about those issues that they would inevitably face in practical situations. With respect to the latter, we were especially keen for students to consider how and why they might address the everyday issues and dilemmas that they may experience in practice. Additionally, we wanted to design the module in a way that encouraged our students to give thought to their career aspirations and how the experiences they would gain from completing a work placement might impact on such decision-making.

When planning the module around our desired learning objectives, it became increasingly apparent that we might be able to encourage reflective thinking through a method of assessment that would provide our students, and their thought processes, with clear conceptual guidance. We constructed assignment guidelines for the generation of a 5,000-word reflective portfolio that was submitted following the completion of a 20-day work placement in a coaching or a sports-related teaching setting. The portfolio was segregated into two distinct sections, parts A and B. In Part A the students were required to provide contextual information regarding their work placement, outline any positive and negative experiences encountered, consider whether or not the placement identified any knowledge or skills gaps, and to articulate how the opportunity impacted on future career aspirations.

Following this, we decided to construct Part B of the assessment guidelines around Gilbert and Trudel's (2001; 2005) model of experiential learning. Our intention here was to provide a framework that we hoped would facilitate our students' engagement in reflective conversations, in a way that was empirically and theoretically supported. In light of Gilbert and Trudel's (2001; 2005) work, it was determined that students would be required to identify two coaching issues, and to discuss, in detail, each phase of the reflective conversations that they engaged in. Here, the students were asked to utilize the subheadings informed by Gilbert and Trudel's (2001) model.

Within the *Coaching Issue and Issue Setting* subheading, the assignment guidelines stipulated that students were expected to describe the identified coaching issue, as it related to their own personal practice or the actions of the placement supervisor. This entailed highlighting whether it was personally or jointly constructed, considering how the setting of the issue was influenced by their own and/or their supervisor's role frame, and discussing how the issue could be situated in relation to Van Manen's (1977) three levels of reflection (i.e., technical, practical and critical). In the *Strategy Generation* section of the assignment, students were required to describe a plan for how they would deal with the identified issue, should it arise again. Here, students were asked to outline a strategy informed by appropriate theory, empirical research evidence and, where appropriate, the advice of the supervisor and/or other experienced practitioners. At the *Experimentation* phase students were permitted to write about either a 'real-world' (i.e., the implementation of the strategy in practice) or 'virtual-world' (i.e., discussion with supervisor about possible consequences of the proposed strategy) experiment. Finally, the *Evaluation* section of the assessment guidelines encouraged students to consider the effectiveness of their strategy. While it was acknowledged that the evaluation presented would depend on the type of experiment completed, in both instances students were advised to collate evidence from discussions with their supervisors.

In addition to the above assessment guidelines, it was also decided that students would receive a number of lectures and one-to-one support sessions throughout the module. It was agreed that four lectures would be delivered in total. In the opening session students were provided with a broad module overview, an introduction to the various documents that students and supervisors were required to complete before being permitted to start their work experience, and information about their responsibilities while on placement. During the second lecture the students were presented with a detailed overview of Gilbert and Trudel's (2001; 2005) work and informed about how their experiential learning model underpinned the assessment for this module. Finally, two additional sessions were planned to aid the students' writing of a cover letter and curriculum vitae, and essential interview skills. These topics were considered particularly pertinent as numerous local placement providers stipulated that they would implement a selection process. One-to-one support sessions with the module leader were also timetabled to ensure that students were provided with ongoing support in relation to not only the process of reflection, but writing up such reflections in accordance with the guidelines discussed.

Staff and student perspectives on the module

Having provided an overview of the module's structure, aims and method of assessment, we would now like to outline the experiences of the module leader (Phil Marshall) and those of a student, Mark, who recently completed the degree programme. In recruiting our student participant, we intentionally sought a First-Class honours student whose work suggested that he had thoroughly engaged with, and critically reflected upon, his work experience placement and had utilised relevant theoretical frameworks to interpret and explain how he dealt with both coaching issues. We will begin by contrasting the work of this student with Phil's experience of another student, Danielle, who appeared to have misunderstood the module aims and who failed to achieve any true level of critical reflection. Phil's recollection is as follows:

> As Danielle sat down opposite me, she had a look of real concern on her face. She had booked in to one of the support sessions offered to students taking this module. The student in question had completed their placement at a local sports club and had chosen to focus her reflection on her practices, behaviours and choices in the club setting. Her underlying motivation for taking the degree programme was to aid entry into a full-time career in coaching or, as an alternative, teaching physical education in a secondary school. Danielle felt that she hadn't encountered anything that represented a 'critical incident' while on placement.

Before discussing this further I reviewed the student's paperwork for the placement. This included a feedback sheet from her placement supervisor. In this instance the supervisor had been the head of coaching at the sports club. The feedback was diplomatically presented but suggested that Danielle wasn't suited to a career in coaching and, instead, went on to suggest a range of alternative career options that she may wish to consider.

Danielle was aware of this feedback, and so I began my discussion with her by highlighting these points and asking why she didn't think these comments were evidence of a critical incident occurring while she was on placement. As we talked two things became apparent to me. Firstly, there had been a whole host of potential incidents, which she could discuss in her assignment. Secondly, this student clearly hadn't engaged in any level of reflection on her placement experience! As we talked 'the penny seemed to drop', and we discussed a range of possible theoretical frameworks that she could use to explore some of the issues that had clearly arisen while she was on placement. I hoped that by engaging in reflection on these matters Danielle may achieve some self-realisation and make meaningful progress in addressing some of the problems that had been raised by the placement supervisor.

I encouraged Danielle to consider the feedback from her supervisor and other colleagues at the sports club to aid her in making sense of these experiences. In addition, I explained that this would help her to address these issues.

Despite several additional meetings the final coursework submission barely achieved a pass mark. The theoretical frameworks were present, just as we had discussed. However, rather than being used to aid reflection, they had, instead, been used to support a one-way line of argument that suggested that other coaching staff, players and the head of coaching had been totally responsible for the problems that occurred. In contrast, she described how, despite the feedback, she was entirely blameless.

Mark's situation closely resembled that of the student described above. He too had chosen to take the degree programme to offer him an entry into a career in coaching or in teaching secondary school physical education. However, and in contrast to Danielle, the work he presented showed evidence of critical reflection.

For example, he considered his actions and choices within his work-based setting and the ways in which these may have positively or negatively influenced his working relationships with others. Here, he was equally willing to identify the knowledge and skill bases that he thought he needed to develop in order to become a better practitioner. Furthermore, he had made use of a range of interwoven theoretical frameworks, while at the same time considering feedback gained through discussion with a range of colleagues encountered while on placement. To investigate his experiences of this further we asked Mark to recall how he completed the written assignment. Here, Mark spoke about taking a number of steps to ensure that he gave himself the best chance of achieving a high grade. For example, in choosing the two specific coaching issues that he addressed in his written work he revealed that:

> I wanted to choose experiences that I knew would allow me to give critical analysis in terms of relevant theory. . . . I wanted two issues that would allow me to engage with the academic literature. . . . I chose issues that were not necessarily the biggest issues that arose during the placement or issues that I thought were necessarily the worst issues . . . they were the two issues that I felt I could construct an argument around . . . obviously that would help me get a better grade.

Mark explained that he had observed numerous issues in his supervisor's coaching, but chose those that he felt could be easily theorised and in a way that his tutor, Phil, would approve of. As such, he deliberately chose two coaching issues that he felt he could link to theoretical frameworks that he was familiar with. Mark had already received high marks in the Level 5 and semester-one Level 6 module assignments, where he had drawn heavily on the same theories. In justifying this approach, he explained that:

> I didn't choose a completely new (theoretical) framework, as it takes a lot more time to develop that knowledge, especially just for one module. I probably wouldn't have been able to go that deep into the theory and actually critiqued the theory.

> Furthermore, although he felt that Phil would have 'no problem' if he had utilised alternative theoretical frameworks appropriately, Mark chose to use theories that 'tied in with the underlying beliefs and values of the lecturers here'.

Another example of such strategic action arose when we discovered that his accounts of the coaching issues presented in his assignment were not entirely honest or accurate in their portrayal. Here, Mark revealed that he had embellished them slightly in order to make the issues 'seem quite big and important' as he felt that this 'would make my argument seem stronger'. More specifically, Mark had portrayed his placement supervisor as being sometimes verbally aggressive when, in fact, he had been little more than dismissive of some individuals during the coaching sessions. In explaining why he employed this tactic Mark stated that:

> If I said it was negative and abusive it was very much one side of the coin. . . . He also did lots of positive things. . . . I had my issue and it was like how can I make this issue tie in with the literature so I can get the best grade possible. . . . Within the theory I knew that negative and abusive ties in quite nicely.

These comments from Mark were (and continue to be) a source of significant concern to us. On one level, the selective representation of the placement supervisor's practice is something that we do not condone from both ethical and academic perspectives. Equally, while we were aware of the concept of studentship, we were disappointed to retrospectively discover Mark's actions here, as they were, from our perspective, the antithesis of the critically reflective mind-set that we had been attempting to develop with our students.

We discovered a further act of studentship when Mark revealed that he had selectively used certain interview quotes (and ignored others) from his placement supervisor so that he could more effectively map his findings against existing empirical research. This strategy allowed him to provide a volume of evidence in support of his strategy generation, experimentation and evaluation. He felt that to achieve a good mark on the assignment he needed to 'show something a little bit different . . . from getting a good grades point of view it shows that you can take an interview and link theory to that interview which is a pretty good analysis'. Indeed, he acknowledged how the module leader had repeatedly stressed the importance of such supporting material as part of a well-balanced and in-depth process of reflection.

Mark's decision to employ these tactics was heavily influenced by his desire to obtain at least a 2:1 classification in his degree. Without this he perceived he would not have had the opportunity of pursuing postgraduate study, something which he saw as essential in helping him to achieve his overall career aspirations. When questioned about how he had learnt this approach, Mark revealed that by the second year of the course he was 'beginning to understand how the academic system worked'. He explained how we, his tutors, had repeatedly argued that quality assignments were characterized by a critical perspective grounded in, and supported by, relevant theoretical frameworks. Having discovered in a second-year assignment that he could present field-based data in a strategic manner, his next step was to present his findings in a way that neatly tied in with the theoretical frameworks favoured by his respective tutors. For Mark, this approach became a clear and logical 'recipe' for academic success and ultimately proved effective, as he achieved a first-class mark in this module and the programme overall.

Reflections on our own pedagogy

The two examples given above have much in common from our perspective as tutors. Both students wanted to pursue the same career paths. Both were keen to achieve the grades they required to allow them to follow this career. Both attempted to provide the module leader with what they thought he wanted, to allow them to achieve these grades. On the face of it, one of these students was not able to do this with any evidence of critical reflection on their placement experience, while the other appeared to do an admirable job. In reality it could be argued that neither student engaged in critical self-reflection on their placement. Where Mark did succeed, though, was in reflecting on the nature of the assessment process and in delivering in accordance with the module leader's preferences. This led him to adopt a strategic approach to his studies, ultimately aimed at achieving the outcome he desired. Danielle's failure to engage in introspection, choosing instead to externally attribute blame to colleagues and co-workers, left her ill prepared to achieve the grades that she desired. This was especially frustrating given the importance attached to students placing themselves at the centre of the reflective process, in other modules on the programme. Of course, Danielle was not the first and, in all likelihood, she will not be the last to do this. The issue of critical engagement remains one of our most challenging issues.

What cannot be ignored in the two examples we have explored here are the broader issues, which may have influenced these behaviours. For both of these students the investment of time and money into their respective degree programmes was driven by a desire to realize their career aspirations. Arguably, these motivations strongly influenced the approach they took to this assessment process. Given the significant pressures of the employment market at the present time, it was perhaps unsurprising that the need to achieve a 2:1 degree classification or better was foremost in their minds. With regard to their possible career pursuits, this outcome would help Danielle and Mark to possibly find employment in coaching, while also leaving open the option of becoming a Physical Education teacher. Here we could regard students as consumers, who saw the successful completion of the degree programme as a means of gaining an advantage in a challenging and competitive market place for training and employment (Bauman, 2007; Molesworth, Scullion & Nixon, 2011).

We are aware that this module occurs at a significant point in the lives and studies of our students. It encompasses the whole of their third year and makes an important contribution to their overall degree classification. In the two years that it has run the module average has been in the 2:1 category. Feedback from our external examiners on the quality of student work for this module has been excellent. In addition we have observed a number of pleasing outcomes in terms of students gaining employment, following their placements. These are all desirable outcomes and perhaps, up until this point, we have (understandably, some may say) tended to focus on these results and compliments rather than asking more difficult questions about how they might have been achieved (and we 'get' the irony).

Mark's comments reflect the range of pressures he perceived in terms of possible career options and a related desire to maximize his final degree classification. In the short term, the desired goal was a favourable grade for the module, in the medium term a better overall mark for his degree, and in the long term hopefully improved employment prospects. Set against the backdrop of a national economic recession and high unemployment figures, this makes absolute sense to us all. Indeed, staff engaged in the promotion of critical reflection cannot, in our view, ignore the importance that some students may place on 'getting' a degree, as opposed to 'being' learners.

Such experiences have prompted us to consider the place of critical reflection within our undergraduate-coaching curriculum. While the preceding examples have led us to increasingly problematize the ways in which we strive to further the critically reflective capacities of the students on our programme, we remain convinced of the benefits of our aspiration in this regard. Indeed, we believe that the students who graduate from our programme should not only be technically proficient coaching practitioners, but individuals who are also capable of acting in ethical, caring and socially responsible ways. We very much hope that our graduates will increasingly recognise the value of thinking about themselves, their practices, their relationships and the social world in a critically reflective manner. In a world of increasing individualism and commodification, we believe that this is one of the central tenets of a university education (Bauman, 2007; Bauman & Donskis, 2013). Of course, making this a reality is no easy endeavour, and we have increasingly recognised that students do not engage with critical reflection in a uniform and consistent way. From our experiences, there are varying degrees of willingness to think about actions, choices and thoughts in this regard. Equally, as educators, we believe that it is important to avoid making the same mistake that we ascribed to Danielle earlier in this chapter; that is not to lay the fault at the feet of others. We also need to recognise how our own choices and actions may have contributed to the problems we experienced with Danielle and Mark. This is something that will be explored in the section below.

Final thoughts from the man at the helm

I cannot ignore the fact that I had a significant role to play in these stories of failed critical engagement. Perhaps, like the students discussed above, I too am guilty of failing to engage in true critical reflection. In many ways I have fallen into a means–ends trap. Like the students, my practice and pedagogical approach cannot be divorced from wider social pressures and expectations. I am becoming increasingly aware of the reality that I operate within the confines, and sometimes counterintuitive nature, of various social, political and institutional pressures and expectations. These external factors are driven by the same kind of ideological and economic conditions, which might influence the decision-making of our students; in effect we are all in the same trap. A frequent coffee time discussion that we have on this topic focuses on why individuals (be they teachers, students, employers, employees) choose to act in ways that ultimately reproduce the existing status quo regardless of its apparent issues, problems, paradoxes and contradictions. This remains very much a work in progress!

In an increasingly competitive higher education sector, student attainment is one of several indicators by which academic institutions are being judged, both internally and externally; an environment where the positive outcomes described above are so desirable that the processes are deemed acceptable. However, as I continue to consider Mark's story (and indeed my experiences with Danielle), I am forced to question my own criticality, my own critical engagement with aspects of my own practice and, with that, the relationship between assessment scores and the development of critical reflection in those that I teach. Of course, when trying to grapple with these issues it is easy to overlook the more positive outcomes that I have experienced with students on this module. During tutorial meetings with students and when reading their written reports, I have been both pleased and impressed with the ways in which some students have shown a refreshing willingness and capacity for reflecting on their experiences in a critical, conscientious and indeed ethical manner. I guess the issue that we face as educators is that learners are capable of responding in a multitude of ways to a given pedagogical approach. This is something that I am beginning to increasingly accept in my efforts to promote critical reflection. However, this does not mean that I should avoid giving ongoing thought to 'what I do', 'how I do it' and 'why I act as I do' in regard to my teaching practices.

Conclusion

The aim of this chapter was to provide some insights into the dilemmas, contradictions and challenges that accompanied Phil's efforts to facilitate critical reflection among students enrolled on the *Professional Practice in Coaching and Performance* module. As Mark's and Phil's respective accounts demonstrated, fostering such reflective practice can be a far more intellectually, philosophically and emotionally challenging endeavour than is first appreciated (Cassidy et al., 2009). Perhaps the key point to emerge from our ongoing and shared critical reflection is that our pedagogical endeavours certainly do not exist in a social and political vacuum (Hussey & Smith, 2010; Molesworth et al., 2011). Indeed, we have come to better appreciate how our pedagogical practices may be considered to operate at the nexus between the multifaceted, and sometimes competing, demands of our pedagogical selves, our students, our institutions and, indeed, our wider society. On one level, it could be contended that our decisions and actions as teachers, and the students' subsequent responses to them, are influenced by the respective goals, expectations and the learning biography of the individual student and teacher (and indeed organization). On another level, however, it could be suggested that it is perhaps impossible to separate these from the dominant discourses surrounding individual achievement and failure in society, be it as a student, a teacher or as an institution in the higher education sector (Jones-Devitt & Samiei, 2011; Molesworth et al., 2011).

Arguably, we live in a society where increasing individualization and an emphasis on consumption have led to a situation where outcomes are seen to matter more than the processes that are used to achieve them (Molesworth, Nixon & Scullion, 2009). For example, press headlines (e.g., Frean, 2008; Wignall, 2006) have noted that students are increasingly viewing a university education as a principal means of gaining well-paid employment. In one such article, Wignall (2006) suggested that university students are no strangers to the pressures and demands of target-led, performance obsessed education – university isn't an adventure playground for learning or licentiousness, but a business transaction, an exchange for money for a guaranteed leg-up in the post-graduation 'real world'.

From our perspective, this helps us make some sense of Mark's, and potentially other students, choice to engage in selected acts of 'studentship' (Graber, 1991). Equally, given the uncertainty and individualization that is a pervasive feature of contemporary society (Bauman, 2007), it is perhaps unsurprising that some students, like Danielle, may be unwilling to highlight, describe and critique their own views, choices and actions. Instead, in the quest to achieve personally desired outcomes, it may be easier for some people to blame others rather than to critically reflect upon their own choices and actions (Bauman, 2007). Rather than discounting the value of critical reflection, or abandon it as being too hard to implement in our practice, such philosophical dilemmas and practical difficulties further reinforce our belief in the importance of encouraging educators and students to critically reflect upon their respective contributions to the society in which we live and practise.

9 Facilitating reflective practice in graduate trainees and early career practitioners

Alison Rhodius and Emma Huntley

Introduction

In the literature, several authors have offered support to the role of reflective practice within sport psychology-based early career experiences and associated supervision (e.g., Cropley, Miles, Hanton & Niven, 2007; Knowles, Gilbourne, Tomlinson & Anderson, 2007; Tod, Andersen & Marchant, 2009). Teaching reflective skills to practitioners and the sharing of techniques associated with this process is, however, lacking commentary and discussion. In this chapter we draw upon our experiences of using reflective practice techniques within our teaching of students, supervising graduate interns, mentoring graduates, peer consultations, and experience of its use as practitioners. Our aim is to illustrate ways in which reflective practice can be embraced to increase awareness and facilitate both learning and growth for students, teachers, and practitioners alike.

We write this chapter as a US-based supervisor (Alison) and a UK-based trainee (Emma), with a focus on neophyte groups. We also note, however, the usefulness of our reflections to the more experienced practitioner in the field of sport psychology and other sport and exercise sciences. Despite differences in terms allowed in the US and UK (and elsewhere), for example, the use of the term 'psychologist', a prominent theme is that we are talking about trainees (both pre-award and early career).

We define reflective practice as an intentional process that enhances self-awareness and understanding through thinking about applicable 'events'. These events vary widely from reflecting on our own professional practice, to that of reading a journal article or news report. Further, we believe reflective practice can be used by athletes to increase their own awareness of training and performance and 'close the loop' on the process of goal setting. In essence, we propose that reflective practice can change one's understanding of self, others, and the environment can elicit change itself or confirm original thoughts and intentions.

Setting the scene

Despite originally hailing from the same part of England and being in the same professional domain, as authors, we have never worked together or met. It is interesting to note that we are now working remotely on the same project under-pinned itself by principles of engaging in reflection, yet represent two different institutions on different continents. Throughout this chapter, we comment on training within different pathways in the US and UK. The first author (Alison) is at John F. Kennedy University (JFKU) in California and the second (Emma) is at Edge Hill University in Lancashire, UK.

In terms of encounters with reflective practice, Alison has incorporated her interest in the topic by including it in her role as administrator, teacher, supervi-sor, and mentor with students and graduates, peer support group member with colleagues, and as a consultant with athletes. Emma has used reflective practice while engaged in BASES (British Association of Sport and Exercise Sciences) supervised experience (SE) as a trainee sport scientist (practitioner), with ath-letes in applied practice when reviewing performances and interventions, as a lecturer within Higher Education (HE) and, most recently, as a PhD student studying reflective practice within sport psychology.

Training and development of reflective practice in sport psychology: the US and UK training systems

In the US, there is little conversation among the literature as to the use of reflec-tive practice in sport psychology. Some discussion exists from US-based authors (e.g., Tonn & Harmison, 2004; Watson, Lubker & Van Raalte, 2011), but most notable contributions in this field have been mainly from the UK (e.g., Ander-son, Knowles & Gilbourne 2004; Cropley, Miles, Hanton & Niven, 2007). These contributions have paralleled the training pathways in the UK, where there are now two training routes to becoming sport and exercise psychology practitioners. The first is through BASES (BASES, 2009), and the second through the British Psychological Society (BPS, 2011).

Each of these routes requires the trainee 'Sport and Exercise Scientist' (BASES) or trainee 'Sport Psychologist' (BPS) to engage in, and give evidence of, reflective practice as a mandatory competency. For example, practitioners engaged in the BPS training scheme are required to undertake tasks linked with education/dissemination, continued professional development (CPD), and a research project. This is completed on either on a full-time (3,680 hours or 460 days) or part-time (equivalent) basis. On completion this allows the respective candidates to identify themselves as a Chartered Sport and Exercise Psychologist. Within the stipulated hours, consultancy work (1,200 hours or 150 days) is also required, and reflective practice is largely evident within this programme through suggested techniques such as practice diaries and reflective logs with the aim to demonstrate practice competence.

Despite the importance of reflective practice and inclusion of it in the accredi-tation criteria for BASES and the BPS, the US-based Association for Applied Sport Psychology (AASP) does not currently feature it within certification crite-ria, and Div 47 (Exercise and Sport Psychology) of the American Psychological Association (APA) does not address it in any guidelines either.

Reflections from a US-based supervisor and practitioner: Alison's journey

Inclusion of reflective practice into applied training did not exist when I undertook BASES SE in the UK in 1993. I was introduced to reflective practice through the use of a 'reflective piece' at the end of my doctoral thesis. In these writings I discussed the process of the research journey, and referred to Schön's (1983) 'swampy lowlands' as I navigated the field of sport psychology. Initially I used a very structured approach to reflective practice and followed Gibbs' (1988) model, but have since adapted this.

Currently, at JFKU in the US (www.jfku.edu), reflective practice is now firmly embedded into the master's curriculum. We teach students in both traditional classes and via supervisory meetings face-to-face and/or online. Within the applied sport psychology curriculum, the students are taught specifically about reflective practice skills and encouraged to spend time addressing and critiquing the literature. Lecturers then subsequently guide students on its use to enhance their class-based learning experiences, in their research practice and/or in the field as interns.

Integration into students' research

Students who choose to do a master's thesis at JFKU are required to keep a reflective journal and include elements of those entries or a summary of their reflections on completion. This aspect of their thesis is not currently assessed, but is used as a formative piece of work to inform the final submission. Maintaining a journal reminds the students why they are doing the research, helps to monitor their own biases and assumptions, and increases their awareness of certain key factors to pay attention to in their own research style. Woodcock, Richards and Mugford (2008) discuss a similar notion of supporting early career practitioners, and argue that reflective practice can help in the learning process alongside quality supervision. These same sentiments are also applicable to the work of neophyte *researchers*.

Integration into students' applied practice work at JFKU

Tod, Marchant and Andersen (2007) touch on the topic of reflective practice for students' training in Australia and suggest it may be useful, but do not discuss its use in any depth. The typology of reflective practice at JFKU is that of, at first, a guided process, and we invariably use the model from Gibbs (1988) to initiate the reflective process. During the four to five internship periods, which vary from 11 weeks to eight months, interns meet weekly with their individual supervisor, all of whom have their own private practice and several are AASP-certified. The interns are required to send to their supervisor an audio recording of a session and also keep a written or audio-based reflective journal. We ask the interns to keep these journal entries separate to their case notes. Case notes are focused on the

client, whereas reflections are consultant-focused, and there may be legal implications if the case notes are subpoenaed. Journal entries focus on issues such as
their own goals, their consulting style and impact on consultations, any issues of
transference or countertransference, and any ethical concerns.

Audio reflections can be completed immediately following the client session,
several hours later or even a day or two after. Indeed, Knowles et al. (2007) refer
to this as 'staged reflection' where the reflection may be immediate or delayed.
As a supervisor, I prefer the first reflective piece to be completed on the same
day as the session with the client with the subsequent audio reflections a day
or two after. I find it helpful to listen to interns' reflective audio after listening
to their client sessions and making some notes on my own evaluation of their
consulting and reflective work to inform the assessment. It is interesting to hear
how interns' immediate and then delayed reflections can change over time. If
the intern is relatively self-aware, he/she can 'hit' many of the main aspects of
consulting (at their stage of development) that I want to give in my feedback. On
conclusion of the process, their own appraisal will often match that of my own
as their supervisor.

In addition to weekly individual supervision, the interns are required to attend
a weekly two-and-half hour group supervision class led by an AASP-certified
consultant, for the duration of their internships. As noted by Knowles et al.
(2007), 'reflection can be an individual or shared task' (p. 113). Within this class
the interns use oral reflections, which are sometimes supervisor-led, and they
share their thoughts, feelings and experiences (initially based on the Gibbs [1988]
model) with their peers and the group supervisor. Although these oral reflections
do not represent documented evidence of using reflective practice, the process
facilitates what the interns are experiencing, thus enabling feedback and support
from both their peers and other members of the supervisory team. This group
process helps to minimize limitations associated with personal reflections (which
may include being restricted by an individual's knowledge and skills), facilitates
the development of a wider knowledge base (Knowles, Gilbourne, Borrie &
Neville, 2001) and allows another 'layer' of reflective activity into the process via
supervision (Knowles et al., 2007).

In preparing for writing this chapter I asked the interns at JFKU to tell me
what they believed the perceived benefits of using reflective practice were on
their training. One intern stated that it was about:

> . . . be[ing] able to maintain consistent progress in developing my skills.
> Reflective practice gives me immediate insight on each interaction I have
> with a client; it allows me to be systematically critical of my own work so I
> can observe myself, learn from any mistakes, and maintain professionalism.

'Immediate insight' is characteristic of staged reflection (Knowles et al., 2007)
where by the reflection can be initiated immediately after a client session and can
continue to take place in stages across time, so the intern revisits their thoughts
and feelings about it in a formalized systematic way once or multiple times.

Practising what I teach

I was invited to reflect about my experiences of working at the Olympic Games in Athens in 2004 with the US archery team for a BPS publication (Rhodius, 2006). After reflecting on my reflections in this publication (or, in other words, using 'staged reflection' [Knowles et al., 2007]), reading others' reflections in the same publication and learning about other 'levels' of reflection (i.e., technical, practical and critical [Knowles & Gilbourne, 2010]), my reflective style has evolved. I now use reflective practice more instinctively, with a less formalized structure and factor in the 'bigger meaning' of what just happened beyond the impact on me as the supervisor or consultant. This might now be considered what Knowles and Gilbourne describe as 'critical reflection'. I now more readily address my own biases and assumptions, I challenge myself in new ways, use my peer support group to challenge me and have come to realize that we can all reflect in very different ways (Rhodius, 2009).

As a practitioner I have used reflective practice with athletes to help them increase awareness of their thoughts, feelings and actions, therefore using a cognitive behavioral approach. It is also a productive way of 'closing the loop' on the process of goal setting by providing balance to post-training/competition thinking/attributions. This development also enables athletes to see a direct link between their reflective process and the direction in which they wish to pursue.

Peer consultations are an essential aspect of high-level practitioner work, and reflective practice plays an important role. Peer consultation can take place during training among students (which we have in place at JFKU), but it is also essential to have regular peer consultations with other practitioners after leaving formal education and training. After moving to the US in 2000, and having been actively involved in peer support practice in the UK, I felt my own need for such a group and established a peer consultation group with local practitioners in 2001. We meet on a regular basis throughout the year (about every six weeks). The logistical and philosophical aspects and how we have been able to include reflective practice into this group are described by Rhodius et al. (2011), and Rhodius (2012).

Reflections from a UK-based trainee practitioner: Emma's journey

I have recently been engaged in a UK-based training programme to become a Sport and Exercise Scientist through BASES. Although the title lacks specificity per se, my specialism is sport psychology. Throughout BASES supervision, alongside my full-time position as a senior lecturer within HE, I have used reflective practice. However, if entirely honest, I was initially only driven to do so because it was a requirement of the SE curricula, not because I saw value in it. Four years later I am now engaged in doctoral research on reflective practice, having seen its value and impact on my own development. Allow me to explain...

My views of reflective practice have not always been favourable, or positive; indeed, like many trainees, I too believed that reflection was a 'tick-box' exercise

(Cropley, 2009). This was probably due to not knowing or understanding the concept or its associated benefits. I soon realized that I did not have all the answers, nor had I been taught them from published studies to date. Reflective practice (along with some other key factors) helped me to address my perceived lack of knowledge and applied practice skills. Evidently, I soon came to the position that there were (and still are) no hard and fast rules about practising applied sport psychology and that one size certainly does not fit all – and as a result reflective practice is essential. However, I also feel that the same conditions apply to reflective practice, which for a process deemed so important can be a major challenge for trainees who are just expected to 'get on with it'.

The supervisory relationship

In recent years, several papers have emerged surrounding supervision within sport psychology, including the optimal supervisory relationship and its implications on practice (e.g., Anderson, Knowles & Gilbourne, 2004; Cropley et al., 2007; Knowles et al., 2007; Tod et al., 2009; Woodcock et al., 2008). Reflecting back on my own supervisory relationship, after commencing the BASES SE programme in 2008, this dyad did not take long to develop. My supervisor and I worked in the same department, within similar roles, could empathize with each other's workloads and commitments, and logistically communication was very easy: I could simply walk down the corridor and initiate an impromptu meeting or discussion about concerns, ideas or an ongoing case study. For example, 'in person' contact meant that I received the full attention of my supervisor, and often spent more time communicating in person than we would have by email or telephone. I feel this provided the conditions for an interpersonal relationship to develop more quickly, and consequently I found it easy to chat about or disclose concerns and worries about my practice. Additionally, I did not experience the same issues as other supervisees such as time, cost of travel and using annual leave to attend meetings/observations. However, although I felt that in personal contact was valuable, a distance-friendly option, such as Skype, could address the concerns of cost and travel (as utilised at JFKU), while still maintaining face-to-face contact and personal supervision.

However, distance-based supervision also proved fruitful and was illustrated while at an international competition with a squad, where I recall struggling with a situation where players raised concerns about my role being too broad. I felt alone and out of my depth, questioning and doubting myself, and not knowing what to do for the best, so I decided to telephone my supervisor back home to voice my concerns and ask for some advice. She asked me what sense I could make of the situation, empathized with my desire to help out where I could, and agreed that plans should be put into place to prevent such issues (e.g., role clarity) arising in future events. My supervisor in this context challenged me to evaluate the situation more objectively by encouraging me to reflect, but also provided a safe forum to share my concerns (Andersen, 1994).

Although the supervisory relationship was mostly positive, a potential limitation included the difficulty in protecting formal time (e.g., organized supervision/meetings with a structure, objectives and action points). Working within the same institution, it was sometimes challenging to separate the supervisory relationship from being work colleagues. The cost of this sometimes resulted in supervisory conversations blending into those about subjects irrelevant to sport psychology, which then could impact on productivity. Furthermore, it became easier to cancel or reschedule a meeting because of the assumption that the other party would understand. Therefore this could pose questions around the quality of the contact and is a potential 'obstacle' to be mindful of when engaging in supervision.

Additionally, I feel being restricted to one supervisor could be limiting for professional development. This has been recognised and discussed by Woodcock et al. (2008), who stated that 'different perspectives enable [trainees] to contrast approaches and styles and helps them recognise the need to develop their own style and not emulate that of a single supervisor' (p. 502). This is also acknowledged within the BASES and BPS guidelines for supervision, which allow the scope for interaction with other supervisors (BASES, 2009; BPS, 2011). Multiple supervisors also provide extended opportunity to experience different philosophical positions, approaches, techniques and client groups, therefore increasing the potential for a more rounded, robust practitioner once qualified or accredited.

Group reflection

Within my BASES SE programme, I was part of a group of four trainees and one supervisor, who was BASES-accredited but had not previously supervised other practitioners. Our supervisor had been accredited for three years and had six years' experience of applied work in elite sport. All the group members had different backgrounds regarding education, applied experience and employment, and ranged in age between 24 and 40 years at the start of the process (in 2008). On average, we met for a formal supervision meeting once every four to six weeks. This was related to the travelling distance required by some members (e.g., one lived approximately 180 miles away from the supervisor). As I was fortunate to work within the same department as my supervisor, I had increased opportunity for access as explained above.

An advantage of our group included the fact we all began supervision at a similar time (within six months of each other). Therefore, regardless of our different experiences, we began to forge relationships quickly and established a solid rapport as we developed our expertise and skills simultaneously. After several meetings, a common theme of sharing reflections began to emerge at the start of each meeting. Each trainee brought a recent example of a case study to the group whereby feedback or action points could be obtained or shared within a confidential and supportive environment.

One particular example that was shared was an ethical dilemma I faced while working with a team at an international competition (see Huntley & Kentzer, in press). The situation related to a female athlete, aged under 18, who was discovered one evening in the room of a male coach from another squad. The circumstances raised several ethical issues that, as a trainee, I believed I was unable to cope with, including safeguarding and child protection. I reflected on the situation immediately post-event, in a solitary environment (individual), which is akin to the introspective reflections required for professional development purposes. I then reflected again when writing an official report for the international governing body (shared with the coach), which demanded a more formalized, objective approach (similar to critical incident report writing within nursing). It was only after using reflective practice that I concluded there was nothing more I could have done (within my role) upon hearing about the incident. My main individual reflections were centred on future actions and how I could have prevented the situation happening in the first place. Questions emerged such as, 'was it my fault as the person providing sport psychology support?'; 'should we have provided tighter boundaries?'; 'was this a coaching issue?'; and 'should the athlete's parents have been there?'

On return from the competition, I engaged in staged reflection verbally with my supervisor who confirmed my actions as being appropriate. We further discussed how a similar situation could be avoided in future through the critical reflection process. It was agreed that this situation, like many faced in applied sport psychology practice, was unlike any 'typical' situation found in a textbook or professional practice article, and therefore could be beneficial to share and reflect upon this with my fellow trainees so that further learning could be achieved. The sharing of this experience through group reflection not only allowed me to provide them with real-life material from which to learn, but I also felt a sense of relief and reassurance in sharing the experience with them, as the astonishment they displayed (and verbalized) demonstrated that they too would not have expected to face such a situation as a trainee.

The supervisory group was a safe environment where we could share experiences with one another (peers and supervisor) and use reflective practice as a tool to learn from these experiences. Ground rules were implemented, such as being critical but constructive, adhering to confidentiality and encouraging open, honest communication while tolerating mistakes (Ghaye, 2005). It was only in this setting that I was able to see the value of reflective practice for my development, and learn from initial anxieties felt about practice. Additionally, action plans in moving forwards were devised, both as the member sharing the experience and those reflecting on the experiences of others.

Consequently, Huntley and Kentzer (in press) developed a model (Figure 9.1), which outlined the conditions and attributes required for group reflection to be effective as trainee practitioners within sport psychology based on their own experiences. These include individual skills such as self-awareness, empathy, self-confidence, critical thinking and communication, and consideration of group conditions such as confidentiality, trust, openness, equality, group size, the utilization of individual strengths and being non-judgemental.

Four years later, outside of the original supervisory group environment, I had the opportunity to attend an applied sport psychology event where several trainees were invited to observe military training and consider the application of sport psychology to this domain. Each trainee also had the opportunity to discuss

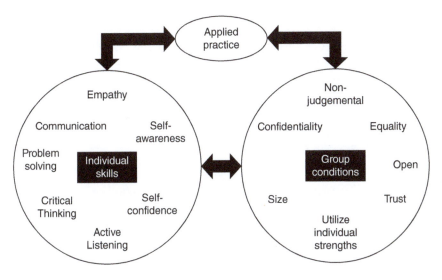

Figure 9.1 Group-based reflective practice model (Huntley & Kentzer, in press)

a recent case study of their own within a confidential, safe environment with the aim of obtaining feedback and support from other trainees. After spending a few hours with the other trainees, it soon felt very similar to my supervisory group, even though the sense of 'knowing' each other was completely different. Therefore, it could be suggested that setting the 'key conditions' for sharing (Figure 9.1) allows practitioners to communicate in a way that is conducive for reflective practice. Overall this type of peer event was beneficial for all involved, and more events of a similar nature are scheduled to take place in the near future. In response to the criticisms of individual reflective practice, this type of event could be recommended to formally exist both within pre-accreditation training curricula and during post-accreditation, which would allow for broader networking, sharing of best practices and group reflection.

On reflection . . .

Reflecting on my reflections, that is, the staged reflection that took place earlier in my training, I now recognise that they were very superficial, technical and descriptive in nature, only adhering to the tick box exercise previously mentioned. However, as demonstrated in these experiences, I now believe I am much more proficient in the 'art' of reflective practice, using more innovative methods, continually seeking opportunities to reflect with peers and mentors, where norms are challenged and more effective practices are developed. In essence I now naturally use critical reflection, even when it is not formally required, but perhaps now necessary for me to be competent and effective in all aspects of my professional (and sometimes personal) life.

Conclusion

In constructing this chapter and drawing upon our experiences within sport psy-chology applied practice, supervision and education within and between two very different systems, we agree that reflective practice is beneficial at several levels, and can be facilitated through different mediums. At the conclusion of this shar-ing and writing process we wish to summarize some ideas and recommendations that may prove useful to both trainees and educators alike.

Recommendations/top tips

1   Reflective practice should be embedded in professional training and practice curricula. This can be in the form of self and group reflection and facilitated by a supervisor and, later, trusted peers.
2   Post-graduation supervision should be underpinned by reflection, as observed in other practitioner domains. This could fulfil accountability and CPD requirements, and consequently bring about increased credibility to the role of the reflective practitioner.
3   Where post-graduation supervision is not needed or required, regular peer consultations are a must for practitioners. Formalized group reflec-tion, both within training curricula and post-accreditation/certification, is recommended.
4   Create time to reflect. Available time to reflect can be a significant barrier to reflective practice (Knowles, Tyler, Gilbourne & Eubank, 2006). There-fore, more innovative, efficient methods of evidencing reflective practice are required in order to overcome such mindsets, such as consistent (e.g., weekly) oral reflections given to the supervisor.
5   Distance does not have to be a barrier to effective supervision if remote media, e.g., online chat facilities like Skype, Google Hangout, etc. are utilised. The key is to keep any reflective practice requirement consistent for all trainees and make sure they have already been guided on purposeful reflecting.

10 Reflective practice and the realms of physiotherapy

Linda Hollingworth, Lindsey Dugdill and Sarah Prenton

Introduction

Learning to become an accomplished reflective practitioner is an integral part of training for the allied health professions. Indeed, reflective practice (RP) is well embedded in such curricula and educators see reflection as vital (Prenton, Dugdill & Hollingworth, 2013). In this chapter, experiences of learning the 'craft' of becoming a reflective practitioner, as experienced by physiotherapy students, will be critically explored in conjunction with current literature. Focus group data offered from these students, at different stages of the training experience, will be used to give a 'real voice' to the realities of learning, doing and then reflecting on reflection. The chapter will reveal how RP can contribute to the development of professional and academic skills for the allied health professional and also explore some of the difficulties and dilemmas students may face when attempting to implement reflection during practice. Often students reveal that they reach points of uncertainty, during the reflective process, where they need help and advice, and this then leads them to raise important questions such as 'can I reveal the truth in my reflection?' or 'if I tell the truth will this affect my marks in my assignment?' The chapter will conclude by giving some pointers to help new students to establish effective reflective skills within their work from the outset of training and beyond into their ongoing professional development.

The authors of this chapter have a common interest in teaching students of the allied health professions regarding RP, and they came together to write a chapter on RP for *Tidy's Physiotherapy* (Prenton, Dugdill & Hollingworth, 2013) – the first time the topic has been included in this seminal text for the physiotherapist. Physiotherapy is an important allied health discipline in that it links into the sport and exercise field – and includes complementary sub-disciplines of physiology, biomechanics, injury prevention and health promotion. Students, as developing practitioners, have to learn how to apply their skills in the complex, field setting and hence the importance of embedding RP at all levels of their professional development. Indeed Mann, Gordon and MacLeod (2009) assert that:

> Reflective capacity is regarded by many as an essential characteristic for professional competence. Educators assert that the emergence of reflective practice is part of a change that acknowledges the need for students to act and to

think professionally as an integral part of learning throughout their courses of study, integrating theory and practice from the outset. (p. 595)

Reflections on teaching RP

Some years ago I (Linda Hollingworth) attended a training event where we, as lecturers, were encouraged to consider our teaching practice as being more like a midwife and less like a postman. The midwife assists and encourages in the birth of a baby but only the mother can actually deliver it, just as the postman delivers the letter and then walks away. On good days I can experience 'midwife' moments, when a student grasps a concept, masters a new skill or has that 'light bulb' moment; however, on other days I think it would be easier all around to be the 'postman', deliver my information and leave. To continue the analogy I have come to realize that in the teaching of RP there are no 'postman' short cuts. Some students will succeed, following what can be a long and painful labour, in delivering their own reflective 'baby'. For some students this will be well-formed and robust, a treasured skill which is carried forward into professional practice to be further nurtured and valued; for others it will be a mere embryo, and some will lapse into neglect and leave the baby on the bus! Picture the 'midwife analogy' of RP – you can provide the student with the information (i.e., be the postman!) but that is not enough. Every 'birth' is difficult and complex, so you (as RP mentor or midwife) have to spend time with the student and coax, mentor and coach them through the process so that they build 'layers of learning' over time. The midwife will be there to ask questions, give encouragement and provide an experienced head throughout. This is the role of RP mentor, which we discuss later in the chapter.

One helpful way of persuading students to take the 'ride of RP' is to get them talking with their peer-group. I (Lindsey Dugdill), as an academic, can provide students with the theoretical rationale for embedding RP in their practice – but it is usually when they have spoken to fellow students (who have recently been through the process and already had a light bulb moment) when the value of RP dawns! Statements from peers such as 'I can see things much more clearly now I have had chance to reflect back on how that physio session went and have had chance to discuss it with my mentor' and 'in future I will try and deliver the therapy in this way to try and make it more effective for the client' were much more likely to make novice students, new to the art of RP, take notice. RP is considered vital to learning and development in the professional workplace (Kember, 2001), and Taylor states that RP can 'bring about deeper insights and changes in practice, leadership, clinical supervision and education' (2006, p. 15). Further to this, Plack and Greenberg (2005) assert that 'reflection . . . helps practitioners develop a questioning attitude and the skills needed to update their knowledge and skills, which is essential in today's rapidly changing global health care environment' (p. 1546). However, getting students to persevere and learn the 'craft' of RP takes time, energy and patience on the part of the tutor and/or mentor, and helping students see the inherent value of RP is the start of that that journey. Also, the reality of usefully implementing reflection for physiotherapy students and practitioners brings many challenges for those of us who would be the 'midwives' – issues that are considered below.

Delivering the 'reflective baby' – planting the seed

The initial introduction of students to the concept of RP seems to be a critical component of the process. Much of the pedagogy surrounding RP, especially in health, can emphasize the emotional component of reflection, although this aspect seems to cause many students to be suspicious and negative before they have even started their journey. In our experience, physiotherapy students who are introduced at a very early stage to models of reflection, such as those developed by Gibbs (1988) and Johns (1994), tend to fix on the emotional component of RP and frequently cite this as a barrier to initial engagement with the process:

> we're 'sciencey' people, we took a 'sciencey' course and so to sit down and write on a piece of paper about how something made you feel doesn't make sense . . .
>
> *Salford Graduate Reflective Group 2010 (Student 5)*

> . . . to put an emotional aspect about what I'm doing, what I'm feeling is not in my makeup . . .
>
> *Salford Graduate Reflective Group 2010 (Student 3)*

It is interesting to reflect on how and why students become focused on this particular aspect, the emotional, subjective nature of RP rather than the perceived 'hard', objective reality of the scientific professions. White (2011) recently stated that physiotherapists are still wary of RP because the foundations of RP lie in phenomenology, a philosophical concept relating to personal perceptions rather than hard science.

One of the challenges of using reflection at early stages of clinical skill development is that everything is new, and students do not necessarily know the questions to ask themselves or do not realize the significance. The types of questions that can help novice physiotherapists begin to reflect on practice include: how did you feel that therapy session went?; how did you relate to the patient during the session?; what therapeutic techniques did you decide to apply to the patient and why?; how effective was the session from your perspective?; how did you come to those conclusions about the effectiveness of the session?; what would you do differently in terms of your therapeutic intervention, next time you are faced with that type of diagnosis?

Early reflections on practice may be difficult owing to the limited experience an individual student has to draw upon – however, this may again be the role of the mentor to find examples to augment a student's limited practical experience (through the use of case scenarios). Starting through facilitated reflective discussion rather than solo written attempts seems to be a more effective starting point.

Peer-support of fellow students can give novice reflective practitioners the confidence to engage in RP, especially if they then realize other students feel similar things about certain situations in practice, thus developing 'reflective empathy' between student cohorts.

The two factors identified by most students (in our experience) as significant barriers to engagement in RP are the inclusion of emotion within their reflection and being required to write their reflections. It is tempting, therefore, to avoid these aspects, although the value of expressive writing is well documented (Pennebaker & Chung, in press). Emotional and stressful experiences, such as the death of a patient, are common for students new to a health care environment: if we consider time spent writing reflectively about emotional and stressful experiences as akin to expressive writing documented within psychological research, it is clear that this is an aspect of RP that should not be abandoned. Expressive writing has been identified as having a positive effect on physical and psychological wellbeing, and it also seems to have a role in improving working memory capacity (Klein & Boals, 2001), which is key to effective reasoning and problem-solving (Wickelgren, 1997) – both important skills for effective patient assessment and management in physiotherapy, and skills highly valued by students. In expressive writing it is felt that the process of transforming feelings into a written form allows a cognitive process that enables practitioners to develop a 'story', making links and identifying causality; this then allows the storing of the experience in a more simplified and coherent manner (Pennebaker & Chung, in press).

What motivates students to engage in RP? There are several reasons: because the activity sustains us in some way (physically or mentally); because we gain enjoyment or pleasure from it (intrinsic motivation); or because we are required to engage in it by some external agency (extrinsic motivation). For most students, who are new to the concept, it might be considered unrealistic to be expected to engage with RP relying purely on intrinsic motivation. Students may enjoy the process of learning through facilitated reflection but are likely to need a skilled and supportive mentor for this to be achieved. Engaging in professional reflection alone, in written form is likely to be too much of a challenge for novice practitioners. It is possible for some students to find value in verbal reflection for mental housekeeping and catharsis, even in the early stages of their development; however, this is unlikely to be in the form of written reflection.

Finding a skilled mentor is an essential step for a novice reflective practitioner as the mentor can act as a guide through the processes and difficulties of RP engagement; they can provide encouragement when the student may want to give up and ask important questions to help the student develop their depth and breadth of RP. A good mentor will question and probe aspects of the student's practice without being judgmental or breaking confidences. They will have time to listen and may give professional advice on how to tackle difficult therapeutic situations if necessary.

Extrinsic motivation for RP is being driven by rising professional expectations from national professional bodies who require RP to be part of good practice models. For example, high-profile national organizations such as the National

Institute for Health and Care Excellence (NICE) have stated that there is a need to 'pay particular attention to developing reflective practice as an integral part of professional training for those working with looked-after children and young people' (NICE, 2010: Public Health Guidance 28, Looked-after Children & Young People – Recommendation 50).

These and similar guidelines thus elevate the importance of RP within the health and social care professions and give an added incentive for all such professionals to fully engage with the process. For example, in the UK, early years practitioners (CWDC, p. 7), teachers (QTS standard 29, TDA, 2012), social workers, physiotherapists and psychologists (HCPC, 2012, p. 5) are, by virtue of their training, reflective practitioners and are expected to continually engage in ongoing cycles of RP during their career.

Also within the field of children's safeguarding it has been acknowledged that: 'Managers at all levels must ensure a "learning culture" (Laming, 2003), with an ethos in which reflective practice and self-questioning are accepted and actively promote' (Burton, 2009, p. 2).

Most students need an external motivator at the early stages, although these external drivers can be counter-productive and encourage a 'box ticking' mentality. This may result in reflection that is not 'honest', and written for the benefit of the reader not the writer:

> I may have adapted my writing because I knew that someone would read it and I was uncomfortable with talking about my feelings and this would have impacted on the depth of my analysis . . .
>
> *Final-year reflective assignment (Salford student, 2010)*

This student acknowledges that the documented output of the reflection was not a totally honest account of their experiences. Not documenting feelings within the written account may have impacted on the depth of analysis apparent within it, but it is quite likely that in order to be consciously avoiding the inclusion of this aspect in writing there has been an element of 'mental housekeeping' that may have been of great value to the individual.

Ross (2012) argues that reflective writing for the purpose of assessment brings with it tensions and dilemmas in terms of creating authentic reflective accounts:

> The reality of most reflective writing in an educational context, especially when it is produced for assessment purposes, is one of obligation, tacit and explicit criteria, and an audience in the form of a teacher or assessor which must be catered to. (p. 260)

Online learning environments have been suggested as offering an alternative mode of working where learning and reflecting can be shared safely. They can also offer a potential way of linking disparate practitioners who need to find RP mentors and/or peers to support them in their ongoing development (Ross, 2012). In my (Sarah Prenton's) experience, students often think these online learning environments are referring to social networking sites; however, these do not necessarily create safe or appropriate environments for discussing patient care and personal development. Nationally, the physiotherapy union (Chartered Society of Physiotherapy, CSP) does offer the opportunity to discuss and reflect about practice online (iCSP). However, previous research into an undergraduate physiotherapy online discussion forum (Clouder & Deepwell, 2004) showed that there is a risk that online discussions can become a series of descriptive monologues from a few individuals rather than analytical dialogue among many. Consideration of group size, mix (external versus self-allocation), privacy settings and information governance, timing within a course, clear expectations, as well as sufficient and appropriate preparation and support by tutors all help to dispel fears of judgement. This facilitates the development of individuals as 'opinion givers' rather than simply 'information givers' and/or 'seekers' (Clouder & Deepwell, 2004).

Intrinsic and extrinsic drivers, as mentioned earlier in the chapter, can both be important motivators for RP and should be considered as equally valuable. Students should be encouraged to understand these different motivators and the impact the nature of motivation has on the type of reflection they might engage with:

> . . . when being formally assessed I spent more time asking myself questions of my reflective practice and reflective writing style. I have also discovered that for me to be motivated to do something I need to have some form of praise to encourage me to do it . . .
>
> *Final-year reflective assignment (Salford student, 2010)*

What are we actually assessing? Should that change as the student progresses? We should try to reassure students that the reader will not be judgemental about what they have written, or they will definitely write what they feel the assessor wants to read (rather than a real and true account of their experience); this leads us to assess students on their use of the reflective process rather than the outcome of it (purpose). The risk here is that students become technically able to follow a reflective cycle but fail to value the activity as it has no meaning to them. A crucial aspect of teaching RP is to enable students to understand that they can become more proficient practitioners, that is, more competent (see Cross, Liles, Conduit & Price, 2004; Mann, Gordan & MacLeod, 2009) if they are good reflectors. As Loughran has stated:

> . . . for reflection to genuinely be a lens into the world of practice, it is important that the nature of reflection be identified in such a way as to offer ways of questioning taken-for-granted assumptions and encouraging one to see his or her practice through others' eyes. The relationship between time, experience, and expectations of learning through reflection is an important element of reflection, and to teach about reflection requires contextual anchors to make learning episodes meaningful. *(2002, p. 33)*

Once a basic understanding of RP has been developed, and students have had the opportunity to practice different reflective approaches, it is important to encourage critical evaluation of practice. Critical evaluation is all about having the skills and evidence to judge the value of a service or intervention ('what works and why?'), and test its effectiveness to ensure it is fit for purpose. Knowledge of effective practice is vital as it is these elements of practice we seek to retain and sustain in future professional practice.

Activities that facilitate students to reflect on their own engagement with RP can be useful in developing awareness of their own processing skills and help to develop individual approaches. Students who are about to embark on a professional career need to understand that being a reflective practitioner is more than writing reflective accounts and completing documentation; that the skill of a reflective practitioner is to analyze and evaluate experiences, and to demonstrate that they have learned from them by changing their practice or improving performance. Questions to stimulate self-evaluation (see below) can be a useful prompt:

1 How do you currently view your reflective activity?
   a Why do you think you have these opinions?
2 What methods of reflection are you currently using?
   a Why have you chosen these methods?
3 What function/role does RP play in your learning and development?
4 How effective is reflection at developing/changing your practice?
   a Which activities you currently utilize for reflection are effective and which are not?
   b How do you know this?
5 Can you identify what assists you to use RP effectively and what barriers you have?
6 Can you provide evidence that you have learned or changed your practice as a result of your reflections?
7 Are you able to identify clear actions as a result of your reflections?
8 Do you follow up on your action plans?
9 How coherent is the link between your reflection and your planning activity within your portfolio?
10 What actions can you identify from reflecting on these questions? Are there any different forms of RP you might experiment with?

Developing the 'reflective baby': sustaining RP into the workplace – 'growing up'

Dugdill (2009) has previously described professional practice as:

> the way a practitioner would go about doing their job. . . . It would involve what they said and did with different clients (e.g., delivery of an exercise programme), their use of interpersonal skills (e.g., motivational interviewing

or practitioner–client conversations), their application of inter-professional working with other professionals and services (e.g., in onward referral for example), their use of existing evidence of 'what works' (e.g., from published guidelines), and their ongoing experience of doing the job in the 'real world' setting. *(p. 49)*

Sometimes this may involve trying new ideas and approaches, being innovative and challenging the boundaries of existing practice. This may be of particular importance when a client/patient fails to respond to conventional, tried-and-tested approaches and the practitioner feels the need to try something different. Oelofsen (2012) has described the need to take a whole-systems approach when thinking about integrating RP into workplaces, and stated:

> For reflective practice to make a difference, healthcare organizations need to instill a culture of reflection within their staff. Reflective managers are likely to make better decisions, reflective practitioners to deliver better, more humane care. The need for staff groups who work with vulnerable and complex people to engage in effective reflective practice is being recognised more widely.

New graduates recognise that although they have reached a level of professional qualification their development and learning needs to progress:

> . . . you will always be a work in progress, you will never be the finished article . . . qualifying is like learning to drive, passing your test is only the beginning.
>
> *Salford Graduate Reflective Group 2010 (Student 5)*

Following qualification there should be a move towards more internally motivated practice, although for many the shift from a 'learning-centred' clinical experience as a student to a 'service delivery'-centred expectation as a qualified practitioner can have significant negative effects on their effective use of RP:

> I reflect better as a qualified practitioner as I am now the motivator not because agrade or assignment depends on it. I feel it now has a higher value in my practice and the issues are more real to me.
>
> *Salford Reflective Practice Group, 2013 (Student 4)*

As a student physiotherapist on clinical placement (work-based learning) there is an expectation that all experiences are influential in learning and developing practitioner skills. This is usually reinforced within the workplace by educators who expect students to articulate their reasoning processes and identify clearly what they are learning. Students are supernumerary and expected to dedicate time purely for learning from their experiences. Once qualified, all practitioners identify the need for continuous learning, although the pressure of delivering a service, within an increasingly constrained system, can result in a lack of time and support for these activities. There is a definite change in emphasis as the practitioner moves from a role where they are primarily a 'learner' to being primarily a 'provider of care'. Many new graduates will identify that this adjustment takes time to achieve and, at this transition point, where reflection on practice should be a high priority, it is most likely to be de-prioritized owing to work pressures.

Supporting newly qualified practitioners in this transition is an important role: a skilled workplace mentor can be invaluable in encouraging independence and developing confidence. Ghaye states that

> the principles and processes of inclusivity, of sharing learning, and cultural literacy . . . are the basis for team learning and service improvement. The practice of reflection, where the 'we' is the team is an emerging practice and policy imperative.
>
> *(2005, p. 65)*

However changing employment patterns in recent years have resulted in a greater number of new graduates moving into posts which offer little or no RP supervision or mentorship, either through workplace staff shortages or because of increased self-employment. With this change in employment it is increasingly important that new practitioners are equipped with the skills to effectively manage their own continuing professional development, or effectively link into professional networks. Some new graduates begin to appreciate the role of reflection in their development later, but only when the support mechanisms provided to them as a student are no longer available:

> . . . you just don't realize how important it (reflection) is . . .
>
> *Salford Graduate Reflection Group 2010 (Student 1)*

Understanding workplace culture and context is a vital step in the road to becoming an effective practitioner:

> Educator: Does the culture of where you are working influence how you engage with reflective practice? If so, how?

> Now that I am working in a community with the diverse culture it has . . . there is a greater need for support with their [the public's] health. You often need to reflect and motivate your clients on why they should engage with the health care system.
>
> *Salford Graduate Reflection Group 2013 (Student 6)*

Those individuals who have experienced some value from their RP as a student are more likely to sustain its use once qualified. However, the workplace culture with respect to RP and staff development is likely to be significant influence in the transition from student to practitioner:

I am currently in my second job and only in the last two months have I experienced what I now call true supervision. I now find it really useful and in hindsight would advise it to be used. I have always had clinical supervision from a senior member of staff and have benefited from their knowledge and experience.

Salford Graduate Reflection Group 2013 (Student 2)

Teams who value reflection and encourage all staff to engage openly in analytical review of practice are an ideal; however, there are many possible contributing factors that prevent the achievement of this ideal. It has already been suggested that in order to value reflection the practitioner needs to learn the processes involved and find their own 'best fit' – to experience, for themselves, that spending time engaging in reflection results in some sort of positive outcome. Many experienced practitioners will have historically been 'required' to complete RP in order to 'prove' competence or skill, and many have a very negative and narrow view of what RP involves. In addition, many more experienced practitioners have experienced educational programmes that did not traditionally include the teaching of the skills required for effective reflection. Practitioners who are forced to engage in an activity for which they are not prepared sufficiently are more likely to perceive little benefit from the time spent, and the negative opinion is perpetuated. Hence reflection may be viewed by some more established therapists as a threatening concept.

The importance of role models at this stage of professional development cannot be over-emphasized. Ghaye (2005) introduces the notion of the healthcare team being a community of learners, and emphasises with caution that in a busy workplace setting gaps may grow between work and learning unless investment in the process of RP is made. Furthermore, Dugdill (2009) also argues that reflection will only become embedded in professional practice and health systems if:

> The time to be reflective is built into service delivery cycles; reflection is both practised by and explicitly valued by managers; staff are rewarded for delivery of a quality service (i.e. a performance management structure that recognizes and measures quality is required) and practitioners are allowed to innovate and try out new ways of working as well as change the practices they no longer believe 'work well'. *(p. 50)*

Moving on: transformational RP in the workplace

As practice moves from 'conscious competence' to 'unconscious competence' in the expert practitioner there is a risk that knowledge and expertise are taken for granted; RP has an important role in bringing the expert practitioner back to conscious consideration of their practice. Facing difficulties and dilemmas in RP can be challenging and include issues to do with levels of disclosure, for example, how much should a practitioner reveal to their manager about a patient consultation process that has not gone well? (Taylor, 2006) Ultimately our students of today may become the exceptional leaders of tomorrow. Polizzi and Frick (2012) argue that transformational professional learning experiences must 'foster RP and processes that elaborate and clarify core professional ideas, experiences and questions within the personal and professional context of . . . leadership' (p. 20). It is by using RP as a transformative learning experience that leaders can make complex decisions about the future organizational agenda for change – which is vital for so many professionals in today's complex work environment.

Part Four

Applied practice

Reflective practice in action

11 'They never bought me flowers'

Storytelling as a means of critical reflection on applied sport psychology practice

Carmel Triggs and David Gilbourne

Introduction

In the present chapter we set out, first of all, to consider scholarly issues that we associate with the broad thematics of critical reflection, of critical social science and storytelling as a means of communicating both. Following on from this discussion the first author illustrates facets of her own 'storied reflections' based on her experiences of 'being around' professional football, first as a young girl growing up on the terraces, watching footballing greats, and latterly, through her present-day applied practice. Through storytelling Carmel shares elements of her time working (behind the terraces) in elite professional soccer in the UK. A summary section includes further thoughts on how the personal medium of reflection and the process of reflective writing can help to disseminate the contextual and cultural nuance of applied practice experience.

Supporting literature and critical debate

According to Knowles and Gilbourne (2010), engagement with critical social science is a process that aligns with the aspirations of critical reflection; further to this, they argue that considering practice as something embedded within a wider and complex societal framework engenders a contesting mindset that might (eventually) challenge aspects of established thinking. In the present chapter the process of critical reflection (within a societal framework) is interpreted through a localized lens (scenes applied practice). The process of writing reflectively via use of creative and/or auto-ethnographic approaches has been differentially stressed through a number of reflective practice communications as a means of realizing a critical reflective mindset (Knowles, Gilbourne, Tomlinson & Anderson, 2007; Knowles & Gilbourne, 2010; Knowles, Katz & Gilbourne, 2012).

Developing a philosophical platform for arguments to follow

It may not be so surprising that the notion of critical reflective practice has interested social science practitioners, particularly as the associated thematic of critical social science has been adopted and debated for some time within social science more generally. It has already been noted that Knowles and Gilbourne (2010) and Knowles et al. (2012) have suggested associations between the assumptions of critical reflective practice and critical social science and, in this introductory discussion, we have opted to briefly revisit and develop these conversations in order to establish a foundation point for the storytelling and discussion to follow.

More specifically, Gilbourne and Knowles (2010) noted that critical social science is thought to encourage creative, critical and evaluative activity (Carr & Kemmis, 1986). In aligning these aspirations with critical reflective practice the present authors identify the potential for these same attributes being present within the mindset of individual practitioners from a range of applied domains. Our specific emphasis in the present text stresses the importance of creative, critical and evaluative thinking within an applied sport psychology setting. Our use of stories to depict practice allows readers a creative and interpretive space in which they might consider how critical reflective practice (and the underpinnings of this provided by the ideals of critical social science) might manifest in their own practice. In this sense we present Carmel's storied reflections in part, and in order, to prompt personal and possibly hidden stories to be reflected upon by those who read our work.

We understand that conveying reflections on applied sport psychology practice in creative form might, at first glance, appear to be at odds with the precision and parameters of science more generally. Furthermore, we are mindful of the challenges faced within pedagogy when, as we suggest later, neophyte sports and exercise scientists are encouraged to engage in reflective practice and, in some cases, critical reflective practice alongside the narrative of dominant and scientific discourse.

Our case in progressing the value of reflective practice generally and critical reflective practice through creative writing is that reflective processes can prove complimentary to science-based practice (in terms of providing a contrast and a real-life feel to issues). We understand that reflective skills are a part of science-based practice but also contend that creative forms of representation can demonstrate and, so, enhance the application of science rather than somehow being in opposition to it. In stressing this notion of symbiosis we accept, at least intuitively, that many readers might feel more comfortable with scientific writing and this, we propose, is ideally suited to technical levels of reflective practice. However, the criteria that come into play when practical and critical levels of reflective practice are attained do require the reflective practitioner to give of themselves, and this tendency invites writing of a more personal and less distal nature. Those points aside, we hope that we can win the day through the ways we have chosen, here, to explore these higher levels of reflection illustration of reflection-in-action.

It has been noted earlier that we have emphasised and tried to illustrate the value of auto-ethnographic texts as a form of critical reflective writing (Knowles & Gilbourne, 2012). In addition to talking 'about it' the process of auto-ethnographic writing has been central to David's research over a number of years (Gilbourne, 2002, 2010, 2011, 2012; Gilbourne, Jones & Sinclair, 2011); in that regard a true attempt to practice before preaching has been undertaken.

In general terms, and in the world of social science, those in favour of auto-ethnographic writing might describe the process of 'writing oneself into text' as a 'revealing' and 'emotive' process, one that might be similarly received by those who read the texts. One aspect of writing auto-ethnographically specifically, and in reflecting and committing thoughts on practice to paper more generally, is that the author becomes vulnerable through the transparency of the text and through their presence within it. It is as though the process of telling others what you have seen, thought and felt that the author exposes 'self' to all who read it. In contrast, writing scientifically exposes only one's theorised ideas and indicates how they might have been linked to the theories or assumptions of others, theories and assumptions that are often shared by their scholarly community. In contrast to this, the exposure of reflecting on the self through writing is rarely undertaken in the hope of providing theoretical explanation; it is, instead, a process of perception sharing and the sense of vulnerability is housed within the intensely personal nature of that.

When auto-ethnographic writing is linked to critical reflective practice and to critical social science more generally, the process is also associated with the exploration of one's own complexities and the multi-layered nature of one's life within a context; and that context is, essentially, within the wider stages of community and politics. It is in these latter descriptors that linkage between elements of an auto-ethnography and the evaluative properties of critical social science become challenging to social scientists, and possibly frightening to those who live and practise closer to the principles and expectations of science. Maybe what is most important here is that critical reflection places self, the complexity of self and the lived experiences of self, as just one localized (yet essential) part of a complex and ever-changing dynamic, and this notion of widening the scope of contemplation is magnified when one's own practice is with similarly complex people living their own complicated lives as best they can. One possible way of illustrating this synthesis is to provide an example of personal challenge through a critique of social science by a social scientist (Carmel in this case). This is, we hope, less confusing, in practice than our explanation of it might first appear; and so after our brief review of critical social science and the potential links to auto-ethnographic writing, we move to the storied landscape of Carmel's practice and to aspects of her sporting world before practice had ever been contemplated.

Reflection as storytelling . . . 'They never bought me flowers'

It was the usual end-of-season awards ceremony. Rows and rows of young boys all kitted out in their club tracksuits, which despite having been worn for every game during the season (and so for most would have seen better days!), it seemed that Mums and Nans had waved their magic and done their usual washing trick of making the tracksuits look brand-new again!

Despite the pristine tracksuits some of the boys had been well and truly weather-beaten themselves. A contrast between some of the younger players and older players, a contrast beyond physical differences in size, could be seen (well, it could if you looked close enough). This sense of 'difference' could also be seen in the respective parents.

Those eager, giddy, giggly and younger players (around 7 years of age) sat at the front; they appeared restless, bodies swaying with excitement. The older boys (16–18 years of age) had all chosen to sit at the back – some looked to be in a world of their own, others looked restless; but not with excitement.

As I watched the older boys I imagined speech bubbles coming from their heads, 'this is bullshit . . . ', 'what a waste of time . . . ', 'what a chore this is . . . ', 'I'm glad I won't be here next year', . . . 'I hate this place'.

I have been selective with these comments because, of course, there were players who didn't mind attending, players who were able to look forward to moving on to the reserve team, maybe then, to the first team. Some players, those whose dreams had come to an end, also seemed able to appear appreciative, and a little solemn. For them it would be a goodbye to the club, the one they had dreamed of playing for. I wondered on their thoughts, their emotions, and concluded it would be melancholic, mainly.

I heard some older players talk about what they 'used to be like'. Looking across at the younger players, a few smiled as they reminisced about different times, maybe happier times, 'remember when' punctuated their conversations. In those moments I felt pleased, pleased they could manage to engage in conversations about happier times, all of this despite their current situation . . . that, I thought, took strength.

I begin to wonder which of those fresh-faced, eager, excited, smiley youngsters will become battered, beaten and weathered. I wonder who out of them will be at the back of the hall one day in the future, facing a similar situation to that faced by some of the older players today. All this, everything in this room, in this space, captures the harsh reality of academy football. But what am I doing/thinking like this, I am about to watch an awards ceremony, I am about to watch a celebration . . .

> I had worked in football for about seven years, but had shared a relationship with the sport for my whole life. Football is directly associated with a catalogue of memories from my childhood. I attended all the home games my team played with my Dad from about the age of seven and was lucky enough to be treated to the odd away game every now and then. I loved being a part of it *all*, being surrounded by people who all wanted the same thing – a win. The banter between my Dad and his friends after the game had always fascinated me. I would listen attentively to their conversations in the pub afterwards with my soft drink and packet of crisps – little did I realize that I was receiving an education of sorts. Most of their conversations would either be about how great some players had done or how badly they had done – there were no grey areas in terms of how players had performed. Sometimes I would be puzzled by their comments, as the players I thought had done quite well and liked were not always spoken about positively. I quickly realized that football was about opinions. I didn't realize then that I would eventually find

myself involved in the game with people whose opinions would inform the lives of others, specifically those of young boys aspiring to be football players. The opinions shared in the pub between fans about players, which of course would have no consequence on the players' lives, was a sanctuary compared to the 'behind closed doors' reality of football, where people's opinions and subsequent decisions on young players mattered. They mattered because they would have life-long consequences for the players concerned and of course on the people who loved, cared and supported them.

The academy manager pays homage to the data analysis boys for putting together the video clips that were played throughout the evening for everyone to enjoy . . . fair play.

The beautiful game is never more beautiful than when carefully selected music plays over carefully selected clips of film. Nevertheless the film and the music harbour a darker message, it tells everyone . . . you have had your opportunities and you have had your playing time . . . it tells everyone . . . 'we have kept our side of the deal'. The younger players are becoming overly excited now, maybe spurred on by seeing themselves on screen. I smile at the naïve nature of it all.

Awards ceremonies were an integral feature of the academy programme, underlining the fact it was the end of another season of football. I must have attended at least six of them during my time at the club, but to my relief the football club had never bought me flowers. I look back on this with intrigue and I have to say a wry smile. I never wanted any moment during my time supporting players (and sometimes staff) at the club to be about me, for me it was always about being ubiquitous but at the same time fading into the background, which I guess is paradoxical but I believed (and still believe) it is possible to practise quietly. I appreciate that this may seem a bit strange to some people, but in a world where many people (and deservedly so in some instances) will eagerly take centrestage or strain to be in the limelight, there was plenty of room and plenty of scope for someone like me to work unseen, to work out of sight, to work backstage.

I have no doubt that there were staff and players alike who may have wondered at times what I actually did and maybe even why I was there, but at the same time I know there were players and staff who had an acute sense of what my role was about. Some never questioned me about it but there was that mutual respect between us – they understood or, I felt they understood. Although many within the club and some outsiders listening in might have had their doubts about what it was I actually did (and this can be a serious issue), I remained secure in the key relationships I had with players and the journeys I was sharing with them. But more than that, I felt appreciated by the players for the role I was playing in their lives.

I was a woman working day-to-day in a man's world, and this, to my way of seeing things, added difficulty. It was an unusual sight for them to see a female out on the training pitches, a women dressed like the coaches with tracksuit and football boots on, standing at the side watching the players train and play in games, in all weathers of course!

One evening when I was at home the doorbell rang. I opened the door and, to my surprise, the lady from across the road was standing outside with her friend who seemed to be holding on to her back with her right hand and leaning slightly forward. She was clearly struggling with some sort of pain. The first thought that come into my mind was that she must have fell over outside the house and they needed help, but before I could act on this assumption, the lady from across the road started talking. 'We're sorry to bother you, it's just that my friend here has been in terrible pain with her back for a while now and she's having to wait for physiotherapy – it's just I've noticed you work for Manley Football Club, and so was wondering if you could just take a quick look at it for her and maybe suggest any exercises or anything like that she could do while she's waiting to be seen.'

I was confused for a second or two, and then it dawned on me that she thought I was a physiotherapist at the club . . . the lady from across the road was not alone in this physiotherapy assumption . . . at away games I have lost count of the number of times a member of staff from the opposition has shown me the medical room and where everything was. I was always impressed and said nice things about the room and the set-up generally, followed by 'I'm not the physiotherapist but I'll go and get him for yer.'

I often thought about what my job entailed when I worked at the club and have continued to think about it since I've left. I tend to ponder on the issue of it having been my job to care – specifically about the young players who were consistently on my radar during the time I spent there. Yet it seems ridiculous to me that it was my job to care, as surely that's like having a job that requires you to breathe. Surely, I would think to myself, 'caring is a natural inescapable and essential process. Care is an interesting issue . . . maybe everyone did care . . . maybe everyone just showed it differently! . . . after all, people's breathing can vary, it can be steady, shallow, deep, depending upon context and so forth . . . so, and in a similar way . . . I would like to think that everyone cared for one another at the club (in their own way).'

For some it was, perhaps, the perception they had of themselves and their own role that acted as a precursor for the ways in which they allowed themselves to overtly and covertly display their care. In my own case and possibly unlike the coaches and many other staff at the club, I had minimal concern for any outward display of authority. I never felt that I was in a position that demanded me to make decisions that would directly have an impact on the boys' futures, I don't believe I was perceived by the players to be in a group of powerful people, those whom they might have hoped would show them approval, aware that their futures depended upon approval from the powerful ones. I did not fall into this category – I think I was an outlet from this, critically and maybe essentially, a trusted outlet from this.

Having been aware by the time I worked in football that I had been fortunate enough to have support from different people, in particular from parents, family and teachers, I was acutely aware that to a degree I was a product of these people, they had informed who I was and who I am. I'm positive though that if I tried to attribute any progression I have had in my life to them, they would quickly try to 'bounce it back to me' and place the emphasis on what I had managed rather than how they had contributed. Gaining plaudits or being centre stage was never on the radar of the people I was close to, and as such has never been on my radar. Playing a 'bit-part' or being an extra in a scene of magnitude or an everyday occurrence and knowing you've contributed in an honest and sincere way is what contentment means for me. This ethos of mine (if you like), had no doubt been nurtured by others, but was also one that I felt deeply attuned to. Evidently it pervaded my practice at the football club I worked for, which is something I consider as more than just 'a good thing'. As I realize now that when I was at work, *I was just being me*, a statement that I believe wouldn't resonate with everyone.

It may have taken the players some time to realize that I was there for them (which was fair enough), and maybe it took some more time to trust me than others; again, that's fair enough. I often thought about this process of gaining trust, reflecting on the relationships and the awareness of me and my role that developed alongside their relationships with their team-mates and coaches and girlfriends, and anyone else who came into their lives. In a match, for example, the players learned who they could trust with the ball during the last five minutes of a closely fought game, one that they were edging by a single goal; who could they trust to ensure they could last it out? Who would run the ball into the corner for them?

I was aware that any time the players 'let me in' to their lives it was precious time, time that I had been given their trust. If this had never happened then I believe I would have failed in my role. In order for the players to 'let me in' I had to position myself strategically. I had, I believed, to be a floater; not someone easily pigeonholed, not located or envisaged by the players within their statements of 'us' and 'them'. Conscious of this, I knew on a daily basis that I needed to overtly mix with everyone to have a variety of contact with players and staff. There was no specific table in communal areas that I assigned myself to for a coffee etc. and I didn't have a 'my chair' in the dining room where everyone ate lunch. A real benefit to me was that most of the staff did, and if for example the groundsmen were up early for lunch before the coaches had finished their training sessions, then the coaches would comment, ' . . . what's going on here, we usually have our lunch on this table'. Of course this always erupted in friendly banter, but the sentiment initially expressed was definitely meant. The players were not as mechanical as the coaches, so it was slightly more difficult to anticipate where they would take their seats, but it was usually in their 'close-knit' groupings. Consequently once one or two players had come through and sat down, I could usually complete the jigsaw of their seating arrangements before the others arrived . . . this kind of thing captured a facet of my practice, my craft-knowledge, my way of being in-practice.

With time I experienced more contact with the players. Notably this increase in contact evolved as a consequence of requests on their part, 'D'ya mind if I drop by at lunch to see you, Carmel?' or 'can I come to speak to you after training, Carmel?' Whilst they were pleasing requests from my perspective, they tended not to be requests made by players who were pleased with themselves or others. Although players did drop by casually simply to say hello and proudly give me an update of their recent progress – usually these were players with whom I'd previously shared their 'downs' with – but what a high I experienced when they did drop by with a smile, connecting with them again but in a different emotional context. A process that tended to require me to be opportunistic and somewhat covert had become increasingly standardized and overt for some of the players. They themselves had informed the nature of my role, and in doing so altered the culture of overtly being able to speak about their own individual circumstances and/or ask for help or support – although this did not transcend all players and nor did it apply to asking all members of staff for help – it was a shift that had occurred, one I believe was a positive one for the players and crucially one they were informants of.

When players asked to see me I often asked if they would prefer to see me in my office or perhaps at the lodge (where some of the players lived), as I was conscious they may want a certain amount of privacy, that they may feel increasingly comfortable in different environments or may not want it to be public knowledge that they were speaking to me. I had a variety of responses to this, but one in particular remains in my mind and serves to reinforce my previous reflection about the cultural shift: 'I don't give a **** where we meet Carm, or if we're seen or not, I'm not bothered who knows I'm talking to yer . . . ' Similar responses were echoed by players after this, and yet I remain cognizant of a time when the majority of players tentatively approached me and seemed extremely conscious and apprehensive about others (players and staff) knowing they were sharing time and information with me . . . I sometimes wonder how best to share these things with those students of sport psychology that I work with now . . . I wonder whose writings might I point them towards?

As a consequence of the players becoming au-fait with me, the staff seemed to respond to this. Some would comment on how they thought I should have a word with certain players, others would ask me questions about what my thoughts were on specific players, and it seemed for some I was associated with needing to 'fix' players, which of course did not reflect my own philosophy or intention and desire to support them. I often found some staffs' comments frustrating and on a few occasions disconcerting. Nevertheless I was pleased there were staff (aware players were coming to see me) who seemed increasingly appreciative and attentive to the intricacies of the players' lives that they were involved in. These were the members of staff who occasionally invited me to offer my thoughts on different matters with players they were experiencing, and to me they seemed keen, respectful of and intrigued by my comments.

I can recall a brief exchange with one member of staff that I had communicated with numerous times before. He was passing me on the corridor and said 'I'm not speaking to you any more' I replied instantaneously, feeling accused of something 'why what 'ave I done?' A response of 'you "prick my conscience" and make me "think" and question myself': I just laughed . . . we both kept on walking. I knew that his comment was referring to conversations we had shared on how he managed the players and decisions he made that involved them – his thought processes had no doubt gone beyond what I perceived as the 'role-restrictive thoughts' that he commonly engaged in (of course he was not alone in doing this). I simply accepted that he perceived this as an uncomfortable place to be and I remained undecided on whether it would have an impact on his coaching behaviour and/or the relationships he had with the players . . . sometimes I found I needed less to 'see' a change . . . I did not hope for revolutions . . . I hoped more that people would 'think' about what they did and ask themselves questions over how they did it.

As my role evolved the purpose of it and my intention to be there for the players as 'a trusted outlet' and someone who cared about them and their futures definitely transpired. I attribute this significantly to being an individual who shared this environment/journey with them and was acutely aware of how desperately they wanted to achieve, but who possessed no preconceptions about what *their* future would or should entail. Consequently, the relationships I shared with the players were void of many complexities that were integral to the relationships they shared with many others, e.g., coaches, parents, and who, for some players, they felt compelled to achieve/perform for. For me such an unconditional approach illuminated the relationships that I shared with the players and enhanced the time and trust they afforded me; whilst also enabling them to allow me to genuinely care.

At some point in all of this it dawned on me that in an environment that required job titles and for those job titles to be displayed on doors, I would love to have had at the time the single term 'miscellaneous' on my door; reflective in my mind (only now) of not only the content of my role but significantly the nature of the relationships I shared. Maybe I was 'miscellaneous' after all, maybe that could explain why the club never bought me flowers, why get flowers when they don't really know what you do? . . . or . . . maybe they knew me all too well, maybe they knew secret agents need to keep a low profile! On the day that I left my role at the club, I did get flowers, a member of staff came up to me and whispered in my ear that two players had collected their expenses from the office and then handed them right back to put into my collection fund . . . the fund that bought me flowers . . . both of those players were leaving the club, they had been sat at the back of the awards ceremony looking melancholic, they had much to be worried over, financially they had very little – that evening I thought about it all a great deal, the trust, the failure for so many, success for so few, about being there for someone else more than for yourself . . . how you practise, I decided, is never about the flowers.

12 Critical reflections from sports physiology and nutrition

Tales from pitch side to ringside

James Morton

Introduction

As an exercise physiologist, my research interests focus on the interactive role of both the training stimulus and nutrient availability in modifying the molecular pathways that regulate how skeletal muscle adapts to exercise training. I am interested in how we can maximize how our muscles respond to training simply by changing what we eat (e.g., carbohydrate, protein and fat) before, during and after each training session. In recent years, our laboratory has challenged existing beliefs in the field of sports physiology and nutrition by demonstrating that deliberately restricting carbohydrate availability actually enhances the oxidative adaptations of human skeletal muscle (Bartlett et al., 2013; Morton et al., 2009), as opposed to conventional wisdom that training should always be completed after carbohydrate loading and with the provision of sports drinks.

As a practitioner, my aim is to subsequently translate the research of my own and others in order to devise practically applicable training and nutritional interventions that will, ultimately, lead to improved athletic performance. In principle, this approach should, of course, be a relatively straightforward process. In practice, however, I have quickly learned that there are many cultural, organizational, financial and political factors that occur in the day-to-day context of professional sport that greatly affect how we may practise. Indeed, unlike the controlled laboratory environment, 'the real world is complex, dynamic, unpredictable and full of emotion, none of which can be interpreted by any two-way ANOVA', (Gilbourne and Richardson, 2006).

As such, this chapter builds upon these sentiments and provides a critically reflective account of my experiences (2008–2013) while working within the real worlds of professional soccer and boxing, two sports that are steeped in tradition but differ very much in culture and organizational structure. Although the tales and reflections contained within have been presented previously in various forms at conferences and lectures, this chapter represents the first documented account. In doing so, I realize that I am now vulnerable to the subjective critique of others who may interpret my reflections in a very different manner from that of how they are intended. Nevertheless, it is noteworthy that published reflective accounts from sports physiologists are sparse within the literature. This is despite the fact that reflection is now a mandatory component of many UK physiology and nutrition-related accreditation programmes (e.g., British Association of Sport and Exercise Sciences, Sport and Exercise Nutrition Register). Furthermore, in my supervisory role of neophyte practitioners, it is my experience that young physiologists often struggle with the basic concept of *what* reflection *is*, let alone what it might look like. For them, the structured reflective cycle of Gibbs (1988) just does not cut it. Despite the potential for critique from my peers, I have therefore reasoned that the present chapter may serve to stimulate further reflection among sports physiologists and perhaps (hopefully) provide an introductory guide and framework for how physiologists may wish to represent their reflections.

Style of chapter

For physiologists, writing reflectively does not conform to the traditional structure of a hypothesis-driven research paper. As scientists, we are not taught to write this way, and as practitioners we are often not encouraged to think this way. The demands of professional sport are such that we are often required to do the job quickly and efficiently, with very little time scheduled, if any, for formal reflection (and importantly, in a non-judgemental environment) of how things could be done better. Although I have written reflectively before based on my early experiences as a lecturer it was, without doubt, the most challenging paper I have ever written (Morton, 2009). Nevertheless, the physical process of documenting my reflections on paper proved a valuable and rewarding experience such that it caused me to completely re-evaluate my teaching practices and philosophy. Although many of us may consider sufficient reflection as simply engaging in corridor and lunch conversations (which I readily acknowledge may indeed contain many elements of technical, practical and critical reflection), for me personally, it is this physical process of *writing* that often leads me to find the most valuable meaning in my practice.

To facilitate my reflections as a practitioner, I have therefore engaged in regular reflective journal writing following both structured and unstructured approaches. While the former helped to facilitate technical and practical elements of reflection, it was often those unstructured elements of writing based on spontaneous events that led to what the reader might consider as the most critical elements of my reflections. Similar to other practitioners (Knowles, Katz & Gilbourne, 2012), my reflections were also based on immediate (i.e., usually on the evening of the day of the event) and staged reflection (i.e., days, weeks and months after the event) and involved many moments of shared reflection. Indeed, this staged reflection with others such as fellow academics and practitioners, both senior and junior to myself, would often lead to re-evaluation and new meaning of those immediate personal reflections *on* and *in-action*. Moreover, my most meaningful reflections were often facilitated by sharing stories with those with no personal attachment or understanding of the environment in question, such as my partner and close friends who work in very different professions. In these moments, I was truly able to off-load my *real* feelings and emotions without fear of judgement from individuals who are influenced by prior knowledge or prejudices of sports science and the specific context in question.

I have chosen to tell my story by writing with an auto-ethnographic tone in the form of a confessional tale where 'I' (the author) am talking directly to 'you' (the reader). In order to promote reader engagement, various elements of my reflections are brought to life through the use of creative non-fiction vignettes. These moments are recognised by indented text and are intended to invite you to experience the same events that I have experienced. Despite being largely unfamiliar with reflective literature, it is clear that reflective writing as an academic genre is still in its infancy (even among sports psychologists), and critical reviews of how best to represent reflective accounts are now appearing within the literature (see Knowles & Gilbourne, 2010). Given that one of the aims of this chapter is to write primarily for a physiology audience in order to represent what 'critical reflection' *might* look like, I was therefore initially very conscious of how this chapter may be received by an unfamiliar target audience. Nevertheless, if the intended emotive nature of my reflections were to be heard and if reflective writing *is* to develop value among sports physiologists, it seemed logical that my writing should lead with an ethnographic tone. In the end, I decided to just write.

Tales from pitch side

To many individuals, professional football is considered as the pinnacle of elite sport. Football remains the most popular sport in the world and, in the modern era, football is glitzy and glamorous. Players and managers are often viewed as superstars, appearing on the back pages of newspapers and television screens almost every day. In my role as a lecturer, undergraduate students often tell me that working in football would be their 'dream job'. I often wonder what *exactly* it is about football that makes them feel that way.

My role as a practitioner in football is a consultant nutritionist and usually involves one or two days per week of physical presence in the football club. Although my responsibilities are primarily with the first team squad, I also provide support to schoolboy, academy and under-21 players. As such, I am responsible for the strategic delivery of a performance nutrition programme to in excess of a hundred players, a major challenge given the part-time nature of the role. To the outsider, it would be reasonable to assume that professional football would be one of the most rewarding and easiest sports to work in. After all, money is no object and the practitioner has a wealth of resources to work from in terms of staffing base and technological capacity.

The application of science in football has evolved considerably in recent years. It is now routine for daily monitoring of workloads during training (through heart rate analysis and GPS technology) as well as collection of regular blood and saliva samples to assess for markers of over-training etc. However, of all the sub-disciplines of sports science and medicine, the application of nutrition (along with psychology maybe) lags behind, perhaps best illustrated by the fact that most nutritionists are still employed on a consultancy basis. Moreover, unlike other team sports such as rugby or individual sports (e.g., running, cycling, boxing), the football culture is one in which nutrition is not often *initially* considered of paramount importance. Indeed, where nutrition can induce measurable and visible changes in performance in the aforementioned sports, optimal muscle glycogen stores or buffering of lactic acid does not immediately translate to more successful passes completed or matches won.

> As I meet the player in reception, he opens the conversation with 'how long is this gonna take?' He is here to have a DXA scan, a type of technology that allows accurate assessment of lean body mass and fat mass. This player was here because (to put it simply) he was fat . . . too fat for an elite footballer. I don't know what it was about that particular day but his comment riled me more than normal. 'You know what, that's a great attitude isn't it?' 'What do ya mean?' came his reply. 'Well, there are people that pay a lot of money to come and watch you play every week – it probably costs them over £100 to come with their sons and watch you play. I'm sure they'd love to know that you've got more important things to do than worry about being in the best shape you can be in.' I think he was quite taken aback by what I said, but I have a good relationship with this player so I didn't regret saying it. In fact, we both had a laugh about my 'biting'. The conversation moved on to how he was playing better than ever so he didn't need to worry about being fat. It was a fair point. Nevertheless, I explained how much sharper he would be over those first few yards if he could shift a few kilos . . . he became a little more interested. I explained that the manager was on to him . . . he perked up even more. However, it wasn't until I joked about getting a 'six-pack' that he really became interested . . . that would mean looking better on the beach in the summer and ultimately, more girls . . . again, I appreciated his thinking but somehow I don't think the winner of the Tour de France feels the same. That was over 6 months ago . . . and the player is still 'fat' . . .

As a football fan and former schoolboy international player, I can fully understand the reluctance to adopt a scientific approach to training and nutrition that is sometimes apparent. Indeed, the top players in the world (e.g., Best, Maradonna, Pele, Zidane, Messi) have not exactly been blessed with athletic attributes. Football is a *skill*-based sport and so changing the culture of professional football to one that also adopts a scientific approach to physical preparation is not easy. Much has been written on the topic of football culture, and the associated fear and insecurities (e.g., Roderick, 2006) that players *may* experience while trying to succeed in what is perhaps the most unpredictable of all sporting environments. In situations such as the above, I often wonder if these fears and insecurities (if indeed they have been experienced at any point in this player's career) have somehow (somewhere) been replaced by the security of a multi-million-pound contract. Footballers may only be as good as their last game, but in the modern era any fears associated with financial concerns for later life can vanish from when they sign their first contract even if injury or loss of form prevents another one.

It is of course unfair to label all players with the attitudes and beliefs such as those described above. Indeed, I have had countless consultations with many players (both young and senior professionals) who have been the complete opposite in their appreciation of how subtle changes in body composition may alter performance. These players display such a professional attitude to issues such as these that they have almost become more skilled than myself in interpreting DXA scan data. Additionally, I often receive late-night phone calls, text messages and emails with requests for nutritional and supplement advice to increase muscle, lose body fat, prevent fatigue, and so on. I consider these individuals as model professionals and who really are great role models to other players in the team. However, the fact remains that with the multicultural backgrounds and diverse personalities and beliefs that make up a professional football team, the capacity to reach and make a difference to *everyone* is more challenging than that associated with working in individual sports and those that are typically more reliant on physical attributes. This challenge of reaching everyone is also further complicated by the fact that my 'face-time' is limited to part-time hours. 'It takes time', I am reminded on a daily basis by my fellow practitioners, and I know they have a point. Indeed, as my face-time increases from season to season and trust and relationships with key individuals develop with both playing and backroom staff, I believe that I *am* (along with the help of other support staff) slowly helping to change practice. As I become more skilled as a practitioner, I have learned to treat players as individuals, adapting my communication strategy according to how best to relate to how that particular player may view the world. Nevertheless, in those days when I witness a half-drunk recovery shake in certain players' supplement 'wall' after training, I am reminded there is much work *still* to do.

Although researchers have focused on describing the football culture from players' point of view (e.g., Parker, 2002; Roderick, 2006), few (if any) have documented the football culture as experienced by the management and support staff. To this end, I would argue that the notion of fear and insecurity that may plague certain players during their career is perhaps more intensely experienced by the actual staff themselves. With the frequency of competition (e.g., two to three games per week), level of public scrutiny (i.e., media intrusion and fan pressure) and demands of club owners, it is hard to imagine another working environment that is so reactive in nature and in which the day-to-day mood can fluctuate so much. For the sports science staff in particular (who are not usually on secure lucrative contracts), job loss may indeed result in *real* financial difficulties. As such, these full-time members of staff may have to resort to a way of working to ensure their survival, an obvious one being the requirement to be seen 'to be important'. Fortunately, the relative safety of the academic world ensures I am not put in such a position.

This requirement to be seen to be important may often result in job conflicts concerning roles and responsibilities and, in this regard, nutrition can often be a common theme. Indeed, given that all of us eat food daily as well as being surrounded by a multitude of contemporary sources of nutritional information (e.g., television, newspapers, magazines, social media), it is only human nature to have some form of opinion on nutritional-related issues. As such, the nutritional programme that is actually delivered day to day is a collective input of key back-room staff that may or may not be always based on good practice. Furthermore, getting people to convey a consistent message is not easy, especially when the nutritional strategy may be very different from that which they are accustomed to. Nevertheless, with the development of sound working relationships and organizational management structures (which may take multiple seasons to really develop), the quality of service provision can only get better and slowly but surely (hopefully), and practitioners can eventually implement a strategy that is perhaps more influenced by their own philosophy. This process, however, does not occur overnight. Indeed, the old clichés of 'this is football' and 'it takes time' are usually brought up in defence here, and just when I consider progress is happening, the rapid turnover of management (which is inevitable in professional football) and associated backroom staff often brings a new set of philosophies and working values to adhere to. Those who 'survived' now begin the process all over again, and those who didn't (but were clever enough to form allegiance with the manager) are likely to follow the manager to his next club.

As I bring my reflections from professional football to a close, I am continually drawn to this theme (and the requirement) of understanding and/or how we can improve the organizational culture in order to really drive improvements in performance. When considering high-performance models of success, it is often said that the *business* world has a fascination with professional sport (Woodward, Chesterfield, Lee & Shaw, 2009). Rather, I would contest that the sport world (and especially football) should have a fascination with business. Indeed, it is in the business world where we could probably all learn valuable lessons on organizational structure, process, team ethos, trust, communication and so on. In recent years, there have been several examples where Performance Directors (with a business background) have achieved great success by lending from the principles of business. In 2003, Sir Clive Woodward led the England Rugby team to become the number one team in the world. Similarly, Sir Dave Brailsford transformed GB Cycling at the Olympic Games in 2008 and 2012, and also achieved victory in the 2012 and 2013 Tour De France with 'clean' British riders. Reflective accounts from these events often refer to the development of a culture that is based on professionalism, trust, respect and togetherness from all staff and athletes (Moore, 2012; Woodward, 2005; Woodward et al., 2009). Egos are set aside in favour of doing what it takes to be the best, even it goes against the grain. Often, these 'leaders in performance' have employed individuals with no experience or understanding of the sport in question (football, in contrast, has a long-standing approach to appoint *within*), but with the *deliberate* aim of recruiting people who *think different*. But then again, those sports were 'ready' for recovery shakes, no matter how they tasted.

Tales from ringside

A professional boxing gym is worlds apart from a professional football club. There are no fancy cars outside, nor is there freshly pressed training kit waiting in the changing rooms. The gym is not found on its own site with security guards and a high surrounding fence. Rather, it is usually an unglamorous building hidden among the working-class back streets of the inner city. The trophies still greet you on your way in, but they are tucked away in an old wooden cabinet as opposed to a shiny and expensive all-glass display. The facilities are basic, usually a couple of rings, multiple bags, a few weights and skipping ropes in the corner.

A boxing gym is a place that has been stripped to the bare essentials, and the fighters would have it no other way. Many of them have been training in the same gym since they were nine years old and in many ways, it is their home. Even the most successful and richest fighters in the world still train in humble surroundings. They say it 'keeps them hungry' and reminds them of 'whom they really are'. When a boxing gym is in full swing, it is a unique atmosphere. There is a degree of authenticity, respect and a work ethic that may not be matched by any other sport. Fighters will be sparring one minute and embracing and encouraging each other the next. There also appears a degree of respect from other athletes towards boxers, and it is not uncommon for major sports stars (footballers included) to be seen ringside at a 'big fight'. After all, the biggest prize in sport is still considered by many to be the heavyweight championship of the world.

A fighter's day usually begins at 6am with a slow, steady-state run in the darkness and quietness of the morning. The fighters return for breakfast and some sleep before arriving at the boxing gym mid-morning for their most important session of the day. Lunch soon follows and, in early evening, they have their third training session, which usually consists of a strength-based workout. This pattern of training two or three times per day is repeated for 8–12 weeks during a typical training camp, and, of course, there is also the arduous task of making weight. The transformation in a fighter's physique from when they begin training camp to when they enter the ring is nothing short of remarkable.

Given the well-known boxing culture and the archaic practices often associated with making weight (Morton, Sutton, Robertson & MacLaren, 2010), it would be reasonable to assume that implementation of sports science and novel practices (similar to the football environment) may also be met by many cultural barriers. However, in my experience of working with boxers ranging from flyweight through to heavyweight as well as what could be considered as 'old school' coaches, I have found this not to be the case. Rather, I have found both coach and athlete all too willing to listen and experiment with new ideas. This initial willingness to listen (which is *sometimes* not present in football), coupled with boxing being an individual and physically dependent sport, can result in an immediately different experience for the practitioner, one in which there is huge potential to make a genuine difference, especially if your personality and craft skills are suited for the 'gym'.

Unlike the footballer, the boxer is not supported by a large support staff but relies on just the coach and usually a conditioning expert. In my case, I operate as both a nutritionist but also the physiologist working closely with the coach to help plan, monitor and deliver sports-specific conditioning. As such, I am provided with the unusual opportunity to simultaneously apply my research knowledge of both training and nutrition. Additionally, the increased contact with the athlete and coach (i.e., increased face-time) inevitably mean (rightly or wrongly) that close personal relationships develop, which can be a lot more meaningful and impactful in the long run.

> He was the first boxer I ever worked with and on a personal level, we clicked immediately. After our very first consultation, I advised him to move up in weight, he was no longer a featherweight. Making 57 kg when you are 5 foot 10 inches was no longer possible, he had 'outgrown' the weight. He moved up to super-featherweight (59 kg) but after another 2 defeats, he quit the game. He had fallen out of love with the sport that he had been doing since he was 9 years old. Making weight and training 2–3 times per day had taken its toll. Once recognised as one of the most talented young boxers in the country . . . he retired at 26 years of age. He soon split from his girlfriend and had to return to live at home. Because we had grown close, it felt like I had taken all those punches with him.

> In the next 12 months, we coached the kids in the local area. It was part of a 'gun crime and knife' project where we used boxing as a means to try and teach value and discipline. During that time, you could see the boxing bug slowly returning. When he announced he was making a comeback, people thought he was crazy. They advised him he would get hurt. Nevertheless, it was clear he needed to do it . . . there was a void without boxing. He came back as a lightweight, a full 9 pounds heavier than when he held a version of the world title.

> His comeback was like starting all over again. A new coach, no longer 'topping the bill' and no glitz of the television. Nevertheless, he was enjoying his day job again. Stronger and more powerful at the new weight, he put together a run of victories and his ranking began to climb . . . people were talking again. In one fight, he boxed the opponent that stopped him when he lost his world title. When his hand was raised in victory, he broke down in the changing room afterward . . . it was as if he had finally let go of all those demons which had haunted him over the last 3 years.

> His winning streak continued and he earned another title shot. He lost the opening two rounds but in the third, the fight changed with a single punch. As his opponent relentlessly came forward, he threw an instinctive upper-cut. His opponent was knocked down for the first time in his career. The atmosphere in the arena changed immediately, and eventually in the sixth round after another hard left hook and a series of unanswered punches, the referee stopped the fight. He had done the unthinkable and that no one said he could do . . . from retirement to champion in the space of 18 months. As I stood in the ring amongst the frenzy, I somehow managed to have a quiet moment to myself . . . 'This is what making a difference *really* feels like . . . '

> I often wonder if I get too close to the fighters personally . . . putting personal emotion ahead of working objectively as a practitioner. I have tried on many

occasions to not get too close, but working at a distance is *not* me . . . and it is hard not to become friends with fighters and coaches when you work with them 5 days out of 7. Unfortunately, this means the highs are high and the lows are even lower. Nevertheless, I have met some of my closest friends in boxing, and that has been more rewarding than being part of any title-winning team. In fact, when my son was born, the above fighter was the *first* person to come and congratulate us in the hospital . . .

To many people, boxing is not nearly as glamorous as the world of professional football. Indeed, unlike footballers, boxers are not normally household names. As sports scientists, our value and ability as a practitioner is often judged by the 'profile' of the athletes we work with. Nevertheless, I often encourage young prac-titioners to learn their trade in a sport and with a level of athlete in which they have the capacity to make a difference. Unfortunately, no one (usually) wants to hire someone who has worked with a relative unknown, regardless of the differ-ence they have made.

The hurt-business

In a recent paper, Gilbourne (2012) challenges the age-old perception that sport is *good*, suggesting that behind the glitz and glamour there are often tales of sad-ness, despair and loneliness. Gilbourne argues that in the absence of qualitative enquiry, these tales remain untold, ultimately leaving us with a one-sided story of sport. For the most part, I would argue that sport (of the kind when we engage in when we are growing up) *is* good. It teaches us many physical skills as well as developing confidence, self-esteem, wellbeing and, of course, many of us have likely met life-long friends through sport. However, in my role as a practitioner, I have also witnessed on many occasions that the world of *professional* sport may *not* always be good. In the professional world, where an athlete's sense of self-esteem is often based on his *last* performance, sport can lead to emotional crisis. As tales from professional sports men and women (e.g., Pendleton, 2012) are now becom-ing increasingly told (even for those who have had highly successful careers), we are learning that the difficulties that arise during a sporting career (such as defeat, injury, retirement, funding cuts, loneliness etc.) can lead to family and marital problems, self-harming, depression, drug addiction, cheating, alcoholism, and in extreme cases, suicide. I often wonder if such individuals would have arrived at these situations if they had never experienced the world of professional sport.

As I sit down and look at the white clock on the wall, I realize its now 4.30 am. This is not where we should be or how I imagined the night to turn out. We should still be out celebrating. This was a fight that he was expected to win . . . he should now be champion. Instead, we have been in the hospital since 1 am. He never looked right from the first bell. His speed wasn't there, his footwork was missing and his punches had no snap. It's known in the game as being flat. Maybe we left it in the gym or maybe his opponent was simply too good . . . not in technical terms . . . but maybe he was just too big, too strong. The coach pulled him out of the fight in the 10th round, it was the right thing to do. There was no point in suffering any more, taking unnecessary punishment. The title may be gone, but that is not important any more. This wasn't just an athlete; it was our *friend* in there.

When we got back to the changing room, I could see he was struggling not just emotionally but also physically. He was dizzy, nauseous and unsteady on his feet. An ambulance was called and so we have ended up here. The coach and myself have been sat bed-side for the last 2 hours while he is kept in for observation, hooked up to a drip delivering fluid and pain-killers. Through the tears and his broken pride, he still manages to have banter with the nurses. His personality is still intact and we still laugh together. He can't remember much about the fight but he talks of retirement, that he has had enough of the fight game.

His Mum arrives. . . . he is glad to see her. We leave the room to give them some time alone, and so now I am sat staring at the clock with his coach. We talk openly about the harsh realities of professional boxing. This isn't just sport . . . this is the hurt-business and make no mistake, it hurts.

Although it is clear to see how a boxer's life is tough, footballers (in contrast) are considered to have it 'easy'. They are paid vast sums of money, have finished 'work' by 1 pm, drive fast cars, and even have their own personal chefs. While many footballers come from working-class backgrounds, it is clear they no longer live a working-class lifestyle. As such, it is probably only human nature to view footballers as *different* from the general population. Yet, for all the glitz and glamour, there are now a growing numbers of footballers who are also publically opening up about their problems. We sometimes forget that footballers are also human beings, who like the rest of us, will also encounter daily experiences that challenge them both professionally and emotionally. It is perhaps only when we understand the way in which they understand the complexities of their world and interpret their lived experiences that we can really intervene as a practitioner. In the world of professional football, however, we may never get the time. It is, after all, a win-at-all-costs business.

It was a bad injury, he would be out for several months. It was such a shame because he had been playing the best football of his career. We were sitting down over lunch to talk about his injury and the nutritional strategies that we could put in place. I much prefer these informal settings as opposed to a quiet consultation room. It tends to work better for both the player and me, it is natural and the conversation flows better. Occasionally, we break from the topic at hand to exchange jokes and banter.

I explain the types of things that we should be doing, it is the usual stuff. Basically, we need to minimize any gains in body fat and loss of muscle mass, an inevitable consequence of physical inactivity and no daily loading of the muscle. As we do a simple dietary recall, he explains that although he wakes at 8 am he doesn't get out of bed until around 10 am because of both difficulty with moving but also nothing to really get up for. He lives alone. As I explain the problems with delaying breakfast until this time in relation to maintaining muscle mass, a passer-by shouts a joke in my direction. I turn around to defend myself and quickly turn back to the player. In the space of seconds, his eyes have filled up . . . he is struggling . . . I need to give him a moment. I am aware that his contract is up at the end of the season, I am sure that is playing on his mind. I return to my previous light-hearted exchange with the passer-by though my mind is now completely elsewhere . . . despite the money, the cars and the houses, even professional footballers can have it tough . . .

Conclusions and final thoughts

As I bring my reflections to a close, it now seems pertinent to shift my reflections from the environments I work in to that of a more intrapersonal perspective (my reasoning for this will hopefully become clear in later sections). As such, the last 12 months have proved particularly challenging both professionally and personally. From a professional perspective, I now seem to be stretched in many different directions, *perhaps* a sign that I am becoming more successful in my career. I am a lecturer, a researcher, a practitioner, an author and a consultant to various sporting organizations. An academic life is, by itself, an extremely demanding job, especially with the growing publish-or-perish culture and the associated pressures of producing high-quality research. Superimposing the demands of professional sport, which in many ways is more taxing than academia, adds another major challenge to maintaining a healthy work–life balance. Additionally, I am now also a father with a one-year-old son who (God willing) is due to have a little brother or sister in October 2013.

In September 2012, I also received the news that my Mum has terminal cancer of the mouth, lung and liver and, at the time of writing (April 2013), probably only has months left to live. I already know what it is like to lose a parent given that my Dad was killed in a car accident in November 2004 (I was a 22-year-old PhD student at the time). The prospect of losing both parents at 30 years of age while also adapting to the demands of becoming a parent has been a particularly challenging time. My Dad is usually my first and last thought of every day and, very soon, I will be adding my Mum to those memories. There have been many nights when I have cried myself to sleep (under the security of knowing that no one is watching) only to realize that I have to 'perform' to my best the next day with my emotions back in check.

I am not telling this story to seek for sympathy, nor am I writing with a self-pity undertone. As a working-class boy from Belfast growing up during the 'Troubles', I am all too aware of how lucky I am to have had a stable family upbringing. I consider myself blessed to have had two wonderful parents to see me through to adulthood and to have had the career opportunities I have been provided with. I have friends who have served in Iraq and Afghanistan, and that is what I consider as *real* pressure. Rather, what I am attempting to illustrate is the multiple roles that many academics and practitioners (and most likely, you the reader) have to fulfil throughout the working day. I have a responsibility to my undergraduate and postgraduate research students, to my athletes, to the organizations I consult for, to my partner, to my son and unfortunately at this time, to my Mum. Although I am attempting to fulfil these roles to the best of my ability each and every day, the harsh reality is that there have been many occasions in which I have not and, ultimately, I have let people down. Perhaps most concerning to me is that more often than not (and despite family being integral to my personal values), it is usually my family and close friends who seem to suffer. Images of his Dad working evenings and weekends are not how I want my son to remember growing up.

The difficulties of maintaining a work–life balance are, of course, not unique to me, and much has been written on this topic (Waumsley, Hemmings & Payne, 2010). Similar to other practitioners, I am certain that my current thoughts are due in part to the transitional period of becoming a parent (Burke, 2009), as well as coming to terms with my Mum's illness. Nevertheless, as a strategy to help with my ability to manage myself (I think I am now gradually learning to say 'no' to say things that I cannot do *well* under the time constraints), it does seem appropriate to constantly remind myself of why I initially entered my chosen profession. My passion for sport and exercise coupled with my desire to advance the understanding of how the human body adapts to exercise were clearly motivating factors. However, perhaps what is most rewarding is the potential to make a difference, that is, a difference to my students, to the research community and to my athletes. To know that you have positively impacted learning, knowledge and performance brings a definite sense of satisfaction despite the fact that there may never be an acknowledgement of gratitude.

Given that the focus of this chapter has been about professional sport, it seems logical to now bring my reflections back to what this means for my work as a practitioner. During the weeks after my Mum got diagnosed, I had a very difficult conversation with one of the coaches I work with, which essentially focused on whether I was still fully committed to the athlete. He noted that I had become a little distant and was perhaps not as forthcoming or innovative in ideas in what I had usually been. 'We're only gonna get one chance at this, ya know . . . ', was the comment that was particularly stinging. Although I was hurting with my own personal struggles, I knew he was right. An athlete *does* only get one career, and in order to make it he needs a fully committed support staff with the ability to switch on and off at key times despite whatever other jobs or struggles they have going on in their own lives. As practitioners, if we suddenly cannot deliver to the scale that we had originally been working at or intended (due to life's evolving transitions), then ultimately it is the athlete who will eventually suffer. Hopefully, the meaning of my personal writing will *now* start to make sense. Indeed, I have hinted throughout this chapter about the necessity to understand (or at least appreciate) the complexities of the environments and lives of those that we work with. However, as practitioners, we too may also experience varying degrees of complexity as our lives unfold, and perhaps it is only when we understand our own way of being (and how that may impact upon others) that we can truly induce meaningful and impactful change.

This brings me to my closing point as to what making a difference really means. For me, it is not about wearing the tracksuit, or seeking public acknowledgement for one's work, or appearing on TV, or becoming content with the current way of doing things. It is not about settling and doing just enough to get by. Rather, it should be about putting the athlete (and student's) development and wellbeing at the forefront of your goals even if this means at the expense of your own ego. It is about carefully navigating your way through the complexities of the real world to speak up at the right moment for what you believe in, but also accepting that you are not always right. It should be about constantly striving to better yourself as a practitioner in order that you can make further improvements to your client, be it an athlete or a student. To really do so, we may need to develop close personal relationships with those involved so that we can truly understand the complexities of their own lives before attempting to intervene with our carefully constructed and unemotional scientific intervention. You may never achieve recognition for your work (and worse still, someone else may publicly take the credit) but at least *you*, who may be your biggest critic, will know you are doing the right thing. In doing so, maybe you can rest easy at night knowing that your work *is* making a difference. I wonder, whatever your line of practice, what does making a *genuine* difference really mean to you?

13 Using critical incident reflection in qualitative research

Transferable skills for sport psychologists?

Nicholas L. Holt, Tara-Leigh F. McHugh,
Angela M. Coppola and Kacey C. Neely

Introduction

Sport psychology is a diverse field. For example, applied sport psychologists work in a range of performance domains, from business to military settings (Gould, 2002), and are increasingly called upon to work with child and adolescent athletes (Knight & Holt, 2012). Some provide services to 'at risk' youth (e.g., children who live in low-income or inner-city neighborhoods) across different types of sport and physical activity settings (Danish & Nellen, 1997). On the other hand, others go into research and spend only a small proportion of their time engaging in applied work.

We have found several skills from our applied sport psychology training have facilitated our ability to conduct qualitative research. An obvious example is interviewing, whereby both qualitative researchers and applied sport psychologists should have the ability to listen, empathize without being judgmental, and respond to participants' needs (Andersen, 2000; Rubin & Rubin, 2012). Another transferable skill is reflective practice. Sport psychologists' skills in using reflective practice have been described with reference to the enhancement of service delivery (Cropley, Miles, Hanton & Niven, 2007), graduate student training (Holt & Strean, 2001), and supervision (Knowles, Gilbourne, Tomlinson & Anderson, 2007). Similarly, qualitative methodologists encourage researchers to compile reflective (or reflexive) journals to monitor their influence on, and involvement with, the research process (Finley, 2002). However, there have been few attempts to link reflective practice with the practice of conducting qualitative research in the sport psychology literature. The purpose of this chapter, therefore, is to show how reflection-on-action can contribute to improving the process of conducting qualitative research using examples from a *participatory action research* (PAR) study.

The research project

A few years ago we interviewed 13 inner-city youth workers plus 59 children and eight staff from a school in one of the lowest-income neighborhoods in Edmonton, Alberta, Canada (Holt, Cunningham, Sehn, Spence, Newton & Ball, 2009).

We found that even though there were numerous sport facilities and physical activity opportunities in the neighborhood, children's access to these facilities was restricted because of concerns about 'stranger danger' (e.g., homeless people, drunks, drug users, prostitutes, and gang members). This led us to believe there was need to provide direct programming to children in these settings, particularly during the after-school period.

The after-school period is sometimes referred to as the 'critical hours' in a child's life. Critical hours are those periods during weekdays from approximately 3.00 pm to 6.00 pm when children are unsupervised following the end of the school day and before parents return home from work. Critical hours programs have the potential to provide children with opportunities to engage in structured and unstructured activities through which they can learn behavioral and movement skills associated with lifelong participation in physical activity (Trost, Rosenkranz & Dzewaltowski, 2008).

The first phase of our project involved developing an understanding of the context and building relationships with community partners. In the second phase, a multi-sport programme involving collaborations between the school board, schools, and provincial sport organizations was created and delivered to 35 children (aged 7–9 years old) at two schools in low-income areas (Tink, 2011). In the third phase, a revised programme (now named TRY-Sport) was created and delivered to an additional 35 children (aged 5–8 years old) attending two schools in low-income areas (Coppola, Neely, McDonald, McHugh & Holt, 2012).

The research was carried out using a PAR approach. PAR is a process of mutual learning by groups of people who come together to create change (Kemmis & McTaggart, 2000). It is necessarily a collaborative process founded on the belief that an understanding of participants' diverse experiences is critical to the outcome of research (Brydon-Miller, Kral, Maguire, Noffke & Sabhlok, 2011). Although there is no singular PAR methodological approach, there is relatively widespread support for the conceptualization of PAR as a spiral of self-reflective cycles that includes planning, acting, and observing. Kemmis and McTaggart (2000) described this self-reflective process in PAR as fluid and responsive. We used concepts and techniques from the 'practitioner' literature to facilitate reflective practice in our research (e.g., Tripp, 1993).

Defining reflective practice

We approached reflective practice, in the broadest sense, as a deliberate process to refine our research and to be more sensitive to participants' needs. More specifically, our approach was consistent with Raelin's (2002) definition whereby reflective practice is 'the practice of periodically stepping back to ponder the meaning of what has recently transpired to ourselves and to others in our environment. Particularly, it privileges the process of inquiry, leading to an understanding of experiences that may have been overlooked in practice' (p. 66).

In the case of our current chapter, we considered issues that may have been overlooked in the practice of conducting our research. Therefore, we viewed reflective practice as an imaginative, creative, and non-linear set of activities through which we recaptured, considered, and evaluated our experiences to improve our research (Ruth-Sahd, 2003). Such reflection is a central feature of PAR as it enables researchers to question their actions as part of an ongoing process that can set a foundation for transformational change (McHugh & Kowalski, 2011).

Consistent with our definition of reflective practice, we engaged in reflection-on-action, which allows individuals to ' . . . make more informed decisions in practice based on the knowledge generated from previous experience' (Cropley, 2009, p. 28). Additionally, we used a 'dual-staged reflection' approach where *immediate* reflection-on-action during the fieldwork and *delayed* reflection-on-action after the fieldwork took place (cf. Knowles, Gilbourne, Borrie & Neville, 2001).

Two of the authors were PhD students responsible for the delivery of the TRY-Sport programme. For immediate reflection-on-action they completed fieldwork journals after each session. These journals contained descriptions of events and personal reflections on their interactions, thoughts, emotions, and concerns. Additionally, the entire research team (the fieldworkers and the 'desk-workers' – both of who were supervisors) engaged in regular debriefing conversations to discuss the progress of the research, challenges faced, and potential solutions. Hence, there were both individual and collective reflections. As we neared the end of our research, to engage in delayed reflection-on-action, the students completed a critical incident reflection (Tripp, 1993), using examples from their fieldwork logs as source material.

A critical incident reflection involves making interpretations about the significance of events, applying a value judgment, and 'the basis of that judgment is the significance we attach to the meaning of the incident' (Tripp, 1993, p. 8). It involves a four-step process: (1) *describe* the phenomenon and attribute meaning and significance to it in terms of your perception of the accepted dominant view; (2) *analyse* and *examine* that view for internal consistencies, paradoxes, contradictions, and counter-instances, including what is being omitted from the viewpoint, the structured silences, and absences; (3) *explain* why the dominant view in step one ignored or exluded what you found in step two: attribute agency and suggest whose interests are best served in step one and who is most disadvantaged in step two; and (4) *search* for an existing structure or create a new alternative structure that is more rational and socially just than step one by utilizing what you found in steps two and three.

Fieldworkers' critical incident reflections

Each fieldworker wrote the first drafts of her critical incident reflections independently. At this time neither fieldworker knew what types of incidents the other was reflecting on. The first drafts were then subjected to scrutiny and editing from the supervisors in order to produce the written accounts provided below, which are written in the first person from each fieldworker's perspective.

Angela's critical incident reflection

Step one (describe): Poor behavior and listening skills

A challenging incident I experienced was setting boundaries with children to enhance their listening, address their aggressive behaviour, and, ultimately, engage them all in physical activity. The following extract from my fieldwork notes described the situation:

> The listening skills of the children are severely lacking and I'm wondering if we can incorporate strategies to enhance their listening skills. For instance, even when you give the children instruction during tag they either don't care or don't understand. . . . Some of the children are extremely physical and don't know when to stop putting their hands on others (January 31).

Some teachers had their own way of addressing poor behaviour, as I further reflected:

> [Name of student]'s behaviour is not getting any better. Today he got in trouble for hitting someone. At one point I saw [name of teacher] physically restraining him on the floor of the gym as he was crying and trying to get away. I'm not really sure why she was doing this. Maybe she was instructed to do so, maybe not. Either way, it was uncomfortable. . . . I am not going to physically restrain children (January 31).

Step two (analyse): Looking for a technical solution

In attempting to address the issue *during* the fieldwork I read an article by Mandigo and Holt (2000) about creating instrinsically motivating contexts in physical education and a booklet about dealing with children with AD/HD (Barkley, 2011). I thought that perhaps giving the children perceptions of choice would improve their behaviour. In my February 9 fieldwork notes I wrote:

> I mentioned [to teacher] that we weren't there to discipline the children and we weren't judging the way that she disciplined. She said when the children are being disruptive, she just takes them out of the activity. I explained we just wanted to get the children more invested in the programme and described some of my ideas to her, but she made a face like it wasn't going to work. She said that it wouldn't register with them. They just won't be able to recognise that a choice is being given to them and will want to do their own thing. . . . She went on to say that her ways might seem 'draconian' but it works for them.

Now apparent was a disciplinary structure that was accepted within the school community, but not clear to me until this session. I was certainly facing an 'inconsistency' in terms of how I viewed motivation and discipline and how the teacher acted.

Step three (explain): Whose interests?

Interestingly, a consequence of the change in structure and student behaviour (which came, in part, from the teacher's 'draconian' discipline) was that I improved as an instructor. I noted this in a fieldwork entry:

> I realized today that I have become comfortable teaching the group because when we arrived late because of road construction, I wasn't nervous or worried about it. I also wasn't worried about how they were going to behave because their behaviour is steadily improving and I also expect a certain level of focus from them. I am able to adapt to it. When we began today's session, I also found it easy to be myself instead of who I thought they wanted to see instructing them.

We had found a balance between my goals of intrinsically motivating the children and providing them with choices and the teacher's (or school's) view of discipline. I have since learned that physical education teachers working in low-income schools may focus more on student discipline and attempting to control their behaviour rather than learning or delivering a skill-based curriculum (Chen, 1999; Ennis, 1995). Thus, it does not appear to be unusual for physical activity programs delivered to children from low-income schools to focus on safety and reduction of negative behaviors as opposed to the promotion of positive behaviors and skills. But I had neglected to consider why I wanted to change the children's behaviour. In some respects my stance may have been a manifestation of Coakley and Donnelly's (2002) viewpoint on the historical development of urban sport programs in Canada. They argued that such programs have regularly been constituted by instrumental goals of social control to instill middle-class values of self-discipline, respect for authority, and the virtues of fair play in 'at risk' youth. Thus, there was the question of whose interests were being served by trying to install values of discipline – perhaps my own, as a middle-class woman and researcher?

Step four (search): Alternatives?

In searching for a structure and solution to the problem of behaviour and discipline, I realized what was in my control and outside of my control. The environment and system we created within TRY-Sport was a compromise between the existing disciplinary system in the school and our belief in keeping the children involved in the programming. In a sense my own learning was about seeing how I fit within the broader structure of the school. But what I had not done (until writing this critical incident reflection) was consider an alternate and more rational/socially just structure. Indeed, as Coakley and Donnelly (2002) suggested, 'it is much easier and, cheaper, to occupy the time of young people identified as "at risk" than it is to deal with the real problems of poverty, impoverished neighborhoods, lack of role models, poor education, and other issues' (p. 12).

What might an alternate structure look like? Broader issues, such as changing the structure of discipline in the school, came to mind. Looking at some of the social inequalities and personal histories of the children was another thought. But ultimately I came back to more controllable issues. While I realize the compromise we reached may not have fully included the children's view, there is another way to look at this. In a study of inner-city physical education, Ennis et al. (1997) suggested students experienced a high level of fear in their lives and they brought this with them into their learning environment. My striving to create a safe space where children could learn may be important in its own right if it contrasts with the children's experiences in other areas of their lives.

Kacey's critical incident reflection

Step one (describe): Lack of fundamental movement skills

It was quite frustrating for me that even the simplest activities were difficult to run because the children lacked the basic fundamental skills to perform them. As I noted on January 12:

> Just from observing this week, their actual physical skills aren't as strong as I would have thought. I'm probably just assuming kids can run, jump, and throw. But I guess if you are never taught properly, you don't really learn – so I guess that's where we come in.

On several occasions throughout the programme I made note of the low skill level of the group. For example:

> Then we had an introductory game where we were in a circle with one ball, catching and throwing. When you caught the ball you said your name and favorite color. . . . I noticed that many of them couldn't catch and had 'interesting' ways of throwing. I guess I just assumed they would be able to underhand toss it – not so much though (January 10).

I realized that some drills or activities would not work simply because of the skills required. I think I was also frustrated because by age six, from all I had learned as a researcher, student, and instructor, children should have developed the basic fundamental movement skills (Gabbard, 1992).

Step two (analyse): These kids can't run, jump or throw

My expectations for the children's fundamental movement skills came from my previous experiences coaching children. These 'other' children of the same age as those in TRY-Sport demonstrated fundamental movement skills at a competent level, and the drills and games I had planned were successful. The obvious 'silence' here was the issue of *why* these children in TRY-Sport had (in my view) poor fundamental movement skills. In reviewing my fieldwork notes I found a specific example of my attempts to analyse the situation. On February 14 I made the following entry:

> I wish I could give running shoes to all the kids. A lot of them have trouble performing the skills because they have poor footwear on. This definitely has an impact on their ability to learn and practice many of the fundamental movement skills. This is something I've actually noticed before, particularly during warm-up, that it looks like some of the kids can't skip or hop and I think it could be because their boots are so heavy.

Step three (explain): Why can't these kids run, jump, or throw?

It is very likely that the children I worked with at TRY-Sport had never been taught the basic skills of throwing and catching, or even running and jumping. Previously I had worked in private organized sport programmes, in which children (or more specifically, their parents) paid to participate. The majority of kids I taught were from middle- to upper-class families where the cost of such programs was not a barrier to participation. However, with TRY-Sport, we were running a free programme in a low-income neighborhood where it is likely that children had not had the opportunity to participate in organized sport before.

In attempting to understand their lack of fundamental movement skills I had to acknowledge there are numerous inequalities in sport participation, most obviously in relation to financial barriers. For example, a national survey conducted in Canada showed sport participation was most prevalent among children from high-income households (68%) and lowest among children from lower-income households, at 44% (Clark, 2008). Most youth sport organizations, in North America at least, exist on a 'pay-to-play' model (Coakley, 2012). Hence, financial expenses relating to registration fees, equipment, and travel limit the sport participation of children from low-income families (Holt, Kingsley, Tink & Scherer, 2011). Perhaps, in a sense, my frustration with the children's skill level was a consequence of my own experiences in the privatized structure of youth sport contrasted with the fact that few of the TRY-Sport children's parents would have been able to pay for organized sport programs outside TRY-Sport.

Step four (search): Giving them shoes is not enough

My frustration was a result of my own interests. I thought that if children were demonstrating their ability to dribble a soccer ball properly or successfully shoot a basketball, it reflected my ability as a coach. In a sense, if the kids look good, it made me look good. Initially, because I was not able to teach them the sport-specific skills (that I had decided on), my own goals for the programme were not being met. It became abundantly clear that the children in the TRY-Sport programme were from extremely disadvantaged circumstances. It is not their fault they have never had the opportunity to be involved in organized sport programs, or that because of limited resources they do not have access to proper sport instruction or even proper footwear. An alternative structure involves more than providing children with equipment. While this may be an important step in providing sport opportunities, children still face a range of barriers (Holt et al., 2011).

Arguably my view that children needed better shoes was a narrow perspective reflecting my middle-class upbringing, experiences in the privatized model of sport, and my beliefs about the promise of sport. Perhaps a more realistic view of sport was provided by Hyman (2012, p. 130), who, in discussing opportunities for children from low-income neighborhoods, wrote:

> For kids who live in suburbia there's usually a second chance. There's always a team to join and a sport in season. It works differently in neighborhoods where money doesn't flow easily, neighborhoods without properly maintained fields, where parents work two even three jobs to give their families the basics. For them, organized sport is what other kids do. The idea of playing soccer in a league with coaches, goal posts and an inflated ball is a nice dream. But it's a dream.

Discussion points

Some of the differences between Angela's and Kacey's critical incident reflections may be attributable to their personal perspectives, biases, and histories. Angela was a less experienced instructor with a strong desire to instill order and motivate the children, which partially reflected how she wanted to be viewed and viewed herself as an instructor. Kacey was a more experienced instructor used to working with children from higher socio-economic backgrounds with sporting aspirations. She wanted to be viewed as a good coach who could run sessions and teach children sport skills. In some ways, Angela's and Kacey's initial views about the children's behaviour and skill level were due to focusing on themselves and their own needs. Perhaps both thought, at some level, 'I've got a Master's degree in sport psychology, I should be able to handle these kids.' Some of these challenges mirror Holt and Strean's (2001) critical incident reflection of a neophyte sport psychology practitioner's early work with a client during which Holt focused on himself to the detriment of seeking to understand his client and her needs.

Van Manen (1997) described three levels of reflection. The first focuses on technical means to reach a given goal, and can be considered as the elementary or rudimentary level of technical reflection. The second is a process of analyzing meanings, assumptions, and perceptions of underlying practices. The third, and most desirable level, relates to questions about moral, ethical, and political aspects of practice. These phases parallel Tripp's (1993) model (with the exception of Tripp's first 'description' step). It can be challenging for individuals to move beyond elementary technical reflections (e.g., reflections like 'that session went well today. The kids were listening,' or 'that session today wasn't great. How can I improve the kids' skill level?') because these types of technical reflections maybe be concrete, obvious, and easiest to identify and address. As Schön (1987) argued, excessive focus on technical-level reflections may lead practitioners to see themselves as instrumental problem solvers who mechanistically apply theory and techniques derived from scientific knowledge. This, in itself, is not problematic, but the point is that a failure to move beyond the elementary level of technical reflection may mean critical assumptions concerning the wider social and cultural context remain taken for granted (Holt, 2001). Thus, reflective practitioners operating within a PAR approach may consider 'technical fixes' to specific problems but also how their practices fit into a broader social framework, the extent to which they reinforce dominant perspectives, and the potential for creating meaningful change. These are critically important aspects of conducting PAR (Kemmis & McTaggart, 2000) and our use of techniques from the reflective practice literature proved to be a useful way of engaging in reflection during the research process.

Conclusion

The conclusion of this chapter leads us to the 'so what?' question (i.e., so what can we learn from engaging in reflection?). Immediate reflection-on-action in the form of field-notes and group discussions enabled us to adapt delivery of the TRY-Sport programme to better suit participants' needs. Some of the issues we identified would have been very difficult for the children to explain or verbalize. For example, it is unlikely the children would even be aware that their fundamental movement skills were not at the level we might expect. Therefore, immediate reflection-on-action was not only useful but necessary, because otherwise we may have failed to identify and address some of the issues we considered.

The benefits of delayed reflection-on-action are more nebulous. These reflections surely provided us with insights that helped with data analysis and manuscript preparation. They also helped us to consider and establish some areas for future research. For example, Angela said that using critical incident reflection helped her recognise and process her biases and assumptions that might have inhibited her understanding and consideration of community and social context when developing future programs. But, by delaying the use of the critical incident reflections until the end of the fieldwork we missed an opportunity to have a greater impact on the quality of the research and, more importantly, the children's experiences. We likely 'delayed too long', and by the time we had more fully considered some of the issues it was too late to address them. In other words, arguably we did not reach or act upon the reflections identified in step four of Tripp's (1993) model in terms of creating a structure that is more rational and socially just. For example, we did not create change in relation to discipline and behaviour but rather reached a workable compromise. As supervisors, Nick and Tara's own reflection-on-action was that we should have emphasised the importance of, and provided more guidance for, engaging in higher levels of reflection earlier in the TRY-sport programme. The lesson we have learned is the value of engaging in 'delayed' reflection-on-action (in this case, operationalized as the critical incident reflections) during the research itself. Rather than wait until the end of the fieldwork, using the critical incident reflection exercise earlier would have been useful. A key issue to consider is the timing of delayed reflection-on-action with reference to the stage of the research.

At the beginning of this chapter we suggested a good sport psychology practitioner has many of the skills needed to be a good qualitative researcher. Our attempt to portray some of the different roles those trained in sport psychology may fulfill is not intended to diminish or devalue the performance enhancement focus in sport psychology. However, we agree with Danish and Nellen (1997, p. 100), who suggested:

> Most of the students entering the field are excited about the possibility of working with elite athletes on performance-enhancement techniques and strategies. Unfortunately, few such opportunities are available. Career opportunities in sport psychology are likely to remain stagnant until we rid ourselves of the restrictive perspective we have adopted about what constitutes sport psychology and recognise its potential to affect athletes of all ages and skill levels.

In addition to considering broader social issues through the critical incident reflections presented, we have tried to position this chapter in a way that allows sport psychologists to consider connections between reflective practice and the practice of conducting qualitative research. More specifically, we hope to have demonstrated some of the benefits of immediate and delayed reflection-on-action and highlighted the need to carefully consider the timing of delayed reflection-on-action (i.e., critical incident reflection) during, rather than at the conclusion of, the research process.

Acknowledgment

The research to which we refer in this chapter was funded by a grant from the Social Sciences and Humanities Research Council of Canada awarded to Drs Holt and McHugh.

14 Mindful supervision in sport and performance psychology

Building the quality of the supervisor–supervisee relationship

Steve T. Barney and Mark B. Andersen

Introduction

Supervision in applied sport psychology has been a topic of discussion since the late 1980s and 1990s (e.g., Andersen & Williams-Rice, 1996). This topic, however, has received only cursory attention by the majority of practitioners and researchers in the field (see Tod & Lavallee, 2011). In the clinical and counselling literature, writings about supervision and supervisory issues can be traced to the early 1920s (Bernard, 2005). Textbooks devoted to supervision began to emerge in the 1950s (e.g., Eckstein & Wallerstein, 1958), and client-centered phenomenological thinking in the 1960s and 1970s provided a different way of looking at supervision. Since that time, research and theoretical writings have burgeoned in the field. Technologies such as digital recordings and video streaming provide opportunities for more scrutiny and real-time supervisory experiences. The way we do supervision has changed dramatically since the early days . . . but has it got any better?

In keeping with the theme of this book, the core business of supervision is reflective practice (see Knowles, Gilbourne, Tomlinson & Anderson, 2007). A major problem with practitioners reflecting on their practice alone is that the stories they tell themselves about practice have only one voice. This insular quality of some self-reflection may often mean that the same stories or narratives emerge over and over again (Watson, Lubker & Van Raalte, 2011). Supervision can become a type of *assisted* self-reflection where another agent enters into the story offering other interpretations, pointing out blind spots, and suggesting further study to help supervisees expand their understandings of themselves and their clients, and to help increase their professional efficacy.

A universal feature of supervision is that the supervisee is reflecting on experiences in sessions with clients. The breadth and depth of that reflective process varies greatly depending on what model of supervision is employed. For example, in behavioral supervision the supervisee is usually relating stories of *doing* (e.g., my client with the phobia and I worked on creating a hierarchy of fears list) and a discussion of what was done and how it all went may ensue. The primary aim of this type of supervision is helping supervisees reflect on their clients' behaviors as well as their own, with client welfare and practitioner growth and development in the area of behaviour modification at the core. In contrast, with cognitive therapy supervision, the reflections and analyses involve the supervisees' and clients' rational and irrational thoughts and patterns of responses to ingrained thinking processes. In other supervision models, the focus may be on reflecting on supervisee and client emotional states and how those may be connected to ontogenetic histories of both the practitioner and the client (and the supervisor; e.g. psychodynamic supervision). Regardless of the model used, supervision is quintessentially a reflective (and self-reflective) process.

We would like to frame, here at the beginning, that what we are writing about is not just reflective practice on what we do in our professional work, but rather, we are talking about living a *reflective life*, similar to many people's individual pathways addressing the Socratic challenge to 'know thyself'. We all have different lenses through which we reflect. For example, in my (Mark's) practice with clients and supervisees, my lenses are psychodynamic and Buddhist philosophical/mindfulness, and when I reflect on my life, my family, my friends, my work, my writing, and so forth, those same lenses are placed before my mirrors of reflection. I tell my students that early in psychologists' careers the professional self and the personal self often seem a bit (or a lot) different, but that over time those two selves begin to coalesce, and in time (with loads of self-reflection and assisted self-reflection), if we are lucky, we will eventually achieve those Rogerian qualities of congruence and authenticity. In contrast, my (Steve's) approach tends to be neurobiological, and I encourage students and supervisees to be mindful of the homeostatic balances that are needed to become reflective and effective students, psychologists, and citizens. Becoming actualized in a Rogerian sense requires sequential and magnificently orchestrated neural circuitry between many brain structures. Interpersonal and intrapersonal awareness and reflection facilitate the development of these circuits.

Approaches to supervision

In the clinical and counselling professions, there are myriad approaches to supervision. Several groups of models or theoretical perspectives are central. The models draw from phenomenological, cognitive-behavioral, psychodynamic, clinical, and developmental approaches (Andersen & Williams-Rice, 1996; O'Connor, 2000). Most models of supervision (we hope) are founded on solid theoretical frameworks (often using behavioral change models, learning theory, or various psychotherapies). For example, in cognitive-behavioral therapy, many of the interventions (e.g., cognitive restructuring, imagery, relaxation, positive self-talk) can be pulled directly from the therapy setting into the practice of supervision. Because psychological skills training (PST) is the dominant approach in applied sport and exercise psychology interventions, it is not surprising that most supervision world-wide has a focus on helping supervisees with the doing and teaching of psychological skills for performance enhancement. PST comes directly from CBT, and it has a decidedly psycho-educational flavor to it. From our experience, it seems that a lot of supervision in applied sport psychology involves reflection on the practice of PST, on what was done in sessions and how to do things better in the future. The reflections are often on acts (doing) and maybe not so often on *self* (being).

In training applied sport psychologists in Australia, reflective practice, supervision, and in-depth reflections on self as the instrument of service take principal roles. Students, from the first days of their postgraduate training in applied sport psychology, know that the task of understanding themselves will be a huge part of their education and that honest (and sometimes compassionately brutal) self-reflection is needed for them to become competent psychologists.

Background to common problems in supervision

Before we launch into the main topic of this chapter, mindful supervision, we thought that some background to problematic issues in supervision would be useful. Once several of these problems have been examined, we will then proceed to the positive effects of supervision. We will discuss the usefulness of mindful supervision later, but wanted to say a few introductory words here about how mindfulness and reflective practice can come together in the supervision experience.

In general, mindfulness is paying attention to self, others, and the environment non-judgmentally in the ever-unfolding present moment. By paying attention to breath, body sensations, thoughts, emotions, hopes, desires, and other people, we begin to become *attuned* to ourselves. Such attunement lays a broad foundation to draw upon for self-reflection. Mindfulness of self then supplies a wealth of data to tap for supervision processes (assisted self-reflection). Often our students can tune into their cognitions, but have trouble accessing their emotions. At this point, the reflective process in supervision stays rather stuck in the limited cognitive realm. With further mindful practice, students begin to experience an increase in the ability to access emotional material, and then supervision can progress beyond the stage of telling cognitive, linear, and rational stories to deeper more meaningful self-reflections on who we are and what we do.

Impact of supervision on counselling trainees

Effective supervision sits at the core of optimal practitioner training. Effective supervisors can help to correct counterproductive behaviors, facilitate new skill development, inspire new approaches, provide supportive feedback, and process personal successes and disappointments in trainees' work with clients or athletes (Watson et al., 2011). Wheeler and Richards (2007) performed a meta-analysis of articles looking at the impact of supervision on trainees. In their review of 448 articles, they extracted 18 that directly addressed this impact. These researchers found that well-timed, theoretically sound supervision facilitates the development of trainee self-awareness (ability to self-reflect), skill proficiency, and counselors' confidence in their therapeutic abilities. They also noted that through transference of supervision to clinical practice, client outcomes were improved. Unfortunately, high-quality supervision may not be readily available (Giddings,

Vodde & Cleveland, 2003; O'Connor, 2000) for many practising applied sport psychologists.

Watson et al. (2011) likened the absence of high-quality supervision to a child instructed to assemble a jigsaw puzzle and then left without any guidance or oversight. Occasionally, the child may succeed through trial and error, but more often than not, pieces are forced together, and contours are distorted. Further, if children are given similar tasks in the future, their approaches may well be haphazard and disorganized, and they may feel unconfident and insecure.

Types of poor supervision

To better understand problematic supervision, Giddings et al. (2003) collected data from over 500 randomly chosen North American clinicians. They found four primary problematic factors: (a) a lack of supervision or deficits in the amount of supervision available; (b) a harsh or unyielding supervisory style; (c) unprofessional behaviour on the part of the field supervisor; and (d) extreme violations of supervisory comportment including ethical or boundary violations. Almost half of their respondents reported encountering problematic supervisory experiences in at least one of these four areas, with lack of supervision being most common. A relatively small subsample (12%) noted that supervisory problems resulted in negative effects on their practice, with a smaller minority reporting more egregious ethical and boundary violations creating significant amounts of distress. Allen, Szollos, and Williams (1986) surveyed doctoral students about their best and worst experiences in supervision. Their respondents reported that their worst experiences were with supervisors who did not have clear theoretical frameworks, were uninterested or inept, were authoritarian or exploitative, and conveyed a subtle or overt disregard of supervisory processes. They found authoritarian denigration, designed to 'encourage conformity and to punish divergence' (p. 98) from supervisors' preferred styles of therapy, was particularly destructive. A small, but alarming percentage of supervisees reported sexual intimacies with their supervisors as well. All of these types of negative, bad, harmful, and poor supervisory experiences are far too common (O'Connor, 2000). With a better understanding of what poor supervision might look like, we turn our attention to research on what comprises good supervision.

Common positive factors in supervision

There is a well-established literature in the clinical and counselling fields outlining common factors that enhance the quality of psychotherapy and optimize client change. Common-factors that researchers seek to understand often relate to the facets of therapy that work for clients, regardless of the theoretic model (Lamprapoulos, 2002; Tod & Lavallee, 2011). They are the 'common mechanisms of change, which cut across all effective psychotherapy approaches' (Sprenkle & Blow, 2004, p. 114). Findings suggested that psychotherapy works best if eight conditions are met. First, there needs to be a clearly delineated situational power difference, with one member of the dyad identified as the expert and the other as the learner or recipient of services. Role clarity seems foundational. Next, the interaction must be built upon a nurturing, supportive, caring, and trusting work-ing alliance or therapeutic relationship. Third, once the trusting and supportive relationship is established, a catharsis and relief from distress can occur. In the absence of the therapeutic relationship, this catharsis may not occur, or could be traumatic to the client. The next common factor is an instillation of hope and raised expectations followed by genuine self-exploration and insight. Providing some rationale or formulations for change and developing skills to effectively confront challenges in the future are next. Finally, acquisition and practice of new learning followed by mastery and control over the problems influence the final outcomes. This process depends on the quality of the therapeutic alliance and working relationship. In its absence, the ability to effectively work through the remaining factors is limited. These theoretical and empirical findings are impressive and provide optimism for the efficacy of psychotherapy regardless of the style or orientation of the therapist. Likewise, theorists and experts in super-vision such as Lamprapoulos (2002), Morgan and Sprenkle (2007), and others are calling for a common-factors approach.

Instead of outlining the specific components of the various models of supervi-sion, common-factors researchers have examined commonalties that might *cut across* effective supervisory practices. As with common factors in psychotherapy, the quality of the supervisory relationship seems to be an essential and 'indispen-sable element of supervision' (Morgan & Sprenkle, 2007, p. 9). A safe, nurturing, empathic, and warm alliance with clear roles, boundaries, direction, and structure that allows for transference, countertransference, and supervision transferences to be explored and worked through in a supportive and nurturing manner seems to be optimal. Some have argued that recent trends in sport psychology are de-emphasizing a commitment to the supervisory process and relationship, and are almost exclusively focusing on skill development and training models (e.g., Wat-son et al., 2011). Tod and Lavallee (2011) have observed what they consider to be an overemphasis on a psychological skills training (PST) approach in sport psychology service delivery. A focus on PST may move supervision away from process-oriented topics and keep them squarely on developing competence in technique, with little attention paid to the supervisory relationship. Andersen (2012) cautioned that 'if practice and supervision stay firmly within one model for years, then the opportunities for professional growth become limited because the one model is reinforced over and over again' (p. 727). Exploring new and innovative models of supervision that serve to enhance reflective processes, increase self-awareness, and facilitate a solid supervisory alliance seems necessary.

The supervisory relationship

Allen, Szollos and Williams (1986) reported that 'the existence of a supportive relationship [is] an essential ingredient of successful supervision' (p. 97). Their participant/supervisees identified several key facets of effective supervision.

Those supervisors who had grounded theoretical orientations, who were able to straddle potentially conflicting roles as supporters and evaluators, and who were perceived as trustworthy and expert were more highly valued than those supervisors who did not have these characteristics. Effective supervisors modeled respect for their trainees and allowed for different ideas, styles, and orientations to enter the supervisory space. They embraced mistakes as learning opportunities and provided safe environments in which to explore anxieties, insecurities, and perceived failings. These supervisors were sensitive to, and confronted, supervisees' resistances in a warm and supportive manner. A solid supervisory relationship is non-judgmental and can facilitate supervisee development at many different levels of experience. A recent trend of bringing mindful practice to supervision seems well suited to promote and develop the types of supervisory relationships that are likely to produce high-quality results regardless of the theoretical model or interactive style of the supervisor.

Mindful supervision

'Mindfulness is the moment-to-moment non-judgmental awareness of thoughts, perceptions, and feelings as they rise and fall away in an unceasing unfolding of conscious experience' (Andersen, 2012, p. 727). There is a detachment between inner awareness and conscious processing (Wells, 2005). Wells argued that this detachment is central in overcoming feelings of anxiety, insecurity, and other self-limiting cognitions and experiences. Mindfulness extends beyond simple self-awareness. For example, people who have extremely negative views of the world and themselves may be exquisitely self-aware, but their awareness may be proscriptively negative in quality. Being aware of the present moment without grasping onto judgments or evaluations is a defining feature of mindfulness (Siegel, 2010). Mindful-based experiencing has been a mainstay of Buddhist traditions for centuries, but the practice was generally ignored by mainstream psychology and educational practitioners until the 1990s (Langer, 1990, 1997). Authors are beginning to merge traditional mindfulness practices with existing psychotherapeutic styles (e.g., Wells & Matthews, 1996; Epstein, 1995) with great success. Neurobiologists and therapists are finding positive neurological correlates to mindful practices (e.g., Badenoch, 2008; Siegel, 2012). It was not until the 2000s that mindfulness emerged on the academic sport psychology scene with any credibility. Since that time, there have been books and articles (e.g., Gardner, 2009) devoted to the practice.

Interpersonal mindfulness

Siegel (2007, 2010) has outlined three key interpersonal phenomena that can occur within a dyadic interaction if one or both participants have a mindful approach: presence, attunement, and resonance.

Presence refers to being in the moment with oneself and one's environment (being aware and conscious of subjective and environmental experience in a non-judgmental way). Being present helps create 'an integrated state of being' (Siegel, 2007, p. 27) that allows the individual to be flexible, adaptive, coherent, energized, and stable. A harmonic pattern of awareness opens our receptive state to environmental and interpersonal input. This type of presence may occur when a supervisor and supervisee are *with* each other. Rogers' concept of congruence, what allows one to be in a 'fully attending and empathic state' (Raskin & Rogers, 1989, p. 172), Yalom's *here and now* experience, and Freud's analytical stance of *evenly suspended attention* are consistent with this idea of *presence*. Being present with another human being has a calming and reassuring effect. Andersen (2012) argued that human beings, having evolved as highly social creatures, are hardwired for being present with one another. We exist and thrive in groups and communities. Those humanoids who were solitary and isolative were easy prey for powerful, nocturnal, and/or pack hunters. Even in modern times, those who tend to be isolated and asocial are the exception and may be identified (in some cases) as pathological (e.g., schizoid personality disorder, avoidant personality disorder).

Recent neurobiological work mapping the mirror neuron systems of the brain gives a preliminary dynamic and organic explanation for *presence*. Mirror neurons (Iacobini, 2008) are those select neural circuits that respond to the actions or emotions of those around us. These networks may be the foundations of empathy and presence. Siegel (2010) and others have suggested that mirror neuron systems are malleable. One can enhance one's empathic capacity through practice and intentionality. Andersen (2012) pointed out that even though mirror neurons provide a functional map for empathic presence, in supervision, they also can interfere with presence. Supervisees, especially early in their professional development, may be anxious, insecure, and seeking reassurance. If they encounter a supervisor who is distant, hurried, punitive, and not interested in the process, the mirror neuron system detects these signals and relates internal messages that may cause the supervisee to recoil and withdraw into self-protection mode. They easily sense the supervisor has 'left the building'. This scenario is particularly true if there is any history of neglect or mistreatment from significant attachment figures in supervisees' early development.

Histories of trauma or neglect may predispose some individuals to being hypervigilant for signs of disapproval or abandonment, perhaps reading them from relatively neutral cues. Badenoch (2008) has observed that at birth, our limbic areas are 'packed with largely undifferentiated neurons' (p. 50). These cells immediately begin to form pathways, circuits, and networks based the nature and quality of experiences. Deficient or chaotic histories establish neural systems that may be highly reactive and predisposed to anxiety, fear, and threat perceptions. These possible interpersonal difficulties are all the more reason for making intentional efforts toward being present with supervisees. Being present creates the essential ingredients for a mindful environment, a space where supervisees can learn to be present with their supervisors and ultimately with their clients in supportive and productive ways. Also, being mindful and non-judgmentally present is itself a reflective practice of watching one's thoughts, emotions, and desires rise and fall away in the ever-unfolding moment. The indented section below is a tale that

Mark tells about being present, losing presence, and then coming back into the room with compassion.

Leaving the building

I (Mark) am sitting with my supervisee, Jesse. We have been doing supervision for 3 years. The story he is telling me is a new and subtle version of 'I was at a loss as to what to do. I am not a good psychologist. I am incompetent and a fraud.' We have heard this story at least once every couple months for the past three years. In supervision, and in therapy, the same story of woe, or hurt, or 'I am not worthy of love' comes up again and again. Even when we think we have a handle on its irrationality and ontogenetic roots, it disguises itself and crops up again with a different costume and a new mask. As I listen to Jesse's tale, my presence collapses into judgment and irritation. 'Here we go again! When is he going to get this? I just want to smack him.'

And then I catch myself. At the root of self-reflection, therapy, and supervision is the process of paying attention to the times we get hooked and drawn out of the present moment by old, automatic patterns of thinking, judgment, and emotional responses. Once we catch ourselves we can then return to the present moment with compassion, care, and curiosity. I (metaphorically) 'come back into the room' and say, 'Jesse, as you're telling me this story and beating yourself up about it all, does it remind you of similar stories we have heard in "soup"'? He slaps his forehead, 'Shit! There it is again. How long am I going to keep falling into this I-am-not-good-enough trap?' I respond with, 'Probably the rest of your life, but you will get better at catching it before it hooks you into despair.'

I then tell Jesse a story about my processes. 'Jesse, as you were telling me this story, I too got hooked and drawn out of the room with judgment and frustration. I was saying to myself, "What a dolt! I just want to smack him" but then I caught myself.' Jesse laughs and says, 'Well, maybe you should just smack me then.' I too laugh and respond with, 'There is a tale of a Buddhist monk asking his lama a simple question, and then the lama hits him over the head with a scroll, and the monk instantly attains enlightenment. Shall we try that?' Jesse laughs again, 'Deal, but can we do the smacking metaphorically?'

Supervisors self-disclosing their fallibilities to supervisees are helpful actions that communicate we are all human. This sort of self-disclosure models compassion and curiosity about what we perceive to be our weaknesses. In the case above, I changed my frustration and judgment into a self-reflective tale about fascination and returning to the present with loving kindness. Jesse already knows how to return to the present moment, come back into the room, and practice directing his deep compassion for others towards himself. But he forgets sometimes and gets hooked, just like the rest of us.

Siegel's (2007, 2010) second condition is *attunement*. When two people are attuned with one another, they feel what the other is feeling (empathy). These types of experiences are common for most all of us, and we don't even have to be attuned to *real* people. Crying at the misfortune of a television character or feeling elation at the successes of a person in a movie are examples of attunement. Being attuned with another person through a distant medium comes fairly natural to most of us. Being attuned in-person, however, may be more difficult. To be attuned, one needs to be able to let go of self-oriented thoughts and feelings, performance anxieties, and interpersonal trepidations. If individuals are concerned about how they are being perceived or evaluated by others, the experience is anxiety-filtered, and attunement may be elusive. Attunement is facilitated when there are strong non-judgmental parameters built into the relationship. Rogers' unconditional positive regard (i.e., non-judgment) is an essential component of therapeutic change and can be a catalyst for attunement (Andersen, 2012). Of course, attunement does not mean we are completely absorbed in the presence of the other person. Being 'over-attuned' can lead to a loss of self and a blurring of boundaries that can cause confusion and enmeshment between two people. Practitioners who experience the emotions of their clients too intensely may consciously or unconsciously lead them away from emotional material. This over-attunement and identification may send the message that clients' feelings or problems may be 'too much for even my therapist to deal with'. A healthy balance between our own emotional world and the emotional worlds of those with whom we are relating is ideal.

Of course, as human beings we are fallible; we all make mistakes. Even those who are highly attuned with their clients or supervisees will tend to slip up and recognise their own histories, assumptions, needs, and desires interfering. This interference is a species of negative countertransference. Attuned supervisors recognise their own problematic reactions and make efforts to identify them with their supervisees, take accountability, and clean things up. Supervisors, especially new ones with blind spots, are less able to catch themselves in these situations. Such negative countertransferential responses is why supervision of their supervision, or metasupervision, is beneficial (Barney & Andersen, in press; Barney, Andersen & Riggs, 1996). By modelling corrective actions for our own mistakes, we create an invitation for our supervisees to be similarly accountable and accepting of their own fallibilities and those of their clients. Recovering from these mis-attuned moments often creates a heightened level of presence, and the relationship may be strengthened. A tale from Steve follows.

In and out of tune

I (Steve) recall one supervision session with Jill. She was a relatively new supervisee with great potential as a psychologist. She had been working with a female golfer, Jackie, who was struggling interpersonally. During our third or fourth session together, after about 30 minutes of discussing her PST work with Jackie, Jill confided that, 'Jackie told me she has an eating disorder; she binges and purges about 3 times a week . . . I have a really hard time working with eating disorders.' Excited at the prospects of sharing some things I had been mulling on for a few weeks, I launched into a discussion of some new ideas I had been developing using catastrophe theory and non-linear change perspectives to facilitate dissonance in people who have eating issues. True to my passion as a teacher, I lectured for about 20 minutes straight, hardly taking time to catch a breath. By the time our session ended, I had developed a comprehensive intervention plan designed to help build emotional regulation and compensatory skills for Jackie. I had it all worked out.

Jill politely said, 'that sounds really good, looks like we are out of time, see you next week' and dismissed herself from the session. Why was she not overwhelmed with my knowledge and enthusiasm for this work with Jackie? I was somewhat astounded. I consulted a colleague with whom I frequently do informal metasupervision. As I recounted my session with Jackie my colleague asked, 'Did you ever find out why it's hard for her to work with people who have eating disorders?' I had assumed it was because she did not yet have my astounding perspective. Then I realized how distant and mis-attuned I had been. My intentions had been pure . . . hadn't they? I began to realize I was more invested in showing Jill how insightful and informative I was rather than being tuned into her experience.

The next week when Jill came in for supervision; the conversation went something like this:

Steve (S):   Hey Jill, I'm glad to see you today.
Jill (J):   Yeah, where should we start today, I have been doing some reading about arousal theory; it's really cool.

It seemed that Jill wanted to guide our discussion to a safe area and meet my interests in intellectual and academic dialogue.

(S):   I would love to visit with you about that, but I wondered, can we talk for a few minutes about our last session? After you left, I realized I hadn't really listened to you at all. I apologize for not being tuned in to what you were saying. No matter how long I do this stuff, I still catch myself screwing up. Can we start over?
(J):   Sure.
(S):   You were talking about how Jackie told you that she was bingeing and purging. You had mentioned that it is hard for you to work with people who have eating issues. Can you tell me more?

I adjusted my seat and leaned in attentively.

(J):   Well, while I was in high school, I thought I was really fat and unattractive . . .

We proceeded to talk about her own struggles with body image, perfectionistic ideas, emotional challenges, and experimentation with bulimic behaviors during that time in her life. She seemed to open up and appeared to have been relieved of a huge burden. As we concluded our session, she commented,

(J): See you next week. Today was a lot better.

And indeed it was.

The keys to recovering from mis-attuned moments seem to be recognition, accountability, and sincere reparation. I believe in my interaction with Jill, recognizing my fallibility and being able to ask for a second chance opened the door to deepening our connection and moving forward with our supervision. Because of my mis-attunement, she thought I wanted intellectual dialogue and was prepared to accommodate my expectations. Once we returned to those things she needed, our process came back on track and her work with Jackie progressed nicely.

Siegel's (2007, 2010) third dimension is *resonance*. Resonance is the coupling of presence and attunement. When resonance occurs, people feel heard, understood, and validated. It is a strong subjective connection with the other person. Andersen (2012) noted that, 'another word for feeling felt and resonance is love' (p. 730). Not love in a romantic context, but unconditional love that sends a strong message that one is valued and cared for deeply, regardless of what one does. Siegel suggested that human beings are neurologically wired for resonance. He has identified *resonance circuitry* that includes activation in the supplemental and premotor areas of the frontal cortex, the ventral and medial prefrontal cortices, and the insula. As this resonance circuitry is activated within the context of an attuned interpersonal experience, dampening signals are sent to the subcortical emotion centers of the brain (e.g., amygdala), resulting in modulation of fear, anxiety, defensive posturing, and other automatic protective mechanisms. Mindfulness strengthens this system and allows us to 'monitor with more clarity, openly attending to the waves of body sensations and not just being bombarded by them, we can modify our internal state with more strength and agility' (Siegel, 2007, p. 59). As we are present and attuned, the conditions are ripe for resonance, which in turn, facilitates our ability to be present and attuned.

Siegel observed that resonance circuits 'permit our joining (attuning and resonating with another person) perhaps long before self-awareness is initiated' (Siegel, 2010, p. 60). Perhaps more importantly, interpersonal experiences are easily moved from automatic pre-cortical levels of processing to the higher brain centers associated with reason and conscious recognition. We become more adept at accurately identifying, labeling, and reacting to interpersonal situations. Supervisees who have experienced resonance with their supervisors may be more likely to resonate with their clients through reducing their negative countertransference enactments and blind spots. They have the potential to be more aware and deliberate about how they relate to clients. Flexibility and plasticity in the resonance circuits are hallmark features of our brains. As mindful conditions are met, Siegel noted, there is a natural release of neuropeptides and trophic factors that 'stimulate neural activation and growth' (2010, p. 84) in these specialized areas.

Of course, for brain systems to function effectively, they need to work together. Mindful and intentional focus and states of attention facilitate this integration (Siegel, 2010). Mindful practice harnesses and exercises integrative brain regions such as the hippocampus, the anterior cingulate, and others. But how can one achieve effective states of mindfulness for oneself and within the supervisory relationship? Most mindful practitioners recommend beginning with the breath (e.g., Andersen, 2012; Ryan, 2007). Deliberate and focused attention on one's diaphragmatic breathing is a simple, but effective initiation to mindfulness. To be mindful, one is aware, but not judgmental, of cognitive or affective intrusions when breathing. As the mind wanders, the mindful breather simply recognizes the deviation and gently brings the focus back to the breath. Intentionally moving focus from the breath onto other body parts and kinesthetic sensations and then back can be helpful as well. Being present with one's breath creates neural pathways that allow one to be present with another person. Attunement exercises in which participants engage in dyadic role plays exhibiting different emotional states can also be beneficial. One participant exhibits or conjures an emotional memory and liberally expresses the facial and body posture manifestations of that emotion, while the other participant tries to be attuned to what the emoter is feeling. The receiver of the emotions then attempts to identify and label for the emoter the quality, intensity, and name of the emotion. Both participants then process their own emotional experience (self-presence and attunement) during the exercise. There are many other exercises designed to promote mindfulness and *mindsight* (the ability to monitor the flow of energy and stimulation within a resonance circuit; Siegel, 2010).

Although these techniques will not guarantee high-quality supervision, the intentional incorporation of presence, attunement, and resonance may provide an overarching 'transtheoretical foundation for many helping professions' (Andersen, 2012, p. 732) including supervision in sport and performance psychology. Mindfulness, presence, attunement, and resonance would also seem to be strong foundations for engaging in almost any reflective practice.

The future of mindful supervision in applied sport psychology

We are hopeful idealists, but we are also realists. We hope that supervision will become a mainstay of training in applied sport psychology, but the evidence of widespread supervision in the field is limited (e.g., Watson, Zizzi, Etzel & Lubker, 2004). Mindfulness has entered the supervision discourse in applied sport psychology only in the past year (i.e., Andersen, 2012). We will have to see where it goes from here.

Once limited to those familiar with Eastern philosophy and practices, mindfulness is now providing a fruitful foundation for many types of human relationships (e.g., relationships in the helping professions). Those professionals engaging in sport psychology supervision may find these practices helpful, enjoyable, and effective in improving the quality of their alliances with supervisees. Enhancing the quality of current supervisory relationships may counteract or repair any damage done by early supervision that was harmful and punitive.

We are also hopeful that the use of mindfulness in applied sport psychology will spread beyond the application of mindful practices for performance enhancement. We think using mindfulness in sport performance situations is a great start, but mindfulness can extend well past this somewhat narrow focus. The mindful sport psychologist and the interpersonal mindfulness of the practitioner–client dyad have much to contribute to what is the core of sport psychology service delivery, the therapeutic relationship. It is a short hop from this relationship to the supervisor–supervisee alliance. Reflective practice in sport and performance psychology enhances the effectiveness of our work with trainees and athletes alike. We also believe that assisted self-reflection in mindful supervision is a part of the warp and weft of the fabric of living a reflective life. So where do we start? It may be as easy as taking that first deep, mindful breath.

15 The utility of reflective practice during the provision of sport psychology support

Tracey J. Devonport and Andrew M. Lane

Introduction

There are many conceptual definitions of reflective practice, an observation found in the study of a number of psychological concepts. However, definitions of reflective practice are not poles apart and each definition tends to contain the same underlying principles. To illustrate this observation, Clouder (2000) defined reflective practice in an educational context as involving 'the critical analysis of everyday working practices to improve competence and promote professional development' (p. 211). In a sport psychology context Anderson, Knowles and Gilbourne (2004) defined reflective practice as 'an approach to training and practice that can help practitioners explore their decisions and experiences in order to increase their understanding of and manage themselves and their practice' (p. 189).

Two common elements across definitions of reflective practice are that it is: (1) a critically analytical process, intended to (2) enhance professional competence. The above two aspects of reflective practice should be welcomed by any practising professional as they sit closely with requirements for continuing professional development. Informed by our research and personal experiences with the use of reflective practice, we define reflective practice as, 'the purposeful but largely informal critical analysis of events past, present or future, the intention being to enhance professional competencies and the attainment of professional objectives.' We do not claim that our definition furthers conceptual clarity, rather we seek to illustrate our interpretation and use of reflective practice within this chapter and, importantly, within our work.

Within this chapter we will outline approaches towards reflective practice, illustrating how these may work in practice. To set the context for our co-authorship, we have worked together at the University of Wolverhampton for over 12 years. This longevity has presented ample opportunities for formal and informal reflections regarding our independent and combined consultancy experiences. When reflecting together, potential strengths are afforded by the different consultancy philosophies, experiences and applied approaches that we each have. So that readers may better understand the influence of our consultancy philosophies on the process of reflection, and indeed the contribution of reflection towards consultancy philosophies, we begin by presenting a consultancy background for each author.

Consultancy background: Tracey Devonport

My first experience as a probationary sport psychologist came in 1994. My client was a female international cricketer. I arranged twice-weekly indoor net sessions that were an addition to her normal training commitments. The aim of these two additional sessions was to introduce and monitor her use of imagery during batting performances. The objective was to utilize imagery to enhance her emotion regulation, decision-making and skill execution. I recall how nervous I was when first working with her, how keen I was to make a positive difference to her game, and how unsure I was that I could make a difference. I selected imagery as the focus of consultancy, not because it was something she had expressed a desire to address, or as a result of a rigorous needs analysis, but because I had researched imagery use as part of my undergraduate and postgraduate dissertation studies. I was confident I knew the theory behind imagery interventions, and as a consequence I felt I knew how to introduce and deliver an imagery intervention. I had a perceived need to be in control of the consultancy agenda in order to stay within my areas of greatest confidence. I placed my faith in the 'truth' of published literature on imagery and performance, and this enhanced my confidence in the intervention I was about to deliver.

Self-assessment through reflection has been identified as a useful method for sport psychologists to manage their own practice, attempt to increase understanding of their practice, and evidence continuing professional development (Cropley, Miles, Hanton & Niven, 2007; Knowles, Gilbourne & Niven, 2011). My consultancy philosophy has evolved as a result of the lessons I have learned having reflected upon formative experiences such as that outlined above. I regularly discuss my applied work with others to ensure that I continue to learn and adapt. I utilize the generic term 'others' as over the years I have discussed carefully selected applied incidents (encountered or anticipated) with other chartered sport psychologists, clinical colleagues, coaches, athletes, teachers, friends and even my partner. In sharing reflections I am mindful of maintaining confidentiality and protecting the identity of clients, and as such, ethical obligations influence the extent to which I divulge information during shared reflections.

An example of a series of critical reflections that were particularly influential on my consultancy philosophy took place during (and following) the British Association of Sport and Exercise Science conference in 2006. Here I heard the phrase, 'the map is not the territory' voiced by Professor Mark Andersen. Prof. Andersen explained that the map represents theories and models of human behaviour. He noted that in many cases the impression given in academia and consultancy is that such maps represent 'some sort of terra firma, a land where things were known, solid, where A precedes B, which leads to C, and the navigation is clear' (Andersen, 2006, p. 10). This observation reflects the beliefs I evidenced in the consultancy scenario described with the female cricketer. I had previously placed my faith in the 'truth' of the maps (imagery theories) concerning imagery and performance. Prof. Andersen suggested that maps (theories) may not accurately reflect the territory (real-world encounters and service delivery issues).

To illustrate that the 'map is not the territory' I will describe a key moment as a new parent. Following the birth of my son I avidly read a well-known parenting book to try and recognise the meaning of different types of crying. I wanted to understand my son's needs and help him, not dissimilar to the aims of consultancy. The book described different types of crying, which represented different needs. This included descriptions of cries for a baby that was tired, overtired, overstimulated, under-stimulated, had wind, hunger, pain, was too cold, too hot, and so the list went on. My partner and I would sit and listen to him, book in hand, trying to map his crying onto one of the cries described. None of the descriptions matched his cries. Exasperated, we put the book down and simply listened to him. We listened for patterns of cries and would then monitor our actions and his reactions. It was the best thing we did; the crying subsided as we learned to understand him, not the generalization of a baby cry as described in a book.

We argue that applied sport psychology (ASP) practitioners should reflect upon and draw meaning from events that occur across professional and personal contexts. In other words, life experiences can, and we emphasize should, be used to inform professional practice. After all, life experiences typically exemplify the application of psychological principles in differing contexts, and moreover, sport is a life experience. As I have gained experience, I have undertaken a personal shift from a steadfast reliance on theory and literature to a more balanced approach. This is not to suggest that I do not value theory and literature, I certainly do. Published work and theory can stimulate thinking and analysis, focus and guide interventions, and help identify expected or anticipated change. However, I now view theory and literature as constructions rather than truths. I consider the application of theory and/or literature where I perceive it to be relevant, useful or appropriate to the context of application. As such, while empirical resources may guide and inform my work, client and situational idiosyncrasies strongly influence my decision-making and ongoing evaluations.

Consultancy background: Andy Lane

The start point for my ASP work is less clear. After completing my first degree, I was a boxing coach at two clubs. One was the university club, which comprised students who liked to box to keep fit and a couple of boxers who would enter the National Student Championship. The second club was an amateur boxing club; this had boxers vying for Olympic selection. I also did a Post-Graduate Certificate in Education, teaching physical education. All of this work involved teaching a number of psychological skills. For example, I encouraged boxers to use imagery, a skill that many would attach to easily because of the link to shadow boxing (boxing on your own into a mirror or looking at your shadow). At the

University boxing club, I learned to mix with an educated largely middle-class group (students) who were doing something out of their comfort zone (boxing). By contrast, club boxers were mainly from working-class backgrounds, some of whom were very poor. They operated a level of seriousness about what they did as though every training session was the Olympic final. Boxing club coaches were initially sceptical of some of the psychology training I used. Their dedication for their athletes to achieve was high, and as such boxing presents an environment where the clientele do not suffer fools gladly (see Schinke & Ramsay, 2009).

At the same time, at school I would be teaching children about goal setting, particularly in cross-country running, a sport I also ran as an after-school club. I structured lessons so that achievement could be recognised and rewarded by giving out 'merits' based on improvement. This approach corresponded with teaching children about how to set specific, measurable, achievable and personal goals. After handing out 20 merits in one class, which meant each child achieved her/ his goal, a Head of Year asked me, 'Was I giving out the merits as it was Christmas?' I had asked the children to set a running goal for the week and said that I would give merits out to those who achieved their goal, and I was prepared to hand out one to every member of the class if that happened.

Over the years my work has become more sophisticated in one way, but many of the characteristics of how I worked initially remain. I like to build on the self-regulation strategies that people already use. One of the main challenges for an athlete is to control emotions, with the idea that emotions invade consciousness and affect priorities in a way that is not consistent with goals (Lane, Beedie, Jones, Uphill & Devonport, 2012). However, emotions are not new concepts, and while sport psychology has undoubtedly contributed to advancing knowledge in emotions, the function of emotion is deep-rooted in human evolution. Just as a giraffe's long neck evolved to help the species survive (the tall ones who could eat the leaves at the top of the tree survived), emotions such as anxiety and depression have done the same. Anxiety acts as a warning to oneself or a means to communicate this message to others that the situation is somehow threatening, and the physiological response to that situation is a fight or flight response. These responses have been embedded into the human psyche over millions of years of evolution. One session with me is going to have less effect. People begin to develop strategies to manage emotions such as anxiety from an early age and across different situations. Exploring what an individual has done and what has worked is how I like to begin working with individuals. I can teach people how to give their mental game a tune-up, or help them reorganize their thoughts, but the start point is a search of what works well in their experience, and therefore the individual is placed at the centre of this process.

Examining the contribution of reflection towards the consultancy agenda

The brief consultancy biographies provide evidence for the development and application of our philosophical and conceptual perspectives. The illustrative examples we offer support the notion of reflective practice as an effective tool for increasing understanding of consultancy practice and/or applied research (Knowles, Gilbourne, Tomlinson & Anderson, 2007; Tod, 2007). Reflecting upon delivery issues and the efficacy of interventions intended to enhance the well-being and performance of clients not only enables practitioners to establish which techniques work under different conditions, but also allows an examination of the processes and factors that influence the effectiveness or ineffectiveness of service delivery (Anderson et al., 2004, Devonport & Lane, 2009). Furthermore, examining how different approaches compare can positively influence the development of consultancy-based interventions, enabling an evaluation of the application of research to applied practice (Grey & Fitzgibbon, 2003).

As practitioners, we engage in self-reflection when assessing an athlete, and subsequently when introducing, developing and refining interventions (Anderson et al., 2004; Knowles et al., 2007). Furthermore, we utilize reflective practice to examine past, present or future experiences, situating theory and professional knowledge into practice in order to enhance our professional competencies and increase consultancy effectiveness (Anderson et al., 2004). Reflecting on past practice in this way is known as *reflection-on-action* (Schön, 1987), the product of which being referred to as *knowledge-in-action*. This process is integral to effective practice as it is proposed to incorporate values, prejudices, experiences, knowledge and social norms (Knowles et al., 2007). *Reflection-in-action*, alternatively, pertains to thinking about a situation while it is occurring in order to clarify thoughts; this then influences decisions made and allows procedures to be implemented in a manner that presents a 'best fit' for the context and individuals involved (Knowles, Gilbourne, Borrie & Nevill, 2001). Consultants should consider reflecting mid-action, acknowledging that they should be flexible to change, and conscious of their own thoughts and feelings. Psychologists are not impervious to experiencing unwanted emotions during consultancy and, as such, it helps to be aware that you are nervous and that these nerves will be influencing your thoughts and actions. Anderson et al. (2004) call reflection-in and -on practical experience *dual-staged reflection*. The resulting insights and understanding gained are used to enhance *craft knowledge* and improve practice (Devonport & Lane, 2009; Grey & Fitzgibbon, 2003; Johns, 1994). Schön (1987) argued that craft knowledge (knowledge-in-action) guides practitioners in dealing with complex practical situations where it is insufficient to simply apply theory to practice. In other words, it assists a practitioner in applying the principle that 'the map is not the territory'.

We have found that reflecting upon practice either independently, or with others, helps to identify and explore effective practice and identify areas for improvement (Knowles et al., 2001). Within ASP, effective practice has been described as the application of psychological theories, principles and techniques to induce psycho-behavioural change in athletes to enhance performance, the quality of the sport experience and personal growth (Anderson, Miles, Mahoney & Robinson, 2002; Poczwardowski, Sherman & Ravizza, 2004). This definition of effective practice supports the notion and importance of *evidence-based practice*. Evidence-based practice refers to the process of applying the best available

Figure 15.1 Image taken at England Women's Volleyball team training, 2/2004: Team
Psychologist Dr Tracey Devonport listens to Volleyball Coach Audrey
Cooper's training session (Photograph©B.M.Totterdell)

research evidence or theory in guiding the selection and implementation of an applied service (McIntosh, 2010). However, as we have identified, it is not always the case that theory clearly situates within applied practice situations. Honesty and openness are prerequisites for advancing effective applied practice and indeed theory via reflection (Devonport & Lane, 2009). It may be that through honest critical reflection regarding applied practice, it transpires that a theory fails to explain phenomena, in which case there may be grounds upon which to challenge or refine theory.

In reality, many applied practitioners take a more balanced approach towards consultancy, wherein theory and literature guide as opposed to prescribe applied work. Some aspects of sport psychology services can involve following a prescribed formula implemented in a manner similar to following a cookbook recipe (e.g., delivering a progressive muscular relaxation intervention). However, many aspects of applied work involve applying techniques that help an athlete become more self-aware and better at solving goal-associated problems. In order to achieve both objectives, the consultant needs to build a relationship with their client, and how this is done is far less formulaic. What should be consistent is that each practitioner should know what they do, why they do it and how they think it works.

It has been suggested that a greater awareness and self-knowledge contributes towards effective practice by enabling an individual to be able to adapt their knowledge to meet the demands of the varying situations experienced in ASP (Cropley et al., 2007; Petitpas, Giges & Danish, 1999). As practitioners accumulate applied experiences they may gather and reflect upon the acquired data as a form of practice-based evidence (Margison et al., 2000). Reflecting upon the usage of practice-based evidence in addition to evidence-based practice serves to improve practice knowledge and practice effectiveness. The use of practice-based evidence in informing future practice is well developed in domains of psychology such as counselling and psychiatry (Barkham, Mellor-Clark, Connell & Cahill, 2006). It affords the practitioner the opportunity to examine their own practice, and the thoughts and feelings that are associated with their actions within the particular context in which they occur. Using such evidence during reflection allows practitioners to think about the whole experience of consultancy rather than a theoretical framework alone. As such, this presents the opportunity for consultancy experiences to inform applied research and vice versa.

Models can be used to guide reflection, and in the sport psychology context Gibbs' model (1988) and Johns' (1994) model are among those commonly used (e.g., Cropley et al., 2007; Knowles et al., 2001). However, for us, these have informed rather than dictated the approach we undertake (Johns, 1994). From our own perspective, we tend to analyse an incident considering pertinent thoughts, feelings and consequences (for ourselves and others). This is accompanied by the development of action points taking into account current research and theoretical propositions. As with any theoretical analysis, we seek alternative explanations cognizant that any one theory is unlikely to be ecumenical. Where appropriate or possible, we seek and consider the reflections of people relevant to the context of consultancy (e.g., athlete, coach, officials, fellow athletes, parents, partners and so on) (Knowles et al., 2001). As such we encourage the same reflective process among our clients. We do so because it helps to inform or triangulate our own reflections and presents clients with the knowledge and performance benefits previously described. Encouraging reflection among clients in itself forms part of an intervention aimed at increasing self-awareness and helping to meet personal goals (performance and well-being). This approach towards reflection acknowledges that many of our realities and truths are social constructions of information. As such this accepts the position that different individuals might perceive the same experiences very differently.

Exemplifying the role of reflection in professional practice, learning and personal development

The following example is intended to offer an insight into the practical application of reflective practice, highlighting its importance in professional practice, learning and personal development. Tracey had been working with a female junior county athlete for over a year, providing individual consultations and group education sessions. During a weekly individual consultation the client described a scenario whereby following a recent performance her dad had criticized her standard of play. This in itself was not the main issue of concern to the client. Her father said that he stayed with her mum; that is, still living together, mainly to support her sports career. He said that because of the sacrifices they were making, they expected returns regarding her sports accomplishments. The client described how she felt upset and angered by this revelation. She also felt guilty that her parents were staying together purely for her and consequently felt tremendous pressure on her game.

Tracey was horrified that any parent would place such a burden on their child, but did not wish to appear judgemental towards her client's parents or seek to understand their perspective. Tracey chose to remain focused on her client's thoughts and feelings. In seeking to help manage her client's emotions, Tracey adopted two main strategies. Firstly, she looked to examine her client's appraisal of the situation and identify situational aspects that she could challenge or change in some way. Secondly, she looked to rationalize her client's emotions and explore ways in which she could seek to regulate these emotions (see Lane et al., 2012). Despite, or perhaps because of the impact her father's comments had on her client, she (the client) did not feel she had the confidence to speak with her parents about the issues raised. Acting as a 'sounding board' for the client by working through her thoughts and emotions appeared to assist with her affective state. However, Tracey was conscious that it had not addressed the underlying problems, and she felt the need to do more. Tracey first spoke with Andy – seeing that he was in office and free, she asked if he was available for a chat.

From Andy's perspective, he listened to what was going on and helped support Tracey in terms of how to address the issue. In situations such as this it is important to be aware of what you can work on and what you cannot influence. It was clear that Tracey could not get involved in the domestic issues of the parents, but she could support her client in seeing and understanding the situation more clearly. In this instance, it was important to help a colleague clarify her thoughts about what was needed and encourage confidence in her decision-making abilities. There are many instances in applied work where the guardian angel of self-confidence is fragile. In such circumstances, helping to build or maintain confidence by using reminders of previous performance needs to be encouraged (Bandura, 1997).

Given the fact that the origins of Tracey's client's concerns sat largely in the home environment, and also given their implications for her well-being, Tracey also sought the advice of a clinical psychologist. Tracey was still considering possible options for broaching (with the client's consent), or encouraging the client to broach the issues raised with her parents. In a phone conversation with a clinical practitioner friend she (the clinical practitioner) explained that confronting the parents may not present a suitable or indeed effective option. Without challenging her parents, how can my client resolve her upset and anger, Tracey asked? The suggestion was that the client writes a letter to her parents expressing and rationalizing her thoughts and feelings, and that she keep this letter hidden and takes time to reflect upon its content. With the passing of time, would she still feel the same way? Would her emotions attenuate as a function of writing them down and better understanding their cause? Could she place the cause of her emotions into perspective or rationalize them? In writing the letter and subsequently revisiting it, would she identify a means of addressing or resolving the issues raised?

In considering the implementation of this intervention Tracey could see how this non-confrontational and reflective approach could be of value to her client. Tracey felt that this strategy offered something tangible in seeking to support her client, something that did not breach her limits of competence or her role as a sport psychology consultant. Tracey suggested that her client pen a letter to her parents, and she discussed the potential value in doing so with her client.

In reviewing the effectiveness of this strategy, Tracey's client felt that writing her thoughts and feelings down, although initially difficult and upsetting, was indeed helpful. She reconciled the causes of the emotions and felt that in doing so they were attenuated. Since this incident, and given the positive outcomes, Tracey undertook reading on the benefits of talking or writing about emotional experiences and the mechanisms of effect. Research indicates that both writing and talking about stressful or emotional events results in improvements in both physical and psychological health among non-clinical and clinical populations (Baikie & Wilhelm, 2005; Davidson et al., 2002). As such, in the consultancy example provided, it could be that using a combination of verbal and written approaches optimized the benefits of examining the emotional experience.

The mechanisms of effect for therapeutic writing/talking are unclear. One possible explanation was proposed by Pennebaker (1985), who developed the emotional inhibition and confrontation theory. This theory proposes that actively inhibiting thoughts and feelings about traumatic events requires effort and presents a stressor (e.g., by resulting in obsessive thinking or ruminating about the event). By contrast, talking or writing about a stressful event acknowledges the associated emotions and is thought to reduce the physiological work of inhibition, gradually lowering the overall stress on the body. Such confrontation involves translating the event into words, enabling the cognitive integration and understanding of it, which further contributes to the reduction in physiological activity associated with inhibition and rumination (Pennebaker, 1985). Writing about and discussing the event may have helped the client organize and structure the stressful event. This may have resulted in a more adaptive and integrated schema about herself, others and the world (Harber & Pennebaker, 1992).

Conclusion

The aim of this chapter was to outline an approach towards reflective practice illustrating how this works in practice. Reflective practice is a shared experience that involves developing trust with the person you are sharing information with. It also involves the confidence to share reflections with the acknowledgement that these might be judged to be incorrect. The notion of correct and incorrect as absolutes stems from feeling judged as part of an accreditation system, and while such decisions on the quality of your work are required for formal accreditation, as you become more experienced you realize that there are multiple ways of doing things, each equally correct in its own way. Reflective practice, especially when sharing with others, helps to accelerate the learning process. Thus, we can say that in our experience reflective practice is helpful.

16 Reflective practice in talent development

A narrative inquiry of a coaching psychology intervention

Reinhard Stelter

Introduction

This chapter is based around my development of a form of intervention that is new and unusual in a sport psychology context. The coaching psychology and group-based intervention had a focus on career development, self-reflection and the personal growth of young sports talents with the intention to integrate demands and challenges from their sports career, their school education and their private lives. Via stimulating co-creative reflective practice and mutual engagement of the participants, the coach presented here aimed to create an environment where all participants could unfold their resources, develop a reflective space and share and discover new perspectives for common or individual challenges. In terms of structure and progression I initially provide a description of the intervention – based on narrative-collaborative theory and practice – before placing emphasis on the narrative and qualitative analysis of the reflections of the young talents and their involvement in the group coaching process. The experienced effect of the coaching process is documented though the analysis of selected participants' reflections, both directly after the end of the intervention and half a year later, and these analyses are presented in narrative form. I conclude the chapter by reflecting on my own practice, comparing the aims and process of the intervention to the experience and understanding of the participants. In this way, the practitioner's reflective path will end with some personal thoughts and the possibility for new insights, also in regard to the usefulness of the approach in other settings.

In a sporting context, coaching psychology (see Palmer & Whybrow, 2007) can be regarded as a new type of intervention and also a supplementation of the repertoire of approaches in applied sport psychology. In this example the novelty of the intervention is even greater, because the intervention is not only directed at individuals, but at groups of young talented athletes involved in different kinds of sports. The intervention aims towards the athlete as a whole person by integrating a broad focus on the athletes' careers, their school education and their private lives as adolescents. In that sense, the athletes' identities, their learning and personal growth in different contexts of their lives is the main developmental objective of the intervention.

With reference to Jarvis (1999) and Lane and Corrie (2006), the inspiration for the development of my own reflective practice has been based on two sources of knowledge: (1) knowledge founded in evidence-based research and academic theory, and (2) knowledge evolved as a kind of *subjective theory* generated from reflective practice. As a reflective practitioner, I am constantly engaged in improving my practice; as a reflective practitioner researcher I am not only interested in improving my practice, but also in understanding possible effects. From these perspectives, the objective of this chapter allows me the space to compare my theoretical foundation and concrete intentions for the coaching intervention with the experiences and reflections of the participants, and with the intention of drawing further conclusions in regard to understanding and developing my practice.

The theoretical foundation and its application in a group-coaching intervention

First the theoretical foundation and some basic guidelines for the application of the intervention are presented. The intervention/interaction is based on a narrative-collaborative approach and is built on the theoretical pillars described briefly in a schematic way (see Figure 16.1); these pillars can be seen as the integrated foundation of intervention methodology (see Stelter, 2014; Stelter, 2010; Stelter & Law, 2010)

A central claim of the narrative-collaborative group coach is to unfold and further develop the coachees' social and personal identity. Identity development can be seen as the pivotal point in all five theoretical pillars, although differently approached by each of them. Developing identity is initiated by the coach in three ways:

1. By focusing on and reflecting about values

The coachees are encouraged to reflect on values inherent in their intentions, wishes, aspirations, etc. as guiding markers to help them organize their careers, education and private lives. These values are no longer timeless and universal, but rather are grounded in the practices and events of local communities and the specific setting. The ultimate aim in the context of the studied coaching intervention was to facilitate the participants' understanding of their involvement in an elite sports career and help them to understand *the why* and *how* of their involvement. This was not necessarily by focusing on specific goals, but by reflecting on key values as a feature of their lived conditions in the three central domains: career, education and private life. This focus on values should give the coachees a better sense of how specific actions and ways of thinking and feeling are connected to their selves and their identities. White (2007) spoke about *landscapes of consciousness*. I prefer to speak about *landscapes of identity*. During the coaching dialogue, the values drawn from intentions, wishes, aspirations, etc. are related to former, present and possible future actions. Here, White (2007) spoke about the unfolding of *landscapes of action*.

Narrative collaborative group coaching
Theoretical pillars for an intervention methodology

Social constructionism	Appreciative inquiry and solution-focused approach	Positive psychology	Narrative approach	Community psychology
It is not the individual with specific traits upon whom the intervention will focus. The social reality of individuals and groups is understood as being shaped in *relationships* between different individuals and through specific contexts (Gergen, 2009).	The coach puts focus on aspects of success, strengths and possible solutions that the coachee has, has had or will find in specific situations and events (Cooperrider & Sekerka, 2003; Orem, Binkert & Clancy, 2007; De Jong & Berg, 1998).	Highlight positive human behaviour that leads to thriving individuals and communities (Seligman & Csikszentmihalyi, 2000). Help the coachee focus on specific strengths and virtues and work towards psychological well-being and moments of happiness (Biswas-Diener, 2010: Seligman & Csikszentmihalyi, 2000).	Through forming alternative, more uplifting stories about events and situations, new connections between the coachee's self-understanding, values, intentions, purposes and goals on the one hand, and the coachee's readiness and possibility to act on the other, will emerge (White, 2007).	Specific attention is drawn towards *empowerment*, where the individual develops new resources through reflective and collaborative processes in the community of practice (in casu: the coaching group) that will enable coachees to think and act in new ways (Orford, 2008).

Figure 16.1 Theoretical pillars of narrative-collaborative group coaching, following Stelter, R. (2014). *A guide to third generation coaching – Narrative-collaborative theory and practice* (Dordrecht: Springer Science + Business Media).

2. By providing opportunities in meaning-making

Meaning-making is considered to be one of the main purposes of facilitating the coaching dialogue (Cavanagh, 2006; Stelter, 2007). Meaning is fundamental, because the young talents ascribe specific values to their experiences, actions and to their interplay with others in their three life domains (career, education and private life). Things become *meaningful* to individuals when they understand their own way of sensing, thinking and acting. This can be achieved by telling certain stories about themselves and significant events they are involved in, or plan to be in. Meaning-making is based on past and present experiences as well as future expectations, and the way coachees relate to the world is holistically incorporated in this timeline.

Meaning evolves from the interplay between acting, sensing, reflecting and speaking. In the process of meaning-making, two dimensions should be highlighted: first, the *personal process of meaning-making* formed through the actual experiences and (implicit) knowledge that an individual acquires in various life contexts; and second, the *social process of meaning-making* shaped through social negotiation and narratives that describe the coachees' involvement in and interplay with different settings and practices. These two dimensions are interwoven.

3. By giving space for the unfolding of narratives

Telling stories to one another and developing and sharing narratives and accounts, either in a coach–coachee relationship or in the group-coaching context, is fundamental to the process of social meaning-making. Narratives serve to structure events and to join them together in timelines and storylines. Narratives bring coherence to stories – the source of meaning-making – and as a result of this process life makes sense and becomes meaningful. Narratives establish temporal coherence and shape how events, actions, other persons and the individual himself/herself can be experienced and perceived as sensible and meaningful.

The plot of every story forms the basis for the development of an inner structure and drama (Sarbin, 1986). By telling stories and listening to one another in the group, the participants cause their life-stories to become meaningful and interrelated. In that sense the story can have an impact both on the storyteller and the group participants who listen to it. The individual participant gains a sense of being part of a cultural context with specific, shared values and meanings. This process of collaborative meaning-making is furthered by applying specific coaching techniques, e.g., *outsider witnessing* (White, 2007), and collaborative reflection on what a group member has said. On the basis of the theoretical foundation a number of guidelines were developed to ensure the greatest possible methodological overlap of the five coaches involved in the project.

Narrative-collaborative practice: some central assumptions and guidelines

- Both coach and coachee(s) are conversational partners. Every participant contributes to the joint process of meaning-making and the production of knowledge.
- All participants strive to be flexible and willing to change, thereby making mutual development possible and allowing them to redefine their perspective and position.
- Being attentive to others and to differences can be very fruitful for one's own development and learning.
- All participants value the contributions of others to the dialogue and the knowledge that unfolds co-creatively, but at the same time value possible and enduring differences.
- *Generous listening* is central for mutual inquiry, where interested and sometimes naïve wondering helps to develop generative conversations.
- Paraphrasing remarks or reflections made by the coachee, and interpreting or shaping these reflections on own premises, including associative comments on specific reflections ('When you say that, it makes me think of . . .').
- Flexible attitudes make it possible to redefine own and other positions; one is thereby open for further development and for learning from others.
- Using questions (as the coach) that invite the participant(s) to a change of perspective. Employing different types of circular questions, as used in systemic coaching.
- Inviting the coachee to use metaphors, and using metaphors as coach to unfold sensual reflections and expand the dimensions of actions, perceptions and thoughts through language.
- Coupling landscapes of action (perspectives of purpose, goals and action) and landscapes of consciousness/identity (values, focus on identity, aspiration, dreams and wishes) and vice versa.
- Coupling specific values that are or might have been important to the coachee. In this process the stories grow in richness and complexity, and can develop in a new direction (alternative storyline). This lets the coach strengthen the coachee's sense of identity – the process of *scaffolding* – to bridge the coachee's learning gap by recruiting lived experiences.
- Encouraging the use of narrative documents: poems, short essays, pictures, concrete reflections or retelling of stories either by the coach or the coachee(s).
- Outsider witness procedure: others reflect on a story told by a coachee in order to cast light on its value and meaning for the storyteller and listeners.

Case study

To illustrate the above ideas and the links from these to the theoretical stance outlined above, a case from a coaching session with altogether six participants from different fields of sport is used. They were all around 16–17 years of age and go to a high school that has a special track for elite sport talents.[1] The coaching session took place in a meeting room at the school. In the following I will focus on a sequence where Maria and Patrick play a central role. The four others are mainly listening in this phase.

The case: 'It's about believing in yourself!'

I perceive 16-year-old Maria as an incredibly goal-oriented and ambitious student, and elite athlete. She is clearly aiming for an international career and has already taken part in several European championships in her age group. In a later coaching session, her classmates say with a smile that the previous year, their first year, she could sometimes be a little 'too intense', almost desperate in her desire to be one of the best students, and best in her sport. At times she was unapproachable. She confirms this assessment now, as the others describe their impressions in a group conversation. During this period in the first year, she had a stress-related breakdown, and the school's Team Denmark coordinator was very supportive of her during this time. As a result of the breakdown, Maria has in fact begun to tone down her ambitions as a student. But she is still uncompromising in her sport. At one point during that day's session, Maria articulates her expectations of her sports coach:

> It's really important for me that my coach considers me a talent. If I'm not told that I am a talent, I'll quit!'

Patrick, a very reflective, talkative and outspoken athlete, responds immediately to Maria's intense statement. He thinks that she is being too defeatist:

> No, you have to believe in yourself. I don't understand why you make yourself so dependent on what your sports coach thinks and says. The main thing is that you think you can make it!

At first, though, Maria sticks to her expectations of her sports coach:

> No, it's just important to me. I need to have the sense that things are working for me, and that my coach can see that I'm doing well, and that I'll be able to compete.

Patrick insists and becomes increasingly engaged:

> But you know it better than anyone. You just have to believe in yourself! No one can tell how things are going to develop…

As coach of the session, I notice Patrick's engagement, which goes beyond merely reasoning about what was said. He almost seems to want to convince Maria to embrace his own conviction. In order to take the conversation in a new direction I say to him:

Patrick, I can tell that you're very involved in Maria's story. What does that involvement say about you and who you are?

Patrick picks up the ball and runs with it; he starts with a detailed and gripping story about his school days when he was in the fourth grade of primary school. His telling is very open and honest, although this is only the third time we have met. I am surprised at this frank revelation and impressed that he dares to be so open with his classmates:

> When I was in the 4th grade, I had a stammer, couldn't read properly, and I was overweight and didn't look too sharp. Not many people believed that I could ever become the person I am today. I didn't really have any support from home, my mother in particular had had a rough childhood, and at a young age I learned to look after myself. I didn't want to trouble her with my problems. For example, if I locked my bike at training and found that I had left the key at home, I would simply carry the bike home. I kept my reading difficulties to myself. I just couldn't bear to burden my parents with it. The same with the stammer: fortunately, there was this speech therapist who said that she could help me with all that. These experiences and the fact that I was able to handle my problems convinced me that I could fend for myself. I came to trust that things would work out for me. I learned that I could rely on myself, so now I think that I can make it if I want to.

There is a moment's silence after this story, which seems to grip everybody in the room. Patrick has impressed me. He seems unafraid that this story might have negative consequences for him and his reputation. Frank, Patrick's best friend, who is sitting right next to him, is the first to break the silence; with admiration in his voice he says:

> . . . and I thought I knew you, Patrick. That's pretty intense! It's hard to imagine that you're the same person now as you were then. (We will hear more from Frank later.)

Maria is fairly astonished by Patrick's story. She is sitting across from him, thinking. The story clearly makes an impression on her. After a while she says, astonished:

> I can't believe that it was something I said that started all this. You make me think. It's amazing that you were able to keep believing in yourself.

Later, it becomes evident that this event had a profound effect on Maria's relationship with her sports coach, herself and her approach to her training. She actually revisits Patrick's story in the final sessions. Everybody says that their perception of training has changed. In this connection, Maria says:

I have a different approach to discipline now. I used to do things because I had to, because the coaches told me to. Now it's self-discipline. I want to do this. When I fail to see the point with something – what the individual training elements are good for – then I ask my coach. Something has happened to me – to us, actually.

Reflection on the case – different views

In the following I will present reflections on and interpretations of the case: Maria's, Patrick's and those of Frank, one of Patrick's good friends and participant in the same coaching group, and finally my own.[2] In doing so, we will get a rich understanding of the case's impact on the process of the meaning-making of the different parties. What has been the impact of their conversions on the other members of the group?[3] How can I as a reflective practitioner, and on the basis of my theory, expound on what happen in the session between Maria and Patrick?

Maria's reflections: My sport is who I am – it's my lifestyle

At first, I was actually a little negative about this process. The idea of sharing a lot of stuff about myself, opening up and sharing things that are really personal, I found it hard. But once we got going, I found it kind of interesting. It was interesting to hear how others deal with their problems. In fact, we've begun to talk more in the group, and I started to pay more attention to the others, like if they're having a bad day, or they've done something great, I ask about it. You could say that we've gotten to know each other in a new way.

I think it was a good process, because I learned to think about why I do things instead of just doing them. If I train really hard, I stop to think about why it is I'm doing this; it's because I want to be really good at it. Or sometimes in school, I think, why is it I bother to pay attention in class right now, when I could be chatting with the others instead; it's because I want good marks. I was surprised to be able to learn so much about myself, because I thought that I knew myself really well.

The conversations with the other athletes also made a big impression on me. Like the one with Patrick, where I said that my sports coach did not expect me to be able to qualify for the world championship. Patrick told me to stop worrying about what my coach said, and that if I wanted to be in that group, I simply had to train to get in. After that, my training was much better than it used to be, and it just sort of became natural for me to train to get in, so I told him, and he said, 'well, do it, then'. That helped me a little.

Also Laura, who had injured her elbow and needed surgery; she was wondering whether sport was really worth it, because she also wanted to be able to hold a baby of her own one day. That got me thinking, like, 'hey, think about how much time you're spending on this; you really have to want it. Just think about what any other teenager would be doing on a normal Tuesday, and there I am, training again tonight.' That has made me more conscious of why I do certain things. For example, I only eat sweets on Fridays, so all the other days, again I might think, why is it that I'm doing this? It's because I have to do it to excel. I have learned to accept that my sport is not just a sport, it's a lifestyle, and you have to acknowledge that. Before the coaching process I used to think that I would just compete until I didn't enjoy it anymore. But now I think that I'm doing this because I love this lifestyle. But that has its drawbacks too, because when I have a poor training round, sometimes it can feel like my world is coming to an end, because I do spend so much time training.

But all the training, a lot of homework and time pressure sometimes stress me out. In the past I would just say, 'fuck it', and then I would go to bed, pull the blankets over my head, and then I wouldn't come out until I couldn't sleep any longer. After group coaching I am better at dealing with my problems, and I try to solve them by making a plan. I've become more aware of what it is that I want to achieve with my sport. So I think that I can use it to make the whole thing more structured, like, make a plan – where I used to be more of a mess. I didn't have the time to think about how to deal with a particular problem. Now I'm better at approaching my sports coach and saying, 'I have a problem, and I need to find a solution.' I think that's pretty cool – that I'm not afraid to admit it when I have a problem now. It's cool to admit that sometimes you don't have everything under control – and then ask for help. It takes some of the pressure off if you tell others about your problem. If I tell people at training that I'm tired, it's nice, because then they have a basis for understanding why I am the way I am.

It's been great to receive feedback and to hear the others' opinions, because they're all my age, and they do more or less the same as I do, instead of talking to a sports coach. Like, I only used to talk to the two girls, but now I've begun to talk to the boys as well, and got to know them, compared with the others in class, because we know each other in more of a sports context and in a different way. I mean, I've learned more about how the others think when they train, or when they do really well.

Patrick's reflections: I have been surprised how I could make a difference

I think the group had a positive influence and helped us to find out what we want – in a way we wouldn't be able to without listening to others. As one says: two minds think better than one. Sometimes one could be quite surprised about some of the conclusions of our conversations, because it has been about you as a person. You could somehow think about how others understand you. So what I want to say is: without the others I would not have been able to open my eyes for some things about myself, but also in regard to life as an athlete in general.

In the process there has been space to speak about what one felt; you could be really honest; we could use each other. That was really good. After we have started to do coaching, four of us started to use each other more on a daily basis. At school we started to talk more about our sport. I think this is what makes sense, also because I feel that I can give something to others; I believe we will continue with that for a long time. For my part it has been super funky to talk with other athletes, because it motivates me to chat about my sports and my life as an athlete. I felt more and more motivated to do my sport every time we met. I had the impression it was similar for the others. I think a lot of others can benefit from it. Sometimes it can be difficult to talk with your parents or some of your other friends who are not involved in sports. It's quite funky to talk to people who know about the same problems you are talking about, and whom you relate to.

I've got something out of the coaching, and could feel that I could help some of the others. The further we got in the process, the more I felt at home. I developed more courage and felt more and more safe. I remember a special situation, where we talked with one of the girls [Maria]. She was irritated about her sports coach, who did not tell her she was a talent. She was afraid whether things would work out for her. So I said to her in the coaching session, that I don't think that way. She should just think for herself, even though there are tons of others who do not regard her as a talent. So I said to her that I got to know the same stuff, and I also had to struggle with that. And I also said to her that she should not fret over what others say, they don't know her. I got a bit excited about that she had to struggle so much with that. And I gave her a long story about different kinds of stuff from my life, and next time she came and said that she really used the things I had said. Also, later people mentioned this episode as a kind of humdinger of an event in regard to how people can benefit from the group. I was actually quite surprised about my own abilities, so to say. I did not expect that I could make a difference.

Frank's reflections – from the perspective of a participant not directly involved in the dialogue

From the beginning I only knew one person in the group. Now I talk with them all. I have got to know them both privately and as athletes. Patrick, who I knew beforehand – I also got to know him better now, even though I thought I knew him completely. It has been really nice to be in the group. Every time after a meeting I thought, it's really nice to be there and to be part of it. I am about 10–20 percent happier at present. We have talked about things we usually might not have talked about. We have opened up. There was not too much focus on me. On one occasion we talked about Maria, because she had a bad day. She got to know from her sports coach that she could not do this and that. But Patrick explained to her: 'there should not be anybody who says that you can do it'. I really took it in, although it wasn't me who he talked to. Patrick is really good at finding words for what he feels, and by that, helping other people when they feel stuck with something. It has been really helpful. Some of the others have also been helpful, but especially Patrick, he has been helpful to get us going if one of us had a negative episode. I did not have a negative episode in this phase, but I have listened to what others have said to Maria, and I took it in, and it kept me going. The coaching process helped me to 'open my mind'. I look more open-minded on my training and my goals. I didn't even know that I had goals before we started this process. I became clear that I have actually been goal-focused through the feedback of others. I actually had goals, but hadn't really thought it over.

My own personal reflections on the case

Maria opens with an honest and open but also rather direct and uncompromising statement. Her statement appears to have a strong spontaneous effect on Patrick, who has proved to be an engaged and active participant in the process, also in the two previous coaching sessions. Patrick's statement, however, can be perceived as equally direct and straightforward. Essentially, this clash of two positions may pose problems for a witnessing process, which has a very different purpose from a discussion. In a discussion each party wants to present their best arguments, and use their rhetorical skills to persuade the counterpart and other discussion participants to embrace their point of view. Group coaching and witnessing, on the other hand, have *nothing* to do with a debate. Witnessing is an invitation to reflect on what is said, based on one's *own values* and the *meaning* and *consequences* that the other person's story might hold for oneself, or the person who told the story. The participants act as a *resonance* or *sounding board* for each other. They resonate with each other and enrich the dialogue by offering their own reflections without presenting any assessment or judgement of what the other person said. These reflections focus mainly on values and on the way in which the statement makes sense as viewed from the point of view of one's own life universe. Without much complication, this approach can also be applied in larger meetings: the only requirements are that the person chairing the meeting introduces the procedure carefully and that all the participants accept it.

My comment to Patrick and my follow-up question to him should be understood in this perspective. First, I express my basic appreciation of his contribution and engagement. Next, I express my interest in hearing more from him by asking, 'What does that involvement say about you and who you are?' Here I ask him to shift his perspective from assessment to self-reflection – a reflection in the identity landscape where he is invited to focus on personal values, convictions, aspirations, dreams and wishes that form the foundation of his own self-perception and identity. And Patrick accepts the invitation in a way that surprises all the participants. The intensity and the frankness in Patrick's story and its meaning for him, his self-perception and his fundamental action orientation affect all the participants in the coaching session. Patrick's story describes his most fundamental beliefs. His story becomes a living expression of his identity; an identity that has given him confidence, personal strength and goal direction, and which is ultimately the source of his impressive athletic achievements. The other participants know him in many ways but mainly through his more visible actions and achievements. In his reply to my question he presents a story that not even his closest friend is familiar with. In Patrick's engaging and gripping story, the participants perceive a degree of *authenticity* that has a contagious effect on all the participants.

Authenticity means *being real* and *being oneself*; it reflects a personal experience of one's own stance, attitude and behaviour, which others perceive as directly proportional with their own level of reflection in their experience and appreciation of this state. Thus, the more aware one is of one's feelings and goals in relation to others, the more authentic one can be.[4] This type of authenticity forms the basis of *relational attunement*, which I consider a prerequisite of developing reflective processes among two or more participants in a co-creative coaching process. Sharing like this creates a reflective learning and developmental space, where new knowledge is co-created, knowledge that is meaningful to the individual and which can be shared with others. The development of this shared reflection space and co-created universe of meaning is a characteristic feature of the witnessing process.

Final practitioner reflections and concluding remarks

Comparing the reflections of the three participants with my own, the differences in their perceptions of the situation is, maybe, the most interesting. As a reflective practitioner I had been quite absorbed to form the dialogue in a specific way, when Patrick presented his position. My focus was on shaping a context for co-creation of meaning-making (Stelter, 2007). Through my way of asking Patrick questions about him, and how Maria's case affected his own way of thinking about himself, I made his position interesting and meaningful for the other participants. The reflections from the three participants make clear how valuable and meaningful Patrick's story has become (in a sense) from their own differing perspectives. Although my intervention can be seen as a basic invitation for Patrick to tell us about himself, the three only retained the essence and the impact of the whole event on their meaning-making in relation to their own lives and career choices. In their memory the situation appeared to be reduced to the core plot of the story 'Believe in yourself!'

I was fascinated by working with these 'kids'. I was fascinated by their open-mindedness to share their lives. When I worked with this coaching research project, my daughter was about the same age as these young athletes. Although I regard myself as a good father, I hardly ever had had a conversation of such existential significance with my own daughter. When I shared these thoughts in one of the coaching groups during the final session the participants could understand me. They said:

If you want to share issues we reflected on here with your parents, they are either worried or they try to make you change your mind. But with you, Reinhard, we can come up with anything we want, you are always accepting.

As a group coach, I consider myself as a sharing partner, a fellow-human, in the group. On the other side I have a big responsibility by facilitating the dialogical process and giving voice to different position, by inviting the participants to view things from another perspective, by encouraging them to re-narrate their stories after having listened to the stories of others. The participants learn how their life world unfolds in an increasingly multifaceted and meaningful way. They learn to share their life with others in a way that helps them to sense a common core in their attempt to grow as a talented athlete and human being in general.

Finally, I would like to broaden the theoretical stance of my coaching psychological intervention by connecting it to sociological and political theory: group coaching as a narrative-collaborative practice becomes a forum where participants feel empowered and develop a personal strength that is based on the development of *social capital* (Bourdieu, 1983; Putnam, 2000), a form of social coherence, built up by a social network created on the basis of every single coaching session. This approach can be used in many different contexts with young participants with social challenges, to adults trying to improve a healthy lifestyle to patients in their process of recovering from serious illness.

Notes

1 Being a student on this special track means that the students have one extra year of school, so that they have more time for their training, and for travelling to training camps and competitions. The school and Team Denmark, the country's elite sport organization, are cooperating partners.
2 The reflections of the participants are based on interviews conducted by two of my former Master's students, Thomas H. Henriksen and Louis Emil Clausen (2011), who then have transformed the interviews into narratives. I use parts of these narratives in this chapter. Because of my own involvement in the coaching process, it would have been impossible to conduct the interviews with the young sports talents myself. LINK Masters thesis: http://nexs.ku.dk/forskning/sektioner/krop-laering-identitet/projekter-kli/rs_coaching/forskningsprojekter/coaching/thh_lec_speciale.pdf/
3 The narratives of the three athletes are based on their own words – translated from Danish. The narrative form is created by analyzing the interviews via selecting the quotes and by shaping a specific storyline and plot.
4 I would like to thank my good colleague, Ole Fogh Kirkeby, for his insightful reflections on the concept of authenticity, which he has shared with me, and which has inspired this brief description. From a social-constructionist perspective (see Gergen, 2009), the concept of authenticity is controversial. My presentation, however, integrates the individual and the relational perspective.

Part Five

Reflecting forwards

17 Reflecting back and forwards

Zoe Knowles, David Gilbourne, Brendan Cropley and Lindsey Dugdill

Introduction: Lindsey Dugdill

It is my privilege to be able to begin to guide you, as reader, through our final editorial thoughts, and interwoven reflections, on this text. It has been an uplifting 'project' for the four of us, as editors, to have been involved with over this last two years or so. We would like to thank all of our contributors for the time, care and thoughtfulness they have shown in the production of each chapter. Drawing together the multidisciplinary expertise of all our contributors has been a relatively easy task. Their dedication to the subject matter has produced an accomplished text that delivers on our original aims: to bring to you contemporary perspectives about the reality of reflective practice in the sport and exercise science domain. We hoped it would make you think about the value of reflective practice as a life skill and process: an invaluable skill that is worth honing and refining over time and that you then 'carry with you'; forever.

I hope that by reading these chapters the notion of learning the 'craft' of reflective practice has stood out to you, the reader. Each chapter adds something fresh and unique to our insight: whether this relates to pedagogical processes we go through in learning about reflective practice; how we use reflective practice in different settings and contexts – even with children; developing ourselves as reflective practitioners or the challenges we encounter when implementing reflective practice in the real world. Whether you are a novice or experienced reflective practitioner I hope you will continue to dip into this text for years to come – and each time you do so you will probably find a new 'nugget' of experience reflected in the contributions which you can use for your journey. You will see some overlap in the final sections of this concluding chapter, which will finally be drawn together in some messages and points for future work.

Critical perspectives within reflective practice: David Gilbourne

Reflecting back on the chapters in Part Two focused on 'critical perspectives in reflective practice' we can see the content is wide-ranging and yet, in one way or another, makes reference to the challenges of 'allowing' reflective practice to exist as a process. This process can be either methodological or practice-based in a way that it is able to truly bring lived experience to life in both reasoning (for the individual to breath into) and in writing (to share and, so, to engage with and contemplate). The chapters vary in style and pitch, possibly reflecting the critically professional 'space' that the authors sense in their respective domains. For example, Trelfa and Telfer (Chapter 5), in their politically articulate and gloriously direct challenge to institutionalized systems and processes, question whether reflective practice has been embraced and controlled in equal measure by sporting institutions and applied professional accreditation systems. Central to their thesis is the possibility that, through exercising power, hierarchically organized institutions prevent critical engagement and, so, dampen down the contesting processes that might accompany generations of critically reflective thinkers and writers. Trelfa and Telfer propose that reflective practitioners are told to 'get critical' yet are kept nicely *in*-place in their own space and, as editors, we found it interesting that the other chapters illustrate a critical, scholarly yet cautious tone suggestive of difficulties and problems. Whatever the style, the remaining chapters by Porcellato and Knowles (Chapter 4), of Picknell et al. (Chapter 3) and Flannery (Chapter 2) also tell us that life across a range of domains is complex, that people are experts on their own experiences of such complexities and that we should allow them to speak to us about their experiences without constraint.

It is clear from all the chapters that research, or practice, takes place in a uneven swamp typified by inter- and intra-personal complexity. It is also noteworthy that the chapters, in different ways and through different examples, hint towards how the dominance of the mentor/assessor, or the expert nature of the adult practitioner, or the dominance of the accepted protocol might act to stop us truly accessing the knowledge (that is surely) to be found in all this life and messiness. It is interesting also how those who 'do' the reflection provide a constant source of reference or point of debate. For example, Porcellato and Knowles stress the importance of the child-voice while Flannery emphasises the need to listen to what it might be like to be obese (from those who live an obese life day in and day out). In these consistent calls for reflective voices to be free and to be heard there is the scent of empowerment and emancipation, sentiments typically associated with critical social science and critical reflection more specifically.

In more general terms, all the chapters house worries over how much reflective practice can really deliver (or work) in disciplines that rely (for their respective understanding of practice) upon scientific reports. Similarly, concerns over how much we might understand people when, through training and degree programmers, say, *explanations* of how and why practice might work are bound tight in various professional frameworks or in scientifically derived theory. As a consequence of these constant criticisms, we sensed a recurring and subliminal question, one that is understood differently through the language of different contributors, yet is consistently phrased in terms of the chapter's capacity to challenge; the question is straightforward enough: that reflection as a process, risks being, contaminated and downgraded by dominant professionalizing narratives and through personal progression and self-interest. In these questions and observations, whether they are conveyed covertly as worrying sentiments or presented directly as statements of challenge to the status quo, there are concerns here for our reflective liberty to 'tell our own truth' and our freedom to question the unquestionable. Yet, and through critique, we might also find ways to move forward, to raise our own expectations and progress the way we might do reflection.

Pedagogical approaches to reflective practice: Zoe Knowles

Reflecting back on five chapters in Part Three titled 'pedagogical approaches to reflective practice', drawing conclusions from this spectrum of contributions and glancing towards the future is not easy in a few hundred words! Through their representations within the chapters educators, supervisors and students have exposed readers to a landscape of what it is like to design, deliver, consume, evidence and assess reflective practice within a range of pedagogical frameworks. We see within each chapter reference to that of a need to embed reflective practice within curricula driven by prioritization and for the purposes of credibility. Educators have given the reader clear insights from the wide perspectives of programme and module design to that of their own specific practice in individual sessions and supervision meetings. It is hoped that as such this provides stimulus for those educators who may wish to consider the inclusion of reflective practice, in some way, within their own programmes.

So what are the issues we face with the pedagogy of reflective practice? In the spirit of the text the contributors have been both candid and reflective in what they have encountered, and do not claim that reflective practice is pedagogically 'easy'. Indeed, I'm sure the contributors would concur that their journeys to date with reflective practice have at times been both similar and different from those of other contributors in this section. All, however, would concur that the reflective practice journey is not straightforward in direction or without challenge at policy, programme or delivery level. In Chapter 8 Marshall et al. offer one explanation that may be somewhat applicable to all. They note that we live in a society where increasing individualization and an emphasis on consumption have led to a situation where outcomes are seen to matter more than the processes that are used to achieve them. Taking this premise into the context of student/practitioner learning (and dare I say the educational establishments themselves), education itself may be more focused on outcomes and assessment marks rather than the ability to engage in process or reflective thought.

Reflective practice is, however, fundamentally anchored within the process of developing the practitioner for graduate employment and, in the main, is something that is applied within curricula at Level 6 (final-year undergraduate) or beyond, and surrounding that of placement-based learning. The contributors' and students' experiences across this section provide a consistent rationale as to why this is the case within their programmes. A notable exception is that of Hollingworth et al. (Chapter 10) and the early focus of reflective practice within the study of physiotherapy (first-year degree), and the practice of Rhodius and Huntley (Chapter 9) in relation to integration of reflective practice within students' research.

Looking ahead, researchers should perhaps further explore the dissonance and resonance of both student and educator positions and resultant experiences of reflective practice. For example, exploring the timing of when to introduce and apply reflective practice over the course of professional training and relevance/transferability of reflective practice to that of research so that we (educators and students alike) may learn from each other and move the pedagogical debate forward. Researchers across the sport and exercise domain may also glance at the work of Knowles, Tyler, Gilbourne & Eubank (2006), who through a follow-up of their graduates from a coaching science degree programme gained insight into the relevance, techniques and application of reflective practice within postgraduate employment roles. Perhaps it is this evidence that may help to convince students (and those within the educational hierarchy) more widely of the currency and worth of reflective practice and help programmes align with the changing demands of the graduate employment market.

Contributors have continued to debate how reflective practice is facilitated, and useful practice is seen across the chapters including 'priming' lectures, written tasks, use of diaries, audio recording, group-work and supervision processes, thus supporting the notion that reflective practice can be facilitated in a range of ways. Rhodius and Huntley call specifically for the use of technology within supervision, evidencing and also assessment of reflective practice, and this is worthy of further exploration. Littlewood et al. (Chapter 6) note that as is the case with students in the sport and exercise science domain, students are predominantly trained in quantitative research methods and hypothesis-driven research, and therefore writing reflectively does not come easily. Perhaps framing reflective practice as a fundamental skill, essential for learning within the applied or research practice context, and set prominently within core modules may help to counteract this position (I refer readers here to the work of Morton who takes this notion further in Chapter 12). In essence, the candid views of educators and the students allow us to appraise the effectiveness, efficiency and efficacy of reflective practice techniques and methods. Indeed, one size does not fit all!

The practice surrounding assessment of reflection is not a new debate within the journal-based literature (see Knowles, Gilbourne, Borrie & Neville, 2001). Kilgour et al. (Chapter 7) note that reflective practice provides an opportunity to develop imaginative and practitioner-based assessments. Within the chapters in this section we see examples of structured written assessment (Marshall et al.), a 'freer' writing task shaped by narrative markers (Littlewood et al.) and innovative use of audio submissions. The chapters have offered experiences associated with assessment, from that of the educator and student, and it is hoped that educators will engage in further discussion as to 'how best' to assess reflective practice, perhaps linked to the graduate experience gained through follow-up studies and to continue, as have our contributors, to share good practice with the sport and exercise science community.

Finally, it is noted how contributors themselves have overtly commented on their engagement with reflection themselves. To use the words of Rhodius and Huntley, we should 'practise what we teach' and opportunities for this may be a 'coffee time discussion' (see Marshall et al.) or indeed something more formal through peer consultations aligned with practice for CPD requirements. As editors we couldn't agree more and, by virtue of constructing this text, have reflected on our own practices formally and informally between ourselves and also through conversations and drafts with our contributors. At a practical level, we have been inspired to 'try out' techniques and modify our educational practice, exemplifying what we set out to achieve with this section. Finally, we would be interested to know from readers what you changed in your practice, what worked and what were/are your challenges when working with reflective practice.

Applied practice: reflective practice in action: Brendan Cropley

The contributions in Part Four, focusing on 'applied practice: reflective practice in action', provide fascinating insights that detail the potential for reflective practice as an approach to: making sense of practice, personal and professional development, and progressing practice within the field in question. The key messages emanating from these chapters appear clear in one sense, yet problematic in another, which is indicative of themes emanating from research into professional practice in other fields (e.g., pedagogy, management).

The contributions in this section appear to answer calls from authors made over a decade ago to provide more personalized accounts of practice in order to elaborate the nuances of actually 'doing' (e.g., Andersen, 2000). These sources have emanated from the discipline of sport psychology. However, we propose that there is an even greater need for such accounts within other disciplines operating in the sporting domain in attempts to provide practitioners with the opportunities to explore and learn from the intricacies of the contexts, dilemmas, innovation, approaches to problem-solving, and personal and interpersonal conflict that are associated with professional practice in sport. It would appear that the most appropriate way of doing this is through reflective writing. Indeed, as Triggs and Gilbourne (Chapter 11) allude to in their chapter, reflective storytelling provides an appropriate approach to illustrate the synthesis between self and lived experience, and thus offer examples of personal challenge in practice. In light of this, we propose that there is potential through the use of reflection-on-action, as additionally evident in the chapters by Holt et al. (Chapter 13), Morton (Chapter 12), Barney and Andersen (Chapter 14), and Stelter (Chapter 16) to furnish the literature in sport with the detail required to inform and guide the practices of others and thus contribute to the development of effective applied work within the field. The problem that this creates, however, is that these accounts call for practitioners to 'put themselves out there' and, as Morton suggests, 'open themselves up for subjective critique'. However, if practice within the sporting domain is to improve we propose that such feelings of vulnerability brought about by opening the door to our own practice and inviting people inside need to be challenged. These feelings must be viewed positively because we suggest that it is out of this personal conflict that *critical* levels of change can occur that question habitual, taken-for-granted practices and enhance our accountability to the field, those we work with, and ourselves. Such a view is evident within the chapter by Holt et al. where the skills developed in different roles (e.g., practitioner, researcher) complement engagement in professional practice as long as the individual is willing to engage in ongoing reflection-on-action that encourages the questioning of our beliefs, values and prejudices, which may impact, positively or negatively, on the type and quality of work conducted.

On reflection, the professional practice section in this text also highlights a significant change in the perception of reflective practice within sport. Morton and Stelter both refer to the reluctance to engage and often negative connotations associated with a concept that is ontologically and epistemologically 'different' from the tradition of the field. However, the emphasis placed upon the value of reflective practice in these chapters is indicative of the change of significance placed on different types of 'knowing' within traditionally positivistic fields and/ or interventions. If, as the chapters in Part Four profess, reflective practice is integral to the development of effective practice, then: 'how do we make reflective practice a formal part of professional practice throughout the sporting domain?' and, 'how do we change the culture of disciplines to become more accepting of reflective practice?' Barney and Anderson's chapter considers the establishment of a shared reflective culture through the supervision process, and this may be the place to start. By integrating the principles of formal reflective practice as an approach to experiential learning early on in a neophyte's career it is likely that such practices will be maintained. We do feel that in order for any practice in the sporting domain to be classified as professional then a process of planning, acting, reflecting-on-action and reflecting-for-action needs to be established. Consequently, reflective practice becomes a fundamental part of what we do, rather than a bolt-on to what we do, or something that's just done during our periods of training.

The challenge for us all appears to be one of questioning what we actually do, what we need to do and how willing we are to be honest, open and accepting of the potential for change. We mean this in respect of both the journey to becoming reflective practitioners and engaging in reflective practice in attempts to move our professional selves forward. The chapters in this section appear to agree that if we are to be able to meet this challenge we not only have to gain a better understanding of what reflective practice actually is but commit to developing the skills (e.g., problem-solving, critical thinking) and attributes (e.g., self-awareness, honesty) required for effective engagement in the practice that goes beyond mere thinking about what we do.

Reflections for the future

So at the end of this text we leave you with a set of emerging, future challenges for the field. We have situated reflective practice as being a necessary, integral core of our professional practice and central to the development of competency – indeed, it is accepted as such in nursing and allied health disciplines, but perhaps not yet fully accepted in sport and exercise sciences. Reflective practice is also central to many educational curricula – even if continued practice out in the workplace is a challenge. Moving forward the types of issues that are likely to be at the forefront of future debates are:

- The continued need to place reflective practice at the centre of educational and professional processes, at a time when the external world is becoming more outcome- and target-focused. The tensions created between process-versus outcome-focused approaches are considerable and can become insurmountable if there is no space for reflection, and no value given to individual reflection by significant others such as line managers, curriculum leaders or professional practice supervisors.
- Ensuring we hear the voices of the under-represented (children and other marginalized groups) in our reflective practice, which may be part of emancipatory research processes and practice. This is increasingly important as we strive to ensure we meet equality and diversity goals within our practice.
- The role of technology in facilitating reflection – online reflection, for example, may become the future 'safe place' for practitioners to reflect and allow anonymous discussion to take place, thus encouraging more truthful reflection. It may become increasingly important as the lines between our work and non-work worlds are increasingly blurred by technological developments.
- The continued necessity to balance scientific paradigms and the weight of evidence (which value certain types of evidence constructed using specific research approaches) with personal reflective accounts of practice, which underpin a different type of evidence and 'alternative ways of knowing'.
- The continued need to be honest, truthful and free in our discussions, reflections and practice – where we are valued for being different, thinking differently and bringing innovation into what we do.

References

Alderson, P. (2001). Research by children. *International Journal of Social Research Methodology*, 4, 139–153.

Alderson, P. & Morrow, V. (2011). *The ethics of research with children and young people: A practical handbook*. London: Sage.

Allen, D., Bowers, B. & Diekelmann, N. (1989). Writing to learn: A reconceptualization of thinking and writing in the nursing curriculum. *Journal of Nursing Education*, 28, 6–11.

Allen, G., Szollos, S. & Williams, B. (1986). Doctoral students' comparative evaluation of best and worst psychotherapy supervision. *Professional Psychology: Research and Practice*, 17, 91–100.

Andersen, M.B. (1994). Ethical considerations in the supervision of applied sport psychology graduate students. *Journal of Applied Sport Psychology*, 6, 152–167.

Andersen, M.B. (Ed.). (2000). *Doing sport psychology*. Champaign, IL: Human Kinetics.

Andersen, M.B. (2006). What's it like out there? Making the terra incognita more firma. *The Sport and Exercise Scientist*, 9, 10–11.

Andersen, M.B. (2012). Supervision and mindfulness in sport and performance psychology. In S.M. Murphy (Ed.), *Oxford handbook of sport and performance psychology* (pp. 725–737). New York: Oxford University Press.

Andersen, M.B. & Williams-Rice, B. (1996). Supervision in the education and training of sport psychology service providers. *The Sport Psychologist*, 10, 278–290.

Anderson, A., Knowles, Z. & Gilbourne, D. (2004). Reflective practice for sport psychologists: Concepts, models, practical implications, and thoughts on dissemination. *The Sport Psychologist*, 18, 188–203.

Anderson, A., Miles, A., Mahoney, C. & Robinson, P. (2002). Evaluating the effectiveness of applied sport psychology practice: Making the case for a case study approach. *The Sport Psychologist*, 16, 432–453.

Atkinson, T. & Claxton, G. (2000). *The intuitive practitioner: On the value of not always knowing what one is doing*. Buckinghamshire: Open University Press.

Atwal, A. & Caldwell, K. (2006). Nurses' perceptions of multidisciplinary team work in acute health-care. *International Journal of Nursing Practice*, 12, 359–365.

Badenoch, B. (2008). *Being a brain-wise therapist: A practical guide to interpersonal neurobiology*. New York: Norton.

Baecke, J., Burema, J. & Frijters, J. (1982). A short questionnaire for the measurement of habitual physical activity in epidemiological studies. *The American Journal of Clinical Nutrition*, 36, 936–942.

Baikie, K. & Wilhelm, K. (2005). Emotional and physical health benefits of expressive writing. *Advances in Psychiatric Treatment*, 11, 338–346.

Bandura, A. (1997). *Self-efficacy: The exercise of control*. New York: Freeman.

Banks, S. & Nøhr, K. (Eds.). (2003). *Teaching practical ethics for the social professions*. Copenhagen: European Social Ethics Project.

Barkham, M., Mellor-Clark, J., Connell, J. & Cahill, J. (2006). A core approach to practice based evidence: A brief history of the origins and applications of the CORE-OM and CORE System. *Counselling and Psychotherapy Research*, 6, 3–15.

Barkley, R. (2011). *Treating children and adolescents with ADHD: Empirically based treatments*. Retrieved from http://www.continuingedcourses.net/active/courses/course068.php

Barney, S. & Andersen, M.B. (in press). Meta-supervision: Training practitioners to help others on their paths. In G. Cremades & L. Tashman (Eds.), *Becoming a sport, exercise and performance psychology professional: A global perspective*. New York: Routledge.

Barney, S., Andersen, M.B. & Riggs, C. (1996). Supervision in sport psychology: Some recommendations for practicum training. *Journal of Applied Sport Psychology*, 8, 200–217.

Barrett, G. & Kerman, M. (2001). Holding in mind: Theory and practice of seeing children in groups. *Psychodynamic Counselling*, 7, 315–328.

Bartlett, J., Joo, C., Louhelainen, J., Cochran, J., Gibala, M., Iqbal, Z., . . . Morton, J.P. (2013). Reduced carbohydrate availability enhances exercise-induced phosphorylation of p53 in human skeletal muscle: Implications for mitochondrial biogenesis. *American Journal of Physiology*, 304, 450–458.

BASES. (2009). *Supervised experience guidance documents*. Retrieved from http://www.bases.org.uk/Supervised-Experience

Bauman, A. (2004). Commentary on the VERB campaign. Perspectives on social marketing to encourage physical activity among youth. *Preventing Chronic Disease*, 1, 1–3.

Bauman, Z. (2007). *Liquid times: Living in an age of uncertainty*. Cambridge: Polity Press.

Bauman, Z. & Donskis, L. (2013). *Moral blindness: The loss of sensitivity in liquid modernity*. Cambridge: Polity Press.

Berentson-Shaw, J. & Price, K. (2007). Facilitating effective health promotion practice in a public health unit: Lessons from the field. *Australian and New Zealand Journal of Public Health*, 31, 81–86.

Bernard, J. (2005, June). *Tracing the development of clinical supervision*. Paper presented at the First International Interdisciplinary Conference on Clinical Supervision, Amherst, New York.

Bernard, W. (2000). Participatory research as emancipatory method: Challenges and opportunities. In D. Burton (Ed.), *Research training for social scientists* (pp. 167–185). London: Sage.

Bhosekar, K. (2009). Using photographs as a medium to create spaces for reflective learning. *Reflective Practice*, 10, 91–100.

Billsbury, J. & Godrich, S. (2010, June). *Blue sky thinking: Using projective techniques to stimulate discussion, reflection and insight*. Paper presented at the 37th OBTC Annual Conference, University of New Mexico. Retrieved from http://obts.org/content/proceedings-obtc-2010-university-new-mexico

Biswas-Diener, R. (2010). *Practicing positive psychology coaching*. Hoboken, NJ: Wiley.

Blair, S., Kohl, H., Barlow, C., Paffenbarger, R., Gibbons, L. & Macera, C. (1995). Changes in physical fitness and all-cause mortality: A prospective study of healthy and unhealthy men. *Journal of American Medical Association*, 273, 1093–1098.

Bleakley, A. (2000). Adrift without a life belt: Reflective self-assessment in a post-modern age. *Teaching in Higher Education*, 5, 405–418.

Bloom, B. (Ed.) (1956). *Taxonomy of educaitonal objectives: The classification of educational goals. Handbook I: Cognitive domain*. New York: Longman.

Boddy, L., Knowles, Z., Davies, I., Warburton, G., Mackintosh, K., Houghton, L. & Fairclough, S. (2012). Using formative research to develop the healthy eating component of the CHANGE! School-based curriculum intervention. *BMC Public Health, 12*, 710.

Bolton, G. (2005). Narrative writing: Reflective enquiry into professional practice. *Educational Action Research, 14*, 203–218.

Boss, S. (2009). *High tech reflection strategies make learning stick*. Retrieved from http://www.edutopia.org/student-reflection

Boud, D., Keogh, R. & Walker, D. (1985). *Reflection: Turning experience into learning*. London: Kogan Page.

Bourdieu, P. (1983). Forms of capital. In J. Richards (Ed.), *Handbook of theory and research for the sociology of education* (pp. 183–198). New York: Greenwood Press.

Boutilier, M., Mason, R. & Irving, R. (1997). Community action and reflective practice in health promotion research. *Health Promotion International, 12*, 69–78.

Bowes, I. & Jones, R. (2006). Working at the edge of chaos: Understanding coaching as a complex, interpersonal system. *The Sport Psychologist, 20*, 235–245.

Boyd, E. & Fales A. (1983). Reflective learning: Key to learning from experience. *Journal of Humanistic Psychology, 23*, 99–117.

BPS. (2011). Qualification in sport and exercise psychology (stage 2) candidate handbook. Retrieved from www.bps.org.uk/sites/default/files/documents/qsep_candidate_handbook_stage_2_revised_may_2011.pdf

Brown, G., Gilbourne, D. & Claydon, J. (2009). When a career ends: A short story. *Reflective Practice, 10*, 491–500.

Brydon-Miller, M., Kral, E., Maguire, P., Noffke, S. & Sabhlok, A. (2011). Jazz and the banyan tree: Roots and riffs on participatory action research. In N. Denzin & Y. Lincoln (Eds.), *Sage handbook of qualitative research* (4th ed., pp. 387–400). Thousand Oaks, CA: Sage.

Burke, L. (2009). The interview tables are turned: Interview by Marie Dunford. *International Journal of Sports Nutrition and Exercise Metabolism, 19*, 685–688.

Burnard, P. (1991). *Experiential learning in action*. Aldershot: Gower.

Burton, E. & Medcalf, R. (2011). Accessing experiences through 'photo voice': Children's perceptions of motivations and barriers towards physical activity participation in rural and urban environments. *Journal of Qualitative Research in Sports Studies, 5*, 19–36.

Burton, S. (2009). *The oversight and review of cases in the light of changing circumstances and new information: How do people respond to new (and challenging) information?* Retrieved from http://www.c4eo.org.uk/themes/safeguarding/files/safeguarding_briefing_3.pdf

Campbell, M., Fitzpatrick, R., Haines, A., Kinmonth, A., Sandercock, P., Spiegelhalter, D. & Tyrer, P. (2000). Framework for the design and evaluation of complex interventions to improve health. *British Medical Journal, 321*, 694–696.

Campbell, N., Murray, E., Darbyshire, J., Emery, J., Farmer, A., Griffiths, F., . . . Kinmonth, A. (2008). Designing and evaluating complex interventions to improve health care. *British Medical Journal, 334*, 455–459.

Carr, W. & Kemmis, S. (1986). *Becoming critical: Education, knowledge and action-research*. London: Falmer Press.

Carson, F. (2008). Utilising video to facilitate reflective practice: Developing sports coaches. *International Journal of Sports Science & Coaching, 3*, 381–390.

Cassidy, T., Jones, R. & Potrac, P. (2009). *Understanding sports coaching: The social, cultural and pedagogical foundations of coaching practice* (2nd ed.). London: Routledge.

Cassidy, T., Potrac, P. & McKenzie, A. (2006). Evaluating and reflecting upon a coach education initiative: The CoDe of rugby. *The Sport Psychologist, 20*, 145–161.

Cavanagh, M. (2006). Coaching from a systemic perspective: A complex adaptive conversation. In D. Stober & A. Grant (Eds.), *Evidence based coaching handbook: Putting best practices to work for your clients* (pp. 55–67). Hoboken, NJ: John Wiley.

Cesar, G., Habicht, J. & Bryce, J. (2004). Evidence-based public health: Moving beyond randomized trials. *American Journal of Public Health, 94*, 400–405.

Chen, A. (1999). The impact of social change on inner-city high school physical education: An analysis of a teacher's experiential account. *Journal of Teaching in Physical Education, 18*, 312–335.

Chesterfield, G., Potrac, P. & Jones, R. (2010). Studentship and impression management: Coaches' experiences of an advanced soccer education award. *Sport, Education and Society, 15*, 299–314.

Clark, A. (2005). Listening to and involving young children: A review of research and practice. *Early Childhood Development and Care, 175*, 489–505.

Clark, A. & Moss, P. (2011). *Listening to young children: The Mosaic approach.* London: NCB.

Clark, W. (2008). *Kid's sports. Component of Statistics Canada catalogue.* Retrieved from http://www.statcan.gc.ca/pub/11-008-x/2008001/article/10573-eng.htm [7 March 2012].

Clarke, B. (2004). *If this child were a car, what sort of car would it be? The global child: Using appropriate projective techniques to view the world through their eyes.* Retrieved from http://www.kidsandyouth.com/child.pdf

Clegg, S., Tan, J. & Saeidi, S. (2002). Reflecting or acting? Reflective practice and continuing professional development in Higher Education. *Reflective Practice, 3*, 131–146.

Clouder, L. (2000). Reflective practice in physiotherapy education: A critical conversation. *Studies in Higher Education, 25*, 211–223.

Clouder, L. & Deepwell, F. (2004, April). *Reflections on unexpected outcomes: Learning from online collaboration in an online discussion forum.* Paper presented at the Second International Networked Learning Conference, Lancaster University, UK. Abstract retrieved from http://www.networkedlearningconference.org.uk/past/nlc2004/proceedings/individual_papers/clouderanddeepwell.htm

Coakley, J. (2012). *Sports in society: Issues and controversies* (10th ed.). Boston, MA: McGraw-Hill.

Coakley, J. & Donnelly, P. (2002). *The role of recreation in promoting social inclusion.* Retrieved from http://www.offordcentre.com/VoicesWebsite/library/reports/documents/laidlaw/donnelly.pdf

Cooperrider, D. & Sekerka, L. (2003). Toward a theory of positive organizational change. In K. Cameron, J. Dutton & R. Quinn (Eds.), *Positive organizational scholarship* (pp. 225–241). San Francisco: Berrett-Kohler.

Coppola, A., Neely, K., McDonald, R., McHugh, T-L. & Holt, N. (2012). *Children's perceptions of a sport-based critical hours program.* Paper presented at Canadian Society for Psychomotor Learning and Sport Psychology Conference, Halifax, NS, Canada.

Cowan, J. (1998). *On becoming an innovative university lecturer: Reflection-in-action.* Buckinghamshire: Open University Press.

Craig, P., Dieppe, P., Macintyre, S., Michie, S., Nazareth, I. & Petticrew, M. (2008). Developing and evaluating complex interventions: The new Medical Research Council Guidance. *British Medical Journal, 337*, a1655.

Cranton, P. (2002). Teaching for transformation. *New Directions for Adult and Continuing Education, 93*, 63–72.

Cranton, P. (2006). *Understanding and promoting transformative learning: A guide for educators of adults* (2nd ed.). San Francisco: Wiley.

Crone, D. & Baker, C. (2009). Physical activity interventions in the community. In L. Dugdill, D. Crone & R. Murphy (Eds.), *Physical activity and health promotion. Evidence-based approaches to practices* (pp. 110–129). Chichester: Wiley-Blackwell.

Cropley, B. (2009). *Reflective practice and consultant effectiveness: An examination of sport psychology practice* (Unpublished doctoral dissertation). University of Wales Institute Cardiff, UK.

Cropley, B. & Hanton, S. (2011). The role of reflective practice in applied sport psychology: Contemporary issues for professional practice. In S. Hanton & S.D. Mellalieu (Eds.), *Professional practice in sport psychology: A review* (pp. 307–336). London: Routledge.

Cropley, B., Miles, A., Hanton, S. & Anderson, A. (2007). Improving the delivery of applied sport psychology support through reflective practice. *The Sport Psychologist, 21*, 475–494.

Cropley, B., Miles, A., Hanton, S. & Niven, A. (2010). Exploring the relationship between effective and reflective practice in applied sport psychology. *The Sport Psychologist, 24*, 521–541.

Cropley, B., Hanton, S., Miles, A. & Niven, A. (2013). *Developing the effectiveness of applied sport psychology service delivery: A reflective practice intervention.* Manuscript submitted for publication.

Cross, V., Liles, C., Conduit, J. & Price, J. (2004). Linking reflective practice to evidence of competence: A workshop for allied health professionals. *Reflective Practice, 5*, 3–31.

Crossley, M. (2000). *Introducing narrative psychology*. Buckingham: Open University Press.

Cushion, C. (2006). Mentoring: Harnessing the power of experience. In R. Jones (Ed.), *The sports coach as educator: Re-conceptualising sports coaching* (pp. 128–144). London: Routledge.

Cushion, C., Nelson, L., Armour, K., Lyle, J., Jones, R., Sandford, R. & O'Callaghan, C. (2010). *Coach learning and development: A review of literature.* Sports Coach UK, Leeds.

CWDC. (2010). *On the right track: Guidance to the standards for the award of early years professional status.* Retrieved from https://www.education.gov.uk/publications/eOrder ingDownload/EY32-0210.pdf

Danish, S. & Nellen, V. (1997). New roles for sport psychologists: Teaching life skills through sport to at risk youth. *Quest, 49*, 100–113.

Davidson, K., Schwartz, A., Sheffield, D., McCord, R., Lepore, S. & Gerin, W. (2002). Expressive writing and blood pressure. In S. Lepore & J. Smyth (Eds.), *The writing cure: How expressive writing promotes health and emotional well-being* (pp. 17–30). Washington, DC: American Psychological Association.

Davies, H. (1972). *The Glory Game*. Edinburgh: Mainstream.

Department of Health. (1989). *The Children Act*. London: HMSO.

Department of Health. (2000). *NHS Plan: A plan for investment. A plan for reform*. London: HMSO.

Department of Health. (2011). *Healthy people, healthy lives*. London: HMSO.

Department of Health. (2012). *Health and Social Care Act*. London: HMSO.

De Jong, P. & Berg, I. (1998). *Interviewing for solutions*. Pacific Grove, CA: Brooks/Cole Publishing.

De Silva-Sanigorski, A., Bell, A., Kremer, P., Park, J., Demajo, L., Smith, M., . . . Swinburn, B. (2012). Process and impact evaluation of the Romp & Chomp obesity prevention intervention in early childhood settings: Lessons learned from implementation in preschools and long day care settings. *Childhood Obesity, 8*, 205–215.

Devonport, T. & Lane, A. (2009). Reflecting on the delivery of a longitudinal coping intervention amongst junior national netball players. *Journal of Sports Science and Medicine, 8,* 169–178.

Dewey, J. (1916). *Democracy and education: An introduction to the philosophy of education.* New York: Macmillan.

Dugdill, L. (2001). *Evaluation supplement. Framework for action.* London: Health Development Agency.

Dugdill, L. (2009). Evaluating professional practice through reflection: Professionalism in the workplace. In C. Heaney, B. Oakley & S. Rea (Eds.), *Exploring sport and fitness: Work-based practice* (pp. 48–56). Abingdon: Routledge.

Dugdill, L., Graham, R. & McNair, F. (2005). Exercise referral: The public health panacea for physical activity promotion? A critical perspective of exercise referral schemes; their development and evaluation. *Ergonomics, 48,* 1390–1410.

Duke, S. & Appleton, J. (2000). The use of reflection in a palliative care programme: A qualitative study of the development of reflective skills over an academic year. *Journal of Advanced Nursing, 32,* 1557–1568.

Edwards, G. & Thomas, G. (2010). Can reflective practice be taught? *Educational Studies, 36,* 403–414.

Einarsdottir, J. (2005). Playschool in pictures: Children's photographs as a research method. *Early Childhood Development and Care, 175,* 523–541.

Ekstein, R. & Wallerstein, R. (1958). *The teaching and learning of psychotherapy.* New York: International Universities Press.

Ennis, C. (1995). Teachers' responses to noncompliant students: The realities and consequences of a negotiated curriculum. *Teaching and Teacher Education, 11,* 445–460.

Ennis, C., Cothran, D., Davidson, K., Loftus, S., Owens, L., Swanson, L. & Hopsicker, P. (1997). Implementing curriculum within a context of fear and disengagement. *Journal of Teaching in Physical Education, 17,* 52–71.

Epstein, A. (2003). How planning and reflection develop young children's thinking skills. *Beyond the Journal: Young Children on the Web,* Sept., 1–8.

Epstein, M. (1995). *Thoughts without a thinker: Psychotherapy from a Buddhist perspective.* New York: Basic Books.

Eraut, M. (1994). *Developing professional knowledge and competence.* London: Falmer.

Ericsson, K. (2003). Development of elite performance and deliberate practice: An update from the perspective of the expert performance approach. In J. Starkes & K. Ericsson (Eds.), *Expert performance in sports: Advances in research expertise* (pp. 49–83). Champaign, IL: Human Kinetics.

Ericsson, K., Krampe, R. & Tesch-Römer, C. (1993). The role of deliberate practice in the acquisition of expert performance. *Psychological Review, 100,* 363–406.

Evetts, J. (2003). The sociological analysis of professionalism: Occupational change in the modern world. *International Sociology, 18,* 395–415.

Faggiani, F., McRobert, A. & Knowles, Z. (2012). Developing pre-performance routines for acrobatic gymnastics: A case study with a tumbling gymnast. *Science of Gymnastics Journal, 4,* 39–52.

Fargas-Malet, M., McSheery, D., Larkin, E. & Robinson, C. (2010). Research with children: Methodological issues and innovative techniques. *Journal of Early Childhood Research, 2,* 175–192.

Faull, A. & Cropley, B. (2009). Reflective learning in sport: A case study of a senior level triathlete. *Reflective Practice, 10,* 325–339.

Finley, L. (2002). Outing the researcher: The provenance, process, and practice of reflexivity. *Qualitative Health Research, 12,* 531–545.

Finlay, L. (2008). Reflecting on 'reflective practice' PBPL paper 52. Retrieved from http://www.open.ac.uk/pbpl

Flannery, O. (2009). *Childhood obesity: Understanding the user perspective to inform prevention and treatment strategies* (Unpublished doctoral dissertation). University of Salford, UK.

Fleming, P. (2006). Reflection – a neglected art in health promotion. *Health Education Research, 22,* 658–664.

Fletcher, D., Hanton, S. & Mellalieu, S.D. (2006). An organizational stress review: Conceptual and theoretical issues in competitive sport. In S. Hanton & S.D. Mellalieu (Eds.), *Literature reviews in sport psychology* (pp. 321–373). Hauppauge, NY: Nova Science.

Fook, J. (2002). *Social work: Critical theory and practice*. London: Sage.

Forneris, S. & Peden-McAlpine, C. (2006). Contextual learning: A reflective learning intervention for nursing education. *International Journal of Nursing Education Scholarship, 3,* 1–18.

Frean, A. (2008, September 11). Student's prefer studying to socialising, says survey. *The Times*. Retrieved from http://www.thetimes.co.uk/tto/education/article1802499.ece

Freese, A. (2006). Reframing one's teaching: Discovering our teacher selves through reflection and inquiry. *Teaching and Teacher Education, 22,* 100–119.

Friesen, A. & Orlick, T. (2010). A qualitative analysis of holistic sport psychology consultants' professional philosophies. *The Sport Psychologist, 24,* 227–244.

Furlong, J. (2000). Intuition and the crisis in teacher professionalism. In T. Atkinson & G. Claxton (Eds.), *The intuitive practitioner: On the value of not always knowing what one is doing* (pp. 15–31). Buckinghamshire: Open University Press.

Gabbard, C. (1992). *Lifelong motor development*. Bubuque, IA: Brown.

Gadsby, H. & Cronin, S. (2012). To what extent can reflective journaling help beginning teachers develop Masters level writing skills? *Reflective Practice, 13,* 1–12.

Gardner, F. (Ed.). (2009). Mindfulness-and-acceptance-based approaches to sport performance and well-being [Special Issue]. *Journal of Clinical Sport Psychology, 3,* 291–395.

Gergen, K. (2009). *An invitation to social construction*. London: Sage.

Ghaye, T. (2005). *Developing the reflective healthcare team*. Oxford: Blackwell Publishing.

Ghaye, T. (2010). *Teaching and learning through reflective practice: A practical guide for positive action* (2nd ed.). London: Routledge.

Ghaye, T. & Lillyman, S. (2006). *Learning journals and critical incidents: Reflective practice for health care professionals* (2nd ed.). London: Quay Books.

Gibbs, G. (1988). *Learning by doing: A guide to teaching and learning methods*. Oxford Brookes, UK: Further Education Unit, Oxford Polytechnic.

Giddings, M., Vodde, R. & Cleveland, P. (2003). Examining student-field instructor problems in practicum: Beyond student satisfaction measures. *The Clinical Supervisor, 22,* 191–214.

Gilbert, W. & Trudel, P. (2001). Learning to coach through experience: Reflection in model youth sport coaches. *Journal of Teaching in Physical Education, 21,* 16–34.

Gilbert, W. & Trudel, P. (2005). Learning to coach through experience: Conditions that influence reflection. *Physical Educator, 62,* 32–43.

Gilbourne, D. (2000). Searching for the nature of action research: A response to Evans, Hardy and Fleming. *The Sport Psychologist, 14,* 207–214.

Gilbourne, D. (2002). Sports participation, sports injury and altered images of self: An autobiographical narrative of a lifelong legacy. *Reflective Practice, 3,* 71–88.

Gilbourne, D. (2010). 'Edge of darkness' and 'just in time': Two cautionary tales, two styles, one story. *Qualitative Inquiry, 16*, 325–331.

Gilbourne, D. (2011). Just-in-time: A reflective poetic monologue. *Reflective Practice, 12*, 27–33.

Gilbourne, D. (2012). Contemplations on sport, complexity, ages of being and practice. *Sports Coaching Review, 1*, 4–16.

Gilbourne, D. & Richardson, D. (2006). Tales from the field: Personal reflections on the provision of psychological support in professional soccer. *Psychology of Sport and Exercise, 7*, 325–337.

Gilbourne, D., Jones, R. & Sinclair, J. (online, 2011). Applied utility and the auto-ethnographic short story: persuasions for and illustrations of writing critical social science. *Sport, Education and Society*.

Gilbourne, D., Marshall, P. & Knowles, Z. (2013). Reflective practice in sports coaching: Thoughts on processes and pedagogy. In R. Jones (Ed.), *An introduction to sports coaching: From science and theory to practice* (pp. 3–11). London: Routledge.

Gould, D. (2002). Moving beyond the psychology of athletic excellence. *Journal of Applied Sport Psychology, 14*, 247–248.

Gould, N. & Taylor, I. (1996). *Reflective learning for social work*. Brookfield, VT & Aldershot: Arena/Ashgate.

Graber, K. (1991). Studentship in pre-service teacher education: A qualitative study of undergraduate students in physical education. *Research Quarterly for Exercise and Sport, 1*, 41–51.

Grey, A. & Fitzgibbon, K. (2003). Reflection-in-action and business undergraduates: What learning curve? *Reflective Practice, 4*, 11–18.

Grol, R. & Wensing, M. (2004). What drives change? Barriers to and incentives for achieving evidence-based practice. *The Medical Journal of Australia, 180*, s57–s60.

Gustafson, K. & Bennett, W. (1999). *Issues and difficulties in promoting learner reflection: Results from a three-year study*. Retrieved from http://it.coe.uga.edu/~kgustafs/document/promoting.html

Habitch, J., Victoria, C. & Vaughan, J. (1999). Evaluation designs for adequacy, plausibility and probability of public health programme performance and impact. *International Journal of Epidemiology, 28*, 10–18.

Hanrahan, S., Pedro, R. & Cerin, E. (2009). Structured self-reflection as a tool to enhance perceived performance and maintain effort in adult recreational salsa dancers. *The Sport Psychologist, 23*, 151–169.

Hanton, S., Cropley, B. & Lee, S. (2009). Reflective practice, experience, and the interpretation of anxiety symptoms. *Journal of Sports Sciences, 27*, 517–533.

Harber, K. & Pennebaker, J. (1992). Overcoming traumatic memories. In S.Å. Christianson (Ed.), *The handbook of emotion and memory: Research and theory* (pp. 359–387). Hillsdale, NJ: Lawrence Erlbaum Associates.

Hardman, A. & Stensel, D. (2003). *Physical activity and health: The evidence explained*. London: Routledge.

Hardy, L., Jones, G. & Gould, D. (1996). *Understanding psychological preparation for sport: Theory and practice of elite performers*. Chichester: John Wiley & Sons.

Hargreaves, J. (2004). So how do you feel about that? Assessing reflective practice. *Nurse Education Today, 24*, 196–210.

Harris, P. (2012). *The youth worker as improviser: Preparing youth workers to be educators in the moment* (Unpublished M.Ed. dissertation). University of Leicester, UK.

Harwood, C. & Knight, C. (2009). Stress in youth sports: A developmental investigation of tennis players. *Psychology of Sport & Exercise, 10*, 447–456.

Hawe, P., Shiell, A. & Riley, T. (2004). Complex interventions: How 'out of control' can a randomised controlled trial be? *British Medical Journal, 328*, 1561–1563.

HCPC. (2012). *Your guide to our standards of continuing professional development*. Retrieved from http://www.hpc-uk.org/registrants/cpd/

Health Survey for England. (2012). *Statistics on obesity, physical activity and diet: England, 2011*. Retrieved from https://catalogue.ic.nhs.uk/publications/public-health/obesity/obes-phys-acti-diet-eng-2011/obes-phys-acti-diet-eng-2011-rep.pdf

Heaney, C., Oakley, B. & Rea, S. (2010). Reflection in work-based practice. In C. Heaney, B. Oakley and S. Rea (Eds.), *Exploring Sport and Fitness* (pp. 1–3). London: Routledge.

Heath, G., Parra-Perez, D., Sarmiento, O., Anderson, L., Owen, N., Goenka, S., . . . Brownson, R. (2012). Evidence based physical activity interventions: Lessons from around the world. *The Lancet, 380*, 258–271.

Heneghan, C., Wright, J. & Watson, G. (2013). Clinical psychologists' experiences of reflective staff groups in inpatient psychiatric settings: A mixed methods study. *Clinical Psychology and Psychotherapy*. Advanced online publication. doi: 10.1002/cpp.1834

Henriksen, T. & Clausen, L. (2011). *Young elite athletes' experiences and change processes as a result of narrative group coaching* (Unpublished Masters thesis). University of Copenhagen, Denmark.

Higgins, D. (2011). Why reflect? Recognising the link between learning and reflection. *Reflective Practice, 12*, 583–584.

Hill, K. (2001). *Frameworks for sport psychologists*. Champaign, IL: Human Kinetics.

Hillsdon, M., Foster, C., Naidoo, B. & Crombie, H. (2004). *The effectiveness of public health interventions for increasing physical activity*. London: Health Development Agency.

Hinett, K. (2002). *Improving learning through reflection – part one*. Retrieved from http://www.new1.heacademy.ac.uk/assets/Documents/resources/database/id485_improving_learning_part_one.pdf

Hobbs, V. (2007). Faking it or hating it: Can reflective practice be forced? *Reflective Practice, 8*, 405–417.

Holt, N. (2001). Beyond technical reflection: Demonstrating the modification of teaching behaviors using three levels of reflection. *Avante, 7*, 66–76.

Holt, N. & Strean, W. (2001). Reflecting on the initial intake meeting in sport psychology: A self-narrative of neophyte practice. *The Sport Psychologist, 15*, 188–204.

Holt, N., Cunningham, C.-T., Sehn, Z., Spence, J., Newton, A. & Ball, G. (2009). Neighborhood physical activity opportunities for inner city children and youth. *Health & Place, 15*, 1022–1028.

Holt, N., Kingsley, B., Tink, L. & Scherer, J. (2011). Benefits and challenges associated with sport participation by children and parents from low-income families. *Psychology of Sport and Exercise, 12*, 490–499. Huntley, E. & Kentzer, N. (in press). Group-based reflective practice in sport psychology: Experiences of two trainee sport and exercise scientists. *Sport & Exercise Psychology Review*.

Hussey, T. & Smith, P. (2010). *The trouble with Higher Education: A critical evaluation of our universities*. London: Routledge.

Hyman, M. (2012). *The most expensive game in town: The rising cost of youth sports and the toll on today's families*. Boston, MA: Beacon Press.

Iacobini, M. (2008). *Mirroring people*. New York: Farrar, Strauss, & Giroux.

Jagosh, J., Macaulay, A., Pluye, P., Salsbery, J., Bush, P., Henderson, J., . . . Greenhalgh, T. (2012). Uncovering the benefits of participatory research: Implications of a realist review for health research and practice. *Milbank Quarterly, 90*, 311–346.

James, C. & Clarke, B. (1994). Reflective practice in nursing: Issues and implications for nurse education. *Nurse Education Today, 14*, 82–90.

Jarvis, P. (1992). Reflective practice and nursing. *Nurse Education, 11*, 3–11.

Jarvis, P. (1999). *Research: The development of theory and practice*. Copenhagen: Alinea.

Jay, J. & Johnson, K. (2002). Capturing complexity: A typology of reflective practice for teacher education. *Teaching and Teacher Education, 18*, 73–85.

Jayatilleke, N. & Mackie, A. (2012). Reflection as part of continuous professional development for Public Health professionals: A literature review. *Journal of Public Health*. Advanced online publication. doi: 10.1093/pubmed/fds083

Johns, C. (1994). *Becoming a reflective practitioner*. Oxford: Blackwell.

Johns, C. (1994). Guided reflection. In A. Palmer, S. Burns & C. Bulman (Eds.), *Reflective practice in nursing* (pp. 110–130). Oxford: Blackwell.

Johns, C. (1995). Time to care? Time for reflection. *International Journal of Nursing Practice, 1*, 37–42.

Johns, C. (2009). *Becoming a reflective practitioner* (3rd ed.). Chichester: Wiley-Blackwell.

Johnson, G.P., Fister, A. & Vindrola-Padros, C. (2013). Drawings, photos and performances: Using visual methods with children. *Visual Anthropology Review, 28*, 164–178.

Jones, R. (2006). How can educational concepts inform sports coaching? In R. Jones (Ed.), *The sports coach as educator: Re-conceptualising sports coaching* (pp. 3–13). London: Routledge.

Jones-Devitt, S. & Samiei, C. (2011). From Accrington Stanley to academia? The use of league tables and student surveys to determine 'quality' in Higher Education. In M. Molesworth, R. Scullion & E. Nixon (Eds.), *The marketisation of Higher Education and the student as consumer* (pp. 86–100). London: Routledge.

Jonker, L., Elferink-Gemser, M., de Roos, I. & Visscher, C. (2012). The role of reflection in sport expertise. *The Sport Psychologist, 26*, 224–242.

Keegan, R., Harwood, C., Spray, C. & Lavallee, D. (2009). A qualitative investigation exploring the motivational climate in early career sports participants. *Psychology of Sport & Exercise, 10*, 361–372.

Kember, D. (2001). *Reflective teaching and learning in the health professions: Action research in professional education*. Oxford: Blackwell Science.

Kemmis, S. & McTaggart, R. (2000). Participatory action research. In N. Denzin & Y. Lincoln (Eds.), *Sage handbook of qualitative research* (2nd ed., pp. 567–605). Thousand Oaks, CA: Sage.

King, K. & Kitchener, K. (1994). *Developing reflective judgement*. San Francisco: Jossey-Bass.

Kirk, S. (2007). Methodological and ethical issues in conducting qualitative research with children and young people: A literature review. *International Journal of Nursing Studies, 44*, 1250–1260.

Klein, K. & Boals, A. (2001). Expressive writing can increase working memory capacity. *Journal of Experimental Psychology, 130*, 520–533.

Knight, C. & Holt, N. (2012). Working with young athletes. In S. Hanton & S.D. Mellalieu (Eds.), *Professional practice in sport psychology* (pp. 31–53). London: Routledge.

Knowles, Z. & Gilbourne, D. (2010). Aspiration, inspiration and illustration: Initiating debate on reflective practice writing. *The Sport Psychologist, 24*, 504–520.

Knowles, Z. & Saxon, J. (2010). Needs analysis and reflective practice: Two important components of case studies. *The Sport and Exercise Scientist, 25*, 23.

Knowles, Z. & Telfer, H. (2010). The where, what and why of reflective practice. In C. Heaney, B. Oakley & S. Rea (Eds.), *Exploring Sport and Fitness* (pp. 22–36). London, UK: Routledge.

Knowles, Z., Borrie, A. & Telfer, H. (2005). Towards the reflective sports coach: Issues of context, education and application. *Ergonomics, 48*, 1711–1720.

Knowles, Z., Gilbourne, D. & Niven, A. (2011). Critical reflections on doing reflective practice and writing reflective texts. In D. Gilbourne & M.B. Andersen (Eds.), *Critical essays in applied sport psychology* (pp. 59–71). Champaign, IL: Human Kinetics.

Knowles, Z., Katz, J. & Gilbourne, D. (2012). Reflective practice within elite consultancy: Diary on a personal and elusive process. Extracts and further discussion. *The Sport Psychologist*, 26, 454–469.

Knowles, Z., Gilbourne, D., Borrie, A. & Nevill, A. (2001). Developing the reflective sports coach: A study exploring the processes of reflection within a Higher Education coaching programme. *Reflective Practice*, 2, 185–207.

Knowles, Z., Gilbourne, D., Tomlinson, V. & Anderson, A. (2007). Reflective practice in review:Case studies of mentor and practitioner in action. *The Sport Psychologist*, 21, 95–109.

Knowles, Z., Parnell, D., Ridgers, N. & Stratton, G. (2013). Learning from the experts: Exploring playground experience and activities using a write and draw technique. *Journal of Physical Activity & Health*, 10, 406–415.

Knowles, Z., Tyler, G., Gilbourne, D. & Eubank, M. (2006). Reflecting on reflection: Exploring the practice of sports coaching graduates. *Reflective Practice*, 7, 163–179.

Kohl, H., Craig, C., Lambert, E., Inove, S., Alkandari, J., Leetongin, G. & Kahlmeier, S. (2012). The pandemic of physical inactivity; global action for public health. *The Lancet*, 380, 294–305.

Kolb, A. & Kolb, D. (2005). Learning styles and learning spaces: Enhancing experiential learning in Higher Education. *Academy of Management and Learning Education*, 4, 193–212.

Kolb, D. (1984). *Experiential learning: Experience as the source of learning and development*. Englewood Cliffs, NJ: Prentice-Hall.

Kostenius, C. & Ohrling, K. (2008). Friendship is like an extra parachute: Reflections on the way school children share their lived experiences of well-being through drawings. *Reflective Practice*, 9, 23–35.

Laming, Lord. (2003). *The Victoria Climbié Inquiry. Report of an inquiry by Lord Laming*. Cm 5730. London: TSO.

Lamprapoulos, G. (2002). A common factors view of counseling supervision process. *The Clinical Supervisor*, 21, 77–94.

Lane, A., Beedie, C., Jones, M., Uphill, M. & Devonport, T. (2012). The BASES expert statement on emotion regulation in sport. *Journal of Sports Sciences*, 11, 1189–1195.

Lane, D. & Corrie, S. (2006). *The modern scientist-practitioner: A guide to practice in psychology*. London: Routledge.

Langer, E. (1990). *Mindfulness*. Cambridge, MA: Da Capo Press.

Langer, E. (1997). *The power of mindful learning*. Cambridge, MA: Perseus Books.

Lee, I.-M., Shiroma, E., Lobelo, F., Puska, P., Blair, S. & Katzmarzyk, P. (2012). Effect of physical inactivity on major non-communicable diseases worldwide: An analysis of burden of disease and life expectancy. *The Lancet*, 380, 219–229.

Leykum, L., Pugh, J., Lanham, H., Harmon, J. & McDaniel, R. (2009). Implementation research design: Integrating participatory action research into randomised controlled trials. *Implementation Science*, 4, 69.

Livingstone, M., McCaffrey, T. & Rennie, K. (2006). Childhood obesity prevention studies: Lessons learned and to be learned. *Public Health Nutrition*, 9, 1121–1129.

Loughran, J. (2002). Effective reflective practice: In search of meaning in learning about teaching. *Journal of Teacher Education*, 53, 33–43.

Lyle, J. (2002). Coaches' decision making. In N. Cross & J. Lyle (Eds.), *The coaching process* (pp. 210–232). Oxford: Butterworth/Heinemann.

Lyle, J. (2010). Coaches' decision making: A naturalistic decision making analysis. In J. Lyle & C. Cushion (Eds.), *Sports coaching: Professionalisation and practice* (pp. 27–41). London: Elsevier.

Lyle, J. & Cushion, C. (Eds.) (2010). *Sports coaching: Professionalisation and practice*. London: Churchill Livingstone.

Mamede, S., Schmidt, H. & Penaforte, J. (2008). Effects of reflective practice on the accuracy of medical diagnoses. *Medical Education, 42*, 468–475.

Mamede, S., van Gog, T., van der Berge, K., van Saase, J., van Guldener, C. & Schmidt, H. (2010). Effect of availability bias and reflective reasoning on diagnostic accuracy among internal medicine residents. *Journal of the American Medical Association, 304*, 1198–1203.

Mandigo, J. & Holt, N. (2000a). Putting theory into practice: How cognitive evaluation theory can help us motivate children in physical activity environments. *Journal of Physical Education, Recreation, and Dance, 71*, 44–49.

Mann, K., Gordon, J. & MacLeod, A. (2009). Reflection and reflective practice in health professions education: A systematic review. *Advances in Health Sciences Education, 14*, 595–621.

Marcus, B. & Forsyth, L. (2003). *Motivation people to be physically active*. Champaign, IL: Human Kinetics.

Margison, F., Barkham, M., Evans, C., McGrath, G., Clark, J., Audin, K. & Connell, J. (2000). Measurement and psychotherapy: Evidence-based practice and practice-based evidence. *British Journal of Psychiatry, 177*, 123–130.

Martens, R. (1987). Science, knowledge and sport psychology. *The Sport Psychologist, 1*, 29–55.

Martindale, A. & Collins, D. (2007). Enhancing evaluation in applied sport psychology with professional judgement and decision making. *The Sport Psychologist, 21*, 458–474.

McCarthy, P. & Jones, M. (2007). A qualitative study of sport enjoyment in the sampling years. *The Sport Psychologist, 21*, 400–416.

McGarr, O. & Moody, J. (2010). Scaffolding or stifling? The influence of journal requirements on students' engagement in reflective practice. *Reflective Practice, 11*, 579–591.

McHugh, T.-L.F. & Kowalski, K.C. (2011). 'A new view of body image': A school-based participatory action research project with young Aboriginal women. *Action Research, 9*, 220–241.

McIntosh, P. (2010). *Action research and reflective practice: Creative and visual methods to facilitate reflection and learning*. London: Routledge.

McKenna, H., Ashton, S. & Keeney, S. (2004). Barriers to evidence based practice in primary care: A review of the literature. *International Journal of Nursing Studies, 41*, 369–378.

McKenna, H., Cutliffe, J. & McKenna, P. (2000). Evidenced based practice: Demolishing some myths. *Nursing Standard, 14*, 39–42.

McKibbon, K. (1998). Evidence based practice. *Bulletin of the Medical Library Association, 86*, 396–401.

McVittie, E. (2012). Children as reflective learners. In A. McVittie (Ed.), *Reflective learning and teaching in primary schools* (pp. 11–31). London: Sage.

Medical Research Council. (2000). *A framework for development and evaluation of RCTs for complex interventions to improve health*. Retrieved from http://www.mrc.ac.uk/Utilities/Documentrecord/index.htm?d=MRC003372

Medical Research Council. (2008). *Developing and evaluating completes interventions: New guidance*. Retrieved from http://www.mrc.ac.uk/Utilities/Documentrecord/index.htm?d=MRC004871

Mellalieu, S.D. & Hanton, S. (Eds.). (2008). *Advances in applied sport psychology: A review*. London: Routledge.

Mezirow, J. (1985). A critical theory of adult learning and education. *Adult Education, 28*, 100–110.

Mezirow, J. (Ed.). (1990). *Fostering critical reflection in adulthood: A guide to transformative and emancipatory learning*. London: Routledge.

Mezirow, J. (2000). Learning to think like an adult: Core concepts of transformative theory. In J. Mezirow (Ed.), *Learning as transformation: Critical perspectives on a theory in progress* (pp. 3–34). San Francisco: Jossey-Bass.

Miles, G. (2000). Drawing together hope: 'Listening' to militarised children. *Journal of Child Health Care, 4*, 137–142.

Milton, B., Porcellato, L., Dugdill, L. & Springett, J. (2012). My Mum and Dad said it calms you down: Children's perceptions of smoking as a coping strategy. *Children & Society, 26*, 89–99.

Moffatt, K. (1996). Teaching social work as a reflective process. In N. Gould & I. Taylor (Eds.), *Reflective learning for social work* (pp. 47–62). Aldershot: Arena/Ashgate.

Molesworth, M., Nixon, E. & Scullion, R. (2009). Having, being and Higher Education: The marketisation of the university and the transformation of the student into consumer. *Teaching in Higher Education, 14*, 277–287.

Molesworth, M., Scullion, R. & Nixon, E. (2011). *The marketisation of Higher Education and the student as consumer*. London: Routledge.

Moon, J. (1999). *Reflection in learning and professional development*. London: Kogan Page.

Moon, J. (2001). *PDP Working Paper 4: Reflection in Higher Education*. York: The Higher Education Academy.

Moon, J. (2004). *A handbook of reflective practice and experiential learning: Theory and practice*. Abingdon: Routledge.

Moore, R. (2012). *Sky's the limit*. London: Harper Sport.

Morgan, M. & Sprenkle, D. (2007). Toward a common-factors approach to supervision. *Journal of Marital and Family Therapy, 33*, 1–17.

Morris, J., Heady, J., Raffle, P., Roberts, C. & Parks, J. (1953). Coronary heart disease and physical activity at work. *The Lancet, 2*, 1053–1057.

Morton, J.P. (2009). Critical reflections from a neophyte lecturer in Higher Education: A self narrative from an exercise physiologist! *Reflective Practice, 10*, 233–243.

Morton, J.P., Sutton, L., Robertson, C. & MacLaren, D. (2010). Making the weight: A case-study from professional boxing. *International Journal of Sports Nutrition and Exercise Metabolism, 20*, 80–85.

Morton, J.P., Croft, L., Bartlett, J., MacLaren, D., Reilly, T., Evans, L., . . . Drust, B. (2009). Reduced carbohydrate availability does not modulate training-induced heat shock protein adaptations but does up-regulate oxidative enzyme activity in human skeletal muscle. *Journal of Applied Physiology, 106*, 1513–1521.National Institute for Clinical Excellence. (2006). *Obesity: Guidance on the prevention, identification, assessment and management of overweight and obesity in adults and children*. Retrieved from http://www.nice.org.uk/CG43

National Institute for Clinical Excellence. (2007). *Behaviour change at population, community and individual levels: NICE public health guidance*. Retrieved from http://guidance.nice.org.uk/PH6/Guidance/pdf/English

National Institute for Clinical Excellence. (2010). *Public health guidance: Looked-after children and young people – recommendations*. Retrieved from http://publications.nice.org.uk/looked-after-children-and-young-people-ph28/recommendations#training-for-professionals

Nelson, L. & Cushion, C. (2006). Coach education, reflection, and learning from experience: The case of the national governing body coaching certificate. *The Sport Psychologist, 20,* 172–181.

Nesti, M. (2010). *Psychology in football: Working with elite and professional players.* Abingdon: Routledge.

Nesti, M. & Littlewood, M. (2011). Making your way in the game: Boundary situations within the world of professional football. In D. Gilbourne & M.B. Anderson (Eds.), *Critical essays in applied sport psychology* (pp. 233–250). Champaign, IL: Human Kinetics.

Newcomb, J. (2004). Junior aged children as reflective practitioners. *The Journal of Design and Technology Education, 9,* 172–184.

Newman, S. (1999). Constructing and critiquing reflective practice. *Educational Action Research Journal, 76,* 145–161.

Nowicka, P. (2005). Dieticians and exercise professionals in a childhood obesity treatment team. *Acta Paediatrica, 94,* 23–29.

O'Brien, N. & Moules, T. (2007). So round the spiral again: A reflective participatory research project with children and young people. *Educational Action Research, 15,* 385–402.

O'Connor, B. (2000). Reasons for less than ideal psychotherapy supervision. *The Clinical Supervisor, 19,* 173–183.

O'Kane, C. (2008). The development of participatory techniques. In P. Christensen & A. James (Eds.), *Research with children perspectives and practices* (pp. 125–155). London: Routledge.

O'Neill, M. & Rieder, S. (2005). The multi-disciplinary team in the management of obesity: The management of eating disorders and obesity. In D. Goldstein (Ed.), *The management of eating disorders and obesity* (pp. 355–356). Totowa, NJ: Humana Press.

Oelofsen, N. (2012). The importance of reflective practices. *Health Service Journal.* http://www.hsj.co.uk/resource-centre/best-practice/flexible-working-and-skills-resources/the-importance-of-reflective-practices/5048994.article (accessed 22 January 2013).

Orem, S., Binkert, J. & Clancy, A. (2007). *Appreciative coaching: A positive process for change.* San Francisco: Jossey-Bass.

Orford, J. (2008). *Community psychology: Challenges, controversies and emerging consensus.* Hoboken, NJ: Wiley.

Osterman, K. & Kottkamp, R. (1993). *Reflective practice for educators: Improving schooling through professional development.* Newbury Park, CA: Corwin Press.

Paffenbarger, R., Hyde, R., Wing, A. & Hsieh, C. (1986). Physical activity, all-cause mortality, and longevity of college alumni. *The New England Journal of Medicine, 314,* 605–613.

Palmer, S. & Whybrow, A. (Eds.). (2007). *Handbook of coaching psychology.* London: Routledge.

Parker, A. (2000). Training for glory, schooling for failure? English professional football, traineeship and educational provision. *Journal of Education and Work, 13,* 61–76.

Parker, A. (2001). Soccer, servitude and sub-cultural identity: Football traineeship and masculine construction. *Soccer and Society, 2,* 59–80.

Parker, A. (2006). Lifelong learning to labour: Apprenticeship, masculinity and communities of practice. *British Educational Research Journal, 32,* 687–701.

Parrillo, L. (1994). *How to guide for reflection.* Holland, PA: Brighton Press.

Patterson, C., Baarts, C. Launso, L. & Verhoef, M.J. (2009). Evaluating complex health interventions: A critical analysis of the 'outcomes' concept. *BMC Complementary and Alternative Medicine, 9,* 18.

Peake, K. & Epstein, I. (2005). Theoretical and practical imperatives for reflective social work organizations in health and mental health. *Social Work in Mental Health, 3,* 23–37.

Peden-McAlpine, C., Tomlinson, P., Forneris, S., Genck, G. & Meiers, S. (2005). Evaluation of a reflective practice intervention to enhance family care. *Journal of Advanced Nursing Practice, 49*, 494–501.

Peel, J., Cropley, B., Hanton, S. & Fleming, S. (2013). *Learning through reflection: Values, conflicts, and role interactions of a youth sport coach.* Manuscript submitted for publication.Pendleton, V. (2012). *Between the lines: My autobiography.* London: HarperSport.

Pennebaker, J. (1985). Traumatic experience and psychosomatic disease: Exploring the roles of behavioural inhibition, obsession, and confiding. *Canadian Psychology, 26,* 82–95.

Pennebaker, J. & Chung, C. (in press). Expressive writing and its links to mental and physical health. In H. Friedman (Ed.), *Oxford handbook of health psychology.* New York: Oxford University Press.Perry, B. & Dockett, S. (2005, June). *As I got to learn it got fun: Children's reflections on their first year of school.* Paper presented at the Annual Conference of the Australian Association for Research in Education, Sydney. Retrieved from http://www.aare.edu.au/04pap/doc04324.pdf

Perry, W. (1970). *Forms of intellectual and ethical development in the college years.* Austin, TX: Holt, Reinhart, & Winston.

Petitpas, A., Giges, B. & Danish, S. (1999). The sport–athlete relationship: Implications for training. *The Sport Psychologist, 13,* 344–357.

Petrie, H. (1976). Do you see what I see? The epistemology of interdisciplinary inquiry. *Journal of Aesthetic Education, 10,* 29–43.

Philippart, F. (2003). Using Socratic dialogue. In S. Banks & K. Nøhr (Eds.), *Teaching practical ethics for the social professions* (pp. 69–82). Copenhagen: European Social Ethics Project.

Piaget, J. & Inhelder, B. (1969). *The Psychology of the Child.* New York: Basic Books.

Placek, J. & Smyth, D. (1995). Teaching pre-service physical education teachers to reflect. *Physical Educator, 52,* 106–112.

Plack, M. & Greenberg, L. (2005). The reflective practitioner: Reaching for excellence in practice. *Pediatrics, 116,* 1546–1552.

Poczwardowski, A., Sherman, C. & Ravizza, K. (2004). Professional philosophy in sport psychology service delivery: Building on theory and practice. *The Sport Psychologist, 18,* 445–463.

Polizzi, J. & Frick, W. (2012). Transformational preparation and professional development: Authentic reflective practice for school leadership, teaching and learning. *The Journal of Natural Inquiry & Reflective Practice, 26,* 1–34.

Pollard, V. (2008). Ethics and reflective practice: Continuing the conversation. *Reflective Practice, 9,* 399–407.

Porcellato, L., Dugdill, J. & Springett, J. (2002). Using focus groups to explore children's perceptions of smoking: Reflections on practice. *Health Education, 102,* 310–320.

Porcellato, L., Dugdill, L. & Springett, J. (2005). A longitudinal study exploring primary schoolchildren's perspectives on smoking: Results from the early years phase. *Childhood, 12,* 425–443.

Porter, S. (Ed.). (2013). *Tidy's Physiotherapy* (15th ed.). London: Sanders Elsevier.

Potrac, P., Jones, R. & Armour, K. (2002). It's all about getting respect: The coaching behaviours of an expert English soccer coach. *Sport, Education and Society, 7,* 183–202.

Prenton, S., Dugdill, L. & Hollingworth, L. (2013). Reflection. In S. Porter (Ed.), *Tidy's Physiotherapy* (15th ed., pp. 67–82). London: Elsevier.

Price, S., Rogers, Y., Scaife, M., Stanton, D. & Neale, H. (2003). Using 'tangibles' to promote novel forms of playful learning. *Interacting with Computers, 15,* 169–185.

Putnam, R. (2000). *Bowling alone: The collapse and revival of American community*. New York: Simon & Schuster.

Queensland Studies Authority. (2011). *Queensland Kindergarten Learning Guideline (QKLG) professional development (Module 5). Reflective practice: Engaging partners*. Retrieved from http://www.qsa.qld.edu.au

Raelin, J. (2002). 'I don't have time to think!' versus the art of reflective practice. *Reflections, 4*, 65–79.

Raskin, N. & Rogers, C. (1989). Person centered therapy. In R. Corsini & D. Wedding (Eds.), *Current psychotherapies* (4th ed., pp. 155–194). Itasca, IL: Peacock.

Rhodius, A. (2006). Reflections on the Athens Olympics: Working with Olympic archers and what it was like to be there. *Sport and Exercise Psychology Review, 2*, 29–34.

Rhodius, A. (2009, June). *Reflective practice in graduate training and consultation: A U.S. perspective*. In Z. Knowles (Chair), Reflective Practice: Explorations of Process, Applications and Representation. Symposium conducted at the 3rd International Conference for Qualitative Research in Sport & Exercise, Roehampton University, London.

Rhodius, A. (2012, February). *To graduation, certification and beyond: The importance of post-training peer support and reflective practice in sport psychology*. Paper presented at the 2nd National University Performance Psychology Conference, San Diego, CA.

Rhodius, A., Carlson, E., Cheadle, C., Coeshott, R., Johnston, T. & Sugarman, K. (2011, September). *I get by with a little help from my peers: The value of ongoing peer consultation in sport psychology*. Workshop presented at the 26th Association for Applied Sport Psychology (AASP) Annual Conference, Honolulu, HI.

Richards, P., Collins, D. & Mascarenhas, D. (2012). Developing rapid high-pressure team decision-making skills. The integration of slow deliberate reflective learning within the competitive performance environment: A case study of elite netball. *Reflective Practice, 13*, 407–424.

Ridgers, N., Knowles, Z. & Sayers, J. (2012). Play in the natural environment: A child-focused evaluation of forest school. *Children's Geographies, 10*, 55–71.

Roderick, M. (1996). A very precarious profession: Uncertainty in the working lives of professional footballers. *Work, Employment and Society, 20*, 245–265.

Roderick, M. (2006). *The work of professional football: A labour of love?* London: Routledge.

Rogers, C. (2002). Defining reflection: Another look at John Dewey and reflective thinking. *Teachers College Record, 104*, 842–866.

Rolfe, G., Freshwater, D. & Jasper, M. (2001). *Critical reflection for nursing and the helping professions: A user guide*. Basingstoke: Palgrave Macmillan.

Rømer, T.A. (2003). Learning process and professional content in the theory of Donald Schön. *Reflective Practice, 4*, 85–93.

Rosenburg, W. & Donald, A. (1995). Evidence-based medicine: An approach to clinical problem solving. *British Medical Journal, 310*, 1122–1126.

Ross, J. (2012, April). *The spectacle and the placeholder: Digital futures for reflective practices in Higher Education*. Paper presented at the Eighth International Networked Learning Conference, Maastricht, Netherlands. Abstract retrieved from http://www.lancs.ac.uk/fss/organisations/netlc/past/nlc2012/abstracts/ross.html

Rubin, H. & Rubin, I. (2012). *Qualitative interviewing: The art of hearing data* (3rd ed.). Thousand Oaks, CA: Sage.

Russell, T. (2005). Can reflective practice be taught? *Reflective Practice, 6*, 199–204.

Ruth-Sahd, L. (2003). Reflective practice: A critical analysis of data-based studies and implications for nursing education. *Journal of Nursing Education, 42*, 488–497.

Ryan, S. (2007). *Mindful supervision*. In R. Shohet (Ed.), *Passionate supervision* (pp. 70–85). London: Jessica Kingsley.

Ryba, Y. (2008). Researching children in sport: Methodological reflections. *Journal of Applied Sport Psychology, 20*, 334–348.

Rychetnik, L., Frommer, M., Hawe, P. & Shiell, A. (2002). Criteria for evaluating evidence on public health interventions. *Journal of Epidemiology and Community Health, 56*, 119–127.

Sarbin, T. (Ed.). (1986). *Narrative psychology: The storied nature of human conduct*. New York: Praeger.

Schatzki, T., Knorr Cetina, K. & Von Svigny, E. (Eds.). (2001). *The practice turn in contemporary theory*. London: Routledge.

Schinke, R. & Ramsay, M. (2009). World title boxing: From early beginnings to the first bell. *Journal of Sport Science and Medicine, 8*, 1–4.

Schön, D.A. (1983). *The reflective practitioner*. New York: Basic Books.

Schön, D.A. (1987). *Educating the reflective practitioner*. San Francisco: Jossey- Bass.

Seers, K. (2007). Evaluating complex interventions. *Worldviews on Evidence-Based Nursing, 4*, 67–68.

Seligman, M. & Csikszentmihalyi, M. (2000). Positive psychology: An introduction. *American Psychologist, 55*, 5–14.

Shaw, I. (1996). Unbroken voices: Children, young people and qualitative methods. In I. Butler & I. Shaw (Eds.), *A case of neglect? Children's experiences and the sociology of childhood* (pp. 19–36). Aldershot: Avebury Press.

Siegel, D. (2007). *The mindful brain: Reflection and attunement in the cultivation of well-being*. New York: Norton.

Siegel, D. (2010). *The mindful therapist: A clinician's guide to mindsight and neural integration*. New York: Norton.

Siegel, D. (2012). *Pocket guide to interpersonal neurobiology: An integrative handbook of the mind*. New York: Norton.

Smith, B. & Sparkes, A. (2009). Narrative analysis and sport and exercise psychology: Understanding lives in diverse ways. *Psychology of Sport and Exercise, 10*, 279–288.

Sobral, D. (2000). An appraisal of medical students' reflection-in-learning. *Medical Education, 34*, 182–187.

Sparkes, A. (2002). *Telling tales in sport and physical activity: A qualitative journey*. Champaign, IL: Human Kinetics.

SportscoachUK. (2012). *UKCC Level 1–3 support guide*. Retrieved from http://www.sportscoachuk.org/resource/ukcc-level-1-3-support-guide

Sprenkle, D. & Blow, A. (2004). Common factors and our sacred models. *Journal of Marital and Family Therapy, 20*, 113–129.

Stam, H. (Ed.). (2001). Social constructionism and its critics. *Theory & Psychology, 11*, 291–296.

Stelter, R. (2007). Coaching: A process of personal and social meaning making. *International Coaching Psychology Review, 2*, 191–201.

Stelter, R. (2010). Narrative coaching: A community psychological perspective. In T. Ryba, R. Schinke & G. Tennenbaum (Eds.), *The cultural turn in sport psychology* (pp. 335–361). Morgantown, WV: Fitness Information Technology.

Stelter, R. (2014). *A guide to third generation coaching – narrative-collaborative theory and practice*. Dordrecht: Springer Science & Business Media.

Stelter, R. & Law, H. (2010). Coaching: Narrative-collaborative practice. *International Coaching Psychology Review, 5*, 152–164.

Surbeck, E., Park Han, E. & Moyer, J. (1991). Assessing reflective responses in journals. *Educational Leadership*, March, 25–27.

Taylor, B. (2006). *Reflective practice: A guide for nurses and midwives* (2nd ed.). Maidenhead: Open University Press.

Telfer, H. (2002). *Report of the teaching fellowship.* Unpublished manuscript, Centre for the Development of Learning and Teaching, University of Cumbria, UK.

Telfer, H. & Knowles, Z. (2009). The 'how to' of reflection. In C. Heaney, B. Oakley and S. Rea (Eds.), *Exploring Sport and Fitness* (pp. 36–47). London: Routledge.

The Quality Assurance Agency for Higher Education. (2009). *Personal development and planning: Guidance for institutional policy and practice in Higher Education.* Gloucester, UK: QAA..Thompson, N. & Pascal, J. (2012). Developing critically reflective practice. *Reflective Practice*, 13, 311–325.

Thompson, S. & Thompson, N. (2008). *The critically reflective practitioner.* Basingstoke: Palgrave Macmillan.

Tink, L. (2011). 'I've never been in a program after school': A participatory action research approach to sports-based critical hours programs (Unpublished Masters thesis). University of Alberta. Edmonton, Alberta, Canada.

Tinning, R. (1995). We have ways of making you think, or do we? Reflections on 'training' in reflective teaching. In C. Pare (Ed.), *Training of teachers in reflective practice of physical education.* Trois-Rivières, Quebec: Université du Québec à Trois-Rivières.

Tod, D. (2007). Reflections on collaborating with a professional rugby league player. *Sport and Exercise Psychology Review*, 3, 4–10.Tod, D. & Bond, K. (2010). A longitudinal examination of a British neophyte sport psychologist's development. *The Sport Psychologist*, 24, 35–51.

Tod, D. & Lavallee, D. (2011). Taming the Wild West: Training and supervision in applied sport psychology. In D. Gilbourne & M.B. Andersen (Eds.), *Critical essays in applied sport psychology* (pp. 193–215). Champaign IL: Human Kinetics.

Tod, D., Andersen, M.B. & Marchant, D. (2009). A longitudinal examination of neophyte applied sport psychologists' development. *Journal of Applied Sport Psychology*, 21, 1–16.

Tod, D., Marchant, D. & Andersen, M.B. (2007). Learning experiences contributing to service-delivery competence. *The Sport Psychologist*, 21, 317–334.

Toner, J., Nelson, L., Potrac, P., Gilbourne, D. & Marshall, P. (2012). From blame to shame in a coach–athlete relationship in golf: A tale of shared critical reflection and the re-storying of narrative experience. *Sports Coaching Review*, 1, 53–67.

Tonn, E. & Harmison, R. (2004). Thrown to the wolves: A student's account of her practicum experience. *The Sport Psychologist*, 18, 324–340.

Training Development Agency (2012). Retrieved from http://webarchive.nationalarchives.gov.uk/20120203163341/http://www.tda.gov.uk/trainee-teacher/qts-standards/skills/reviewing-teaching-learning/Q29.aspx?_st=911499296

Trelfa, J. (2005). Faith in reflective practice. *Reflective Practice*, 6, 205–212.

Trelfa, J. (2010a). *Emperor's new clothes? Exploring student experiences of reflective practice* (Unpublished M.Ed. dissertation). University of Exeter, UK.

Trelfa, J. (2010b, July). *The Emperor's new clothes? A critical exploration of reflective practice.* Paper presented at the meeting of the Challenging Futures: Youth & Community Work group, Durham, UK.

Trelfa, J. (2011, July). *Are reflective journals fit for purpose?* Paper presented at the Annual Conference of Youth and Community Workers Training Agencies Group, University of Brighton, UK.

Tripp, D. (1993). *Critical incidents in teaching: Developing professional judgment.* London: Routledge.

Trost, S., Rosenkranz, R. & Dzewaltowski, D. (2008). Physical activity levels among children attending after-school programs. *Medicine and Science in Sports and Exercise, 40,* 622–629.

United Nations. (1989). *Convention on the Rights of the Child.* Geneva: UN.

Usher, R., Bryant, I. & Johnston, R. (1997). *Adult education and the postmodern challenge: Learning beyond the limits.* London: Routledge.

Valkanova, Y. (2004). Enhancing self-reflection in children: The use of digital video in the primary science classroom. *Journal of Literacy, 1,* 42–55.

Van Maanen, J. (1988). *Tales of the field: On writing ethnography.* Chicago: University of Chicago Press.

Van Manen, M. (1977). Linking ways of knowing with ways of being practical. *Curriculum Inquiry, 6,* 205–228.

Van Manen, M. (1997). *Researching lived experience: Human science for an action sensitive pedagogy.* London, ON: Althouse Press.

Vaughn, R. (2004). Evaluation and public health. *American Journal of Public Health, 94,* 360.

Veale, A. (2011). Creative methodologies in participatory research with children. In S. Green & D. Hogan (Eds.), *Researching children's experiences* (pp. 253–272). London: Sage.

Ward, J. & McCotter, S. (2004). Reflection as a visible outcome for pre-service teachers. *Teaching and Teacher Education, 20,* 243–257.

Waters, E., De Silva-Sanigorski, A., Hall, B., Brown, T., Campbell, K., Gao, Y., . . . Summerbell, C. (2011). Interventions for preventing obesity in children. *Cochrane Database of Systematic Reviews, 12.* doi: 10.1002/14651858.CD001871.pub3.

Watson, J., Lubker, J. & Van Raalte, J. (2011). Problems in reflective practice: Self-bootstrapping versus therapeutic supervision. In D. Gilbourne & M.B. Andersen (Eds.), *Critical essays in applied sport psychology* (pp. 157–172). Champaign, IL: Human Kinetics.

Watson, J., Zizzi, S., Etzel, E. & Lubker, J. (2004). Applied sport psychology supervision: A survey of students and professionals. *The Sport Psychologist, 18,* 415–429.

Watson, P., Dugdill, L., Murphy, R., Knowles, Z. & Cable, N. (2012). Moving forward in childhood obesity treatment: A call for translational research. *Health Education Journal.* Advanced online publication. doi: 10.1177/0017896912438313

Waumsley, J., Hemmings, B. & Payne, S. (2010). Work–life balance, role conflict and the UK sports psychology consultant. *The Sport Psychologist, 24,* 245–262.

Weinberg, R. & Comar, W. (1994). The effectiveness of psychological interventions in competitive sport. *Sports Medicine, 18,* 406–418.

Wells, A. (2005). Detached mindfulness in cognitive therapy: A metacognitive analysis and ten techniques. *Journal of Rational-Emotive and Cognitive Therapy, 23,* 337–355.

Wells, A. & Matthews, G. (1996). Modeling cognition in emotional disorder: The S-REF model. *Behaviour Research and Therapy, 32,* 867–870.

Wheeler, S. & Richards, K. (2007). The impact of clinical supervision on counsellors and therapists, their practice and their clients: A systematic review of the literature. *Counselling and Psychotherapy Research, 7,* 54–65.

White, M. (2007). *Maps of narrative practice.* New York: Norton.

White, P. (2011). *Using reflective practice in the physiotherapy curriculum.* Retrieved from http://repos.hsap.kcl.ac.uk/content/m10129/1.6/

Wickelgren, I. (1997). Getting a grasp on working memory. *Science, 275,* 1580–1582.

Wignall, A. (2006, September 26). You have passed Go. Pay £3000. *The Guardian*. Retrieved from http://www.guardian.co.uk/money/2006/sep/26/education.students

William, R. & Wessel, J. (2004). Reflective journal writing to obtain student feedback about their learning during the study of chronic musculoskeletal conditions. *Journal of Allied Health, 33*, 17–23.

Wong, F., Kember, D., Chung, L. & Yan, L. (1995). Assessing the level of student reflection from reflective journals. *Journal of Advanced Nursing, 22*, 48–57.

Woodcock, C., Richards, H. & Mugford, A. (2008). Quality counts: Critical features for neophyte professional development. *Sport Psychologist, 22*, 491–506.

Woodward, C. (2005). *Winning!* London: Hodder and Stoughton.

Woodward, C., Chesterfield, G., Lee, S. & Shaw, D. (2009). Reflections from a world champion: An interview with Sir Clive Woodward, Director of Olympic Performance, the British Olympic Association. *Reflective Practice, 10*, 295–310.

World Health Organization. (2001). *Evaluation in health promotion. Principles and perspectives*. Retrieved from http://www.healthknowledge.org.uk/public-health-textbook/disease-causation-diagnostic/2h-principles-health-promotion/health- promotion-evaluation

Wyatt, S., Winters, K. & Dubbert, P. (2006). Overweight and obesity: Prevalence, consequences, and causes of a growing public health problem. *American Journal of Medical Sciences, 331*, 166–174.

Xyrichis, A. & Lowton, K. (2008). What fosters or prevent interprofessional team-working in primary and community care? A literature review. *International Journal of Nursing Studies, 45*, 140–153.

Zeichner, K. & Liston, D. (1987). Teaching student teachers to reflect. *Harvard Educational Review, 57*, 23–48.

Index